Editorial project:
2021 © **booq** publishing, S.L.
c/ Domènech, 7-9, 2º 1ª
08012 Barcelona, Spain
T: +34 93 268 80 88
www.booqpublishing.com

ISBN: 978-84-9936-708-8 [EN]
ISBN: 978-84-9936-703-3 [DE]

© Editions du Layeur
Dépôt Légal : 2021
ISBN : 978-2-915126-79-2
Espagne, en avril 2021

monsa
publications

2021 © Instituto Monsa de ediciones, S.L.
c/ Gravina, 43
08930 Sant Adrià de Besós, Barcelona, Spain
T: +34 93 381 00 93
www.monsa.com
monsa@monsa.com

ISBN: 978-84-17557-35-5

Editorial coordinator: Claudia Martínez Alonso
Art director: Mireia Casanovas Soley
Editor: Marjolein Visser
Layout: Cristina Simó Perales
Translations: **booq** publishing S.L.

Printing in Spain

Is it possible to live with all the necessary comforts in a house that is sometimes the size of a conventional living room? More and more people are sure it is. The trend towards living in small homes is here to stay; it is a social and architectural trend that has become a philosophy of life, not only for economic reasons or lack of space in large cities, but as a way of living a simpler and more sustainable life, with less ecological impact. Having just what we need allows us to feel lighter and make the most of what we have. In addition, having a small house does not mean living cramped for space: an ingenious and minimalist design that helps to optimise space, accompanied by appropriate decoration, will make it possible to create an open, unique and functional environment.

Designing an interior design project for a small space is a great challenge that designers and architects are increasingly facing, as it is not only about creating environments with an attractive aesthetic but also about making the most of the few square metres available.

There are many strategies to achieve a feeling of spaciousness in small spaces: creating longitudinal visual axes, eliminating divisions or partitions to unify rooms, or ensuring the greatest possible entry of natural light through skylights, large windows or floor-to-ceiling glazed panels and/or enclosures are some of them.

All spaces must be functional and have their uses, without giving up on a stylish home with pieces that we love. Therefore, another key strategy is to design made-to-measure furniture on a suitable scale, which, as well as being visually aesthetic, contains everything that is needed in a home: multifunctional furniture, both when it comes to dividing spaces and creating all kinds of storage possibilities, such as drawers under the stairs or folding furniture, for example. A whole series of "tricks" that do not detract from the beauty of the home and that allow it to adapt to the needs and personality of those who live in it.

Through the pages of this book we will travel the world from east to west, from Canada to Australia, passing through the United States, Costa Rica, Norway and China, among other countries, in which an important group of architects and designers with great national and international recognition have developed very varied projects for small dwellings of between 10 and 150 m². They are projects of very diverse typology: from a cabin in the mountains, to a flat in a modern city or a house inside a yacht. But all of them offer intelligent and ingenious design and construction solutions, with a careful aesthetic and with the aim of adapting to the lifestyle of their occupants as much as possible, as well as taking care of the environment and in many cases adapting to the surroundings in which they are located.

Ist es möglich, mit allen notwendigen Annehmlichkeiten in einem Haus von der Größe eines herkömmlichen Wohnzimmers zu leben? Immer mehr Menschen sind sich sicher, dass es so ist. Die Tendenz, in kleinen Häusern zu leben, ist mit Macht ausgebrochen, um zu bleiben; es ist ein sozialer und architektonischer Trend, der zu einer Lebensphilosophie geworden ist, nicht nur aus wirtschaftlichen Gründen oder Platzmangel in Großstädten, sondern als eine Möglichkeit, ein einfacheres und nachhaltigeres Leben zu führen, mit weniger ökologischen Auswirkungen. Nur das zu haben, was wir brauchen, erlaubt uns, uns leichter zu fühlen und das Beste aus dem zu machen, was wir haben. Darüber hinaus bedeutet ein kleines Haus zu haben nicht, dass man vom Platz überwältigt wird: ein ausgeklügeltes und minimalistisches Design, das hilft, den Raum zu optimieren, begleitet von einer angemessenen Dekoration, wird es möglich machen, eine offene, einzigartige und funktionale Umgebung zu schaffen.

Ein Einrichtungsprojekt für einen kleinen Raum zu entwerfen, ist eine große Herausforderung, der sich immer mehr Designer und Architekten stellen, denn es geht nicht nur darum, Umgebungen mit einer attraktiven Ästhetik zu schaffen, sondern auch darum, das Beste aus den wenigen verfügbaren Quadratmetern herauszuholen.

Es gibt viele Strategien, um ein Gefühl von Großzügigkeit in kleinen Räumen zu erreichen: Schaffen Sie visuelle Längsachsen, beseitigen Sie Unterteilungen oder Trennwände, um Umgebungen zu vereinheitlichen, oder suchen Sie den größtmöglichen Einlass von natürlichem Licht durch Oberlichter, große Fenster oder raumhohe verglaste Paneele und/oder Abdeckungen sind einige von ihnen.

Alle Räume müssen funktional sein und ihren Nutzen haben, ohne auf ein Haus voller Stil und mit Stücken zu verzichten, in die wir uns verlieben. Daher ist eine weitere Schlüsselstrategie, maßgefertigte Möbel in einem geeigneten Maßstab zu entwerfen, die nicht nur optisch ästhetisch sind, sondern auch alles enthalten, was in einem Haus benötigt wird: multifunktionale Möbel, sowohl wenn es darum geht, Räume zu unterteilen als auch alle Arten von Aufbewahrungsmöglichkeiten zu schaffen, wie Schubladen unter der Treppe oder Klappmöbel. Eine ganze Reihe von „Tricks", die nicht von der Schönheit ablenken und es erlauben, sich an die Bedürfnisse und die Persönlichkeit derjenigen anzupassen, die im Haus leben.

Durch die Seiten dieses Buches werden wir die Welt von Ost nach West bereisen, von Kanada nach Australien, vorbei an den Vereinigten Staaten, Costa Rica, Norwegen oder China und anderen Ländern, in denen eine wichtige Gruppe von Architekten und Designern mit großer nationaler und internationaler Anerkennung, sehr unterschiedliche Projekte von kleinen Wohnungen, zwischen 10 und 150 m² entwickelt haben. Es handelt sich dabei um Projekte unterschiedlichster Typologie: von einer Hütte in den Bergen über ein Apartment in einer modernen Stadt bis hin zu einem Haus im Inneren einer Jacht. Aber alle bieten intelligente und ausgeklügelte Design- und Konstruktionslösungen, mit einer sorgfältigen Ästhetik und mit dem Ziel, sich so weit wie möglich an die Lebensweise der Bewohner anzupassen sowie die Umwelt zu schonen und sich in vielen Fällen an die Umgebung, in der sie sich befinden, anzupassen.

Est-il possible de vivre avec tout le confort nécessaire dans une maison de la taille d'une salle de séjour classique ? De plus en plus de gens en sont convaincus. La tendance à vivre dans de petites maisons a éclaté avec force pour rester ; c'est une tendance sociale et architecturale qui est devenue une philosophie de vie, non seulement pour des raisons économiques ou de manque d'espace dans les grandes villes, mais comme une façon de vivre une vie plus simple et plus durable, avec un impact écologique moindre. Avoir juste ce dont nous avons besoin nous permet de nous sentir plus léger et de tirer le meilleur parti de ce que nous avons. En outre, avoir une petite maison ne signifie pas vivre en étant submergé par l'espace : un design ingénieux et minimaliste qui contribue à optimiser l'espace, accompagné d'une décoration appropriée permettra de créer un environnement ouvert, unique et fonctionnel.

Concevoir un projet d'aménagement intérieur pour un petit espace est un grand défi auquel de plus en plus de designers et d'architectes sont confrontés, car il ne s'agit pas seulement de créer des environnements à l'esthétique attrayante, mais aussi de tirer le meilleur parti des quelques mètres carrés disponibles.

Il existe de nombreuses stratégies pour obtenir une sensation d'espace dans les petits espaces : créer des axes visuels longitudinaux, éliminer les divisions ou les cloisons pour unifier les environnements, ou chercher à faire entrer le plus de lumière naturelle possible par les puits de lumière, les grandes fenêtres ou les panneaux vitrés du sol au plafond et/ou les enceintes sont quelques-unes d'entre elles.

Tous les espaces doivent être fonctionnels et avoir leur utilité, sans renoncer à une maison pleine de style et avec des pièces dont on tombe amoureux. Par conséquent, une autre stratégie clé consiste à concevoir des meubles sur mesure à une échelle appropriée, qui, en plus d'être visuellement esthétiques, contiennent tout ce qui est nécessaire dans une maison : des meubles multifonctionnels, tant lorsqu'il s'agit de diviser les espaces que de créer toutes sortes de possibilités de rangement, comme des tiroirs sous l'escalier ou des meubles pliants. Toute une série de « trucs » qui ne nuisent pas à la beauté et permettent de s'adapter aux besoins et à la personnalité de ceux qui vivent dans la maison.

À travers les pages de ce livre, nous allons parcourir le monde d'est en ouest, du Canada à l'Australie en passant par les États-Unis, le Costa Rica, la Norvège ou la Chine entre autres pays, où un important groupe d'architectes et de designers de grande renommée nationale et internationale, ont développé des projets très variés de petites habitations, entre 10 et 150 m². Ce sont des projets de typologie très diverse : d'une cabine à la montagne, à un appartement dans une ville moderne ou à une maison à l'intérieur d'un yacht. Mais tous proposent des solutions de conception et de construction intelligentes et ingénieuses, avec une esthétique soignée et dans le but de s'adapter le plus possible au mode de vie de ses occupants ainsi que de prendre soin de l'environnement et, dans de nombreux cas, de s'adapter à l'environnement dans lequel ils se trouvent.

¿Es posible vivir con todas las comodidades necesarias en una vivienda con el tamaño que tiene el salón de una casa convencional? Cada vez hay más personas que están seguras de ello. La tendencia a vivir enviviendas pequeñas ha irrumpido con fuerza para quedarse; es una corriente social y arquitectónica que se ha convertido en una filosofía de vida, no solo por motivos económicos o falta de espacio en las grandes urbes, sino como una manera de vivir una vida más simple y más sostenible, con menor impacto ecológico. Tener lo justo y necesario nos permite sentirnos más ligeros y aprovechar lo que tenemos. Además, el tener una casa pequeña no significa vivir agobiados de espacio: un diseño ingenioso y minimalista que ayude a optimizar el espacio, acompañado de una decoración adecuada harán posible la creación de un ambiente abierto, único y funcional.

Realizar un proyecto de interiorismo para un espacio pequeño es un gran desafío al que cada vez más se enfrentan los diseñadores y arquitectos, ya que no solo consiste en crear ambientes con una estética atractiva sino en sacar el máximo provecho de los pocos metros cuadrados con los que se cuenten.

Son muchas las estrategias para conseguir una sensación de amplitud en espacios reducidos: crear ejes visuales longitudinales, eliminar divisiones o particiones para unificar ambientes, o procurar la mayor entrada posible de luz natural mediante tragaluces, grandes ventanas o paneles y/o cerramientos acristalados de suelo a techo son algunos de ellos.

Todos los espacios deben ser funcionales y tener su utilidad, sin que por ello renunciemos a una casa llena de estilo y con piezas que nos enamoren. Así pues, otra de las estrategias clave es diseñar muebles a medida a una escala adecuada, que además de ser visualmente estéticos, alberguen en su interior todo aquello que se necesita en una casa: un mobiliario multifuncional, tanto a la hora de dividir los espacios como de crear todo tipo de posibilidades de almacenajes, como por ejemplo, cajones bajo la escalera o muebles abatibles. Toda una serie de «trucos» que no resten belleza y que permitan adaptarse a las necesidades y a la personalidad de los que habitan en la vivienda.

A través de las páginas de este libro recorreremos el mundo de este a oeste, desde Canadá hasta Australia pasando por Estados Unidos, Costa Rica, Noruega, o China entre otros países, en los cuales un importante elenco de arquitectos y diseñadores con gran reconocimiento a nivel nacional e internacional, han desarrollado proyectos muy variados de viviendas pequeñas, de entre 10 y 150 m². Son proyectos de tipología muy diversa: desde una cabaña en la montaña, a un apartamento en una moderna ciudad o una vivienda dentro de un yate. Pero todas ellas ofrecen soluciones de diseño y construcción inteligentes e ingeniosas, con una estética cuidada y con el objetivo deadecuarse al máximo al modo de vida de sus ocupantes además de cuidar el medio ambiente y, en muchos casos, adaptarse al entorno en que se encuentran.

COTTAGE IN WOODS

3SIX0 ARCHITECTURE
PRINCIPALS: KYNA LESKI, CHRISTOPHER BARDT
PROJECT ARCHITECT: JACK RYAN

WWW.3SIX0.COM

3SIXØ Architecture was founded in 1997 and has been the recipient of numerous awards and honors. The Rhode Island chapter of the AIA has bestowed its top honors on 3SIXØ nine times in the past decade and The Boston Society of Architects has recognized 3SIXØ with six awards. In 2002 Architectural Record named 3SIXØ one of ten "vanguard" architecture firms emerging worldwide and in 2008 Architectural Record recognized 3SIXØ's STIX Restaurant as one of its annual "Record Interiors." The work of 3SIXØ has also been widely published in magazines including Architectural Record; Dwell; the Korean Magazine; Plus Architecture and Interior Design; the Japanese Journal; SPA-DE; Interior Design; Design New England; Residential Architect; Rhode Island Monthly; The Boston Globe; The Boston Herald; The Providence Journal and The Hartford Courant. Over a dozen books have featured the work of 3SIXØ: Architecture Competition Works; Collection: U.S. Architecture; Stylish Restaurants; Salons and Spas; The Architecture of Beauty; Eat! The Best of Restaurant Design.

3SIXØ Architecture wurde 1997 gegründet und hat bereits zahlreiche Auszeichnungen und Ehrungen erhalten. Die Rhode Island Chapter of the AIA hat 3SIXØ in den letzten zehn Jahren neunmal ihre höchsten Auszeichnungen verliehen und die Boston Society of Architects hat 3SIXØ mit sechs Preisen gewürdigt. 2002 wurde 3SIXØ von Architectural Record als eines von zehn weltweit aufstrebenden „Avantgarde"-Architekturbüros genannt und 2008 wurde das STIX Restaurant von 3SIXØ von Architectural Record als eines der jährlichen „Record Interiors" ausgezeichnet. Die Arbeit von 3SIXØ wurde außerdem in zahlreichen Magazinen veröffentlicht, darunter Architectural Record; Dwell; das koreanische Magazin; Plus Architecture and Interior Design; das japanische Journal; SPA-DE; Interior Design; Design New England; Residential Architect; Rhode Island Monthly; The Boston Globe; The Boston Herald; The Providence Journal und The Hartford Courant. Mehr als ein Dutzend Bücher haben die Arbeit von 3SIXØ vorgestellt: Architecture Competition Works; Collection: U.S. Architecture; Stilvolle Restaurants; Salons und Spas; The Architecture of Beauty; Eat! Das Beste aus dem Restaurant-Design.

3SIX0 ARCHITECTURE

3SIXØ Architecture a été fondée en 1997 et a reçu de nombreux prix et distinctions. Le chapitre de Rhode Island de l'AIA a décerné ses plus hautes distinctions à 3SIXØ neuf fois au cours de la dernière décennie et la Boston Society of Architects a récompensé 3SIXØ à six reprises. En 2002, Architectural Record a désigné 3SIXØ comme l'un des dix cabinets d'architecture « d'avant-garde » émergeant dans le monde entier et en 2008, Architectural Record a désigné le restaurant STIX de 3SIXØ comme l'un de ses « Record Interiors » annuels. Le travail de 3SIXØ a également été largement publié dans des magazines tels que Architectural Record, Dwell, le Korean Magazine, Plus Architecture and Interior Design, le journal japonais, SPA-DE, Interior Design, Design New England, Residential Architect, Rhode Island Monthly, The Boston Globe, The Boston Herald, The Providence Journal et The Hartford Courant. Plus d'une douzaine de livres ont présenté le travail de 3SIXØ : Architecture Competition Works ; Collection : U.S. Architecture ; Stylish Restaurants ; Salons and Spas ; The Architecture of Beauty ; Eat ! The Best of Restaurant Design.

3SIXØ Architecture se fundó en 1997 y ha recibido numerosos premios y distinciones. El capítulo de Rhode Island de la AIA ha concedido sus máximos honores a 3SIXØ nueve veces en la última década y la Sociedad de Arquitectos de Boston ha reconocido a 3SIXØ con seis premios. En 2002 Architectural Record nombró a 3SIXØ uno de los diez estudios de arquitectura de «vanguardia» que están surgiendo en todo el mundo y en 2008 Architectural Record reconoció el restaurante STIX de 3SIXØ como uno de sus «Record Interiors» anuales. El trabajo de 3SIXØ también ha sido ampliamente publicado en revistas como Architectural Record; Dwell; Korean Magazine; Plus Architecture and Interior Design; el Japanese Journal; SPA-DE; Interior Design; Design New England; Residential Architect; Rhode Island Monthly; The Boston Globe; The Boston Herald; The Providence Journal y The Hartford Courant. Más de una docena de libros han recogido el trabajo de 3SIXØ: Architecture Competition Works; Collection: U.S. Architecture; Stylish Restaurants; Salons and Spas; The Architecture of Beauty; Eat! The Best of Restaurant Design.

COTTAGE IN WOODS

49 M² // FOSTER, RHODE ISLAND, UNITED STATES
PHOTOS © 3SIX0 ARCHITECTURE

Our client, a ceramicist, and artist, lives in a loft residence in a renovated manufacturing building in Providence. Although it is large, open, airy, and home to her studio, the loft lacks the outdoor space she desires for a balanced life. The request was simple: a cottage in the woods for our client to retreat from urban loft living, reconnect with nature, and develop a garden landscape with walking trails. The design challenge of this project is tight. The exterior of the cottage, a cubic volume measuring 25' x 25' x 25', is faceted like a gem. Facets are cut to shed water, carved into a protected entry, or shaped for a venting chimney. Like the rocks of the site, the cottage is an understated angular block that opens up in celebration of nature. The cottage's exterior is entirely clad in Alaska yellow cedar—a durable wood that has been left untreated and will weather to a silver-grey.

Unser Kunde, ein Keramiker und Künstler, lebt in einer Loft-ähnlichen Wohnung in einem renovierten Industriegebäude in Providence. Obwohl es groß, offen und luftig ist und ihr Atelier beherbergt, fehlt es an Platz im Freien. Die Anfrage war einfach: ein Haus im Wald für unseren Kunden, um sich vom städtischen Leben zurückzuziehen und sich wieder mit der Natur zu verbinden und eine Gartenlandschaft mit Wanderwegen zu gestalten. Das Äußere des Häuschens, ein kubisches Volumen, ist wie ein Juwel geschnitzt. Profile werden geschnitten, um Wasser abzuweisen, in einen geschützten Eingang eingearbeitet oder zur Abdeckung eines Lüftungsschornsteins geformt. Wie die umliegenden Felsen ist auch das Haus ein unaufdringlicher, kantiger Block, der sich öffnet, um die Natur zu genießen. Das Äußere des Hauses ist komplett mit gelber Zeder aus Alaska verkleidet, einem langlebigen Holz, das unbehandelt ist und mit der Zeit eine silbrig-graue Farbe annimmt.

Notre client, un céramiste et artiste, vit dans une résidence de style loft dans un bâtiment industriel rénové à Providence. Bien qu'il soit grand, ouvert et aéré, et qu'il abrite son studio, il manque d'espace extérieur. La demande était simple : une maison dans les bois pour que notre client puisse se retirer de la vie urbaine et se reconnecter avec la nature et concevoir un jardin paysager avec des sentiers de promenade. L'extérieur du chalet, un volume cubique, est sculpté comme un bijou. Les profils sont découpés pour repousser l'eau, taillés dans une entrée protégée ou façonnés pour couvrir une cheminée de ventilation. Comme les rochers environnants, la maison est un bloc angulaire discret qui s'ouvre pour profiter de la nature. L'extérieur de la maison est entièrement revêtu de cèdre jaune d'Alaska, un bois durable qui n'a pas été traité pour prendre une couleur gris argenté avec le temps.

Nuestra clienta, ceramista y artista, vive en una residencia tipo *loft* en un edificio industrial renovado en Providence. Aunque es grande, abierto y ventilado, y alberga su estudio, carece de espacio exterior. La petición era sencilla: una casa en el bosque para que nuestra clienta se retirara de la vida urbana y volviera a conectar con la naturaleza y diseñar un paisaje ajardinado con senderos para caminar. El exterior de la casa de campo, un volumen cúbico, está tallado como una joya. Los perfiles se cortan para repeler el agua, se tallan en una entrada protegida o se moldean para cubrir una chimenea de ventilación. Al igual que las rocas de su entorno, la casa es un bloque angular discreto que se abre para disfrutar la naturaleza. El exterior de la casa está completamente revestido de cedro amarillo de Alaska, una madera duradera que se ha dejado sin tratar para que con el tiempo adquiera un color gris plateado.

Study models

Scale model view from above

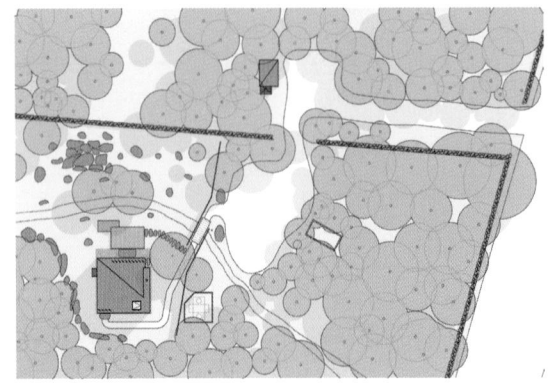

Site plan

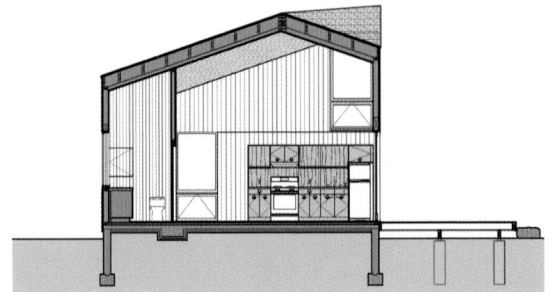

Section

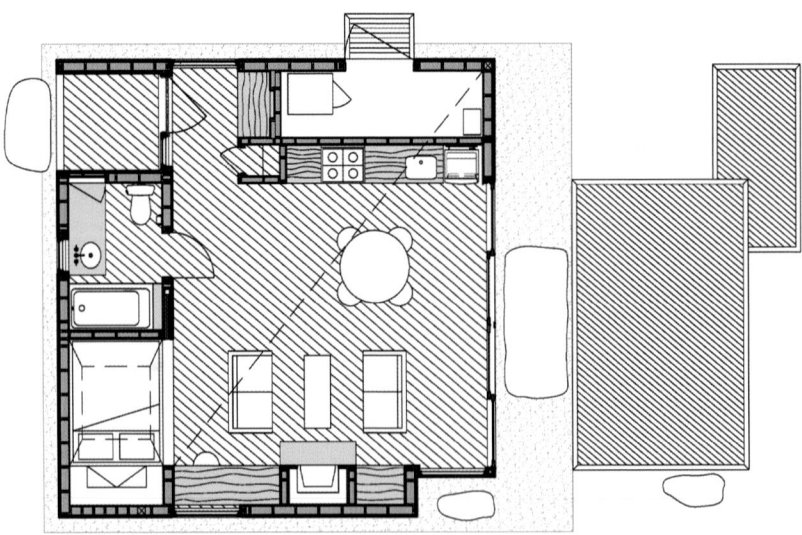

Floor plan

Wall kitchen sketch

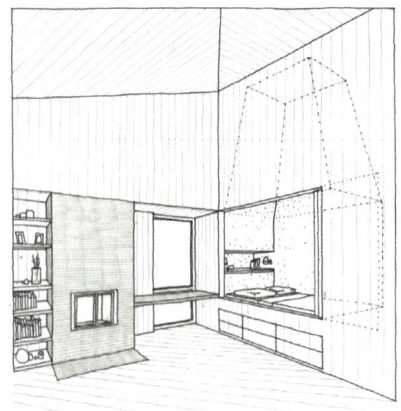

Sleeping nook sketch

ROBINSON HUT

A1ARCHITECTS

DAVID MAŠTÁLKA, LENKA KŘEMENOVÁ

WWW.A1ARCHITECTS.CZ

At first glance insignificant details shape the uniqueness of our life. And we, in our work, look for the magic of these little things in ordinary things around us and in things that inspire us...

First independent projects of a1architects date to the year 2003. Two years later a studio and a creative workshop are formed in Prague. Today this studio is built on the works of architects Lenka Křemenová and David Maštálka who initially studied together at the Academy of Arts, Architecture and Design in Prague.

Interdisciplinary communication and searching for unique solutions are the main characteristics of our studio. All of our projects are solved in a complex way, starting with the whole concept and moving on to the interior details and design of utility objects.

Auf den ersten Blick unbedeutende Details prägen die Einzigartigkeit unseres Lebens. Und wir suchen in unserer Arbeit nach der Magie dieser kleinen Dinge in den gewöhnlichen Dingen, die uns umgeben, und in den Dingen, die uns inspirieren...

Die ersten eigenständigen Projekte von a1architects gehen auf das Jahr 2003 zurück. Zwei Jahre später wurde ein kreatives Atelier und eine Werkstatt in Prag gegründet. Heute baut dieses Studio auf den Arbeiten der Architekten Lenka Křemenová und David Maštálka auf, die gemeinsam an der Akademie für Kunst, Architektur und Design in Prag studiert haben.

Interdisziplinäre Kommunikation und die Suche nach einzigartigen Lösungen sind die Hauptmerkmale unseres Studios. Alle Projekte werden komplex gelöst, angefangen von der Gesamtkonzeption über die Innenraumdetails bis hin zum Design von Gebrauchsgegenständen.

A1ARCHITECTS

À première vue, des détails insignifiants façonnent le caractère unique de notre vie. Et nous, dans notre travail, nous cherchons la magie de ces petites choses dans l'ordinaire qui nous entourent et dans se qui nous inspirent... Les premiers projets indépendants des a1architects remontent à 2003. Deux ans plus tard, un studio et un atelier de création ont été fondés à Prague. Aujourd'hui, cet atelier est construit sur les travaux des architectes Lenka Křemenová et David Maštálka qui ont étudié ensemble à l'Académie des arts, de l'architecture et du design de Prague.

La communication interdisciplinaire et la recherche de solutions uniques sont les principales caractéristiques de notre studio. Tous nos projets sont résolus de manière complexe, en partant de l'ensemble du concept et en passant par les détails intérieurs et la conception d'objets utilitaires.

A primera vista, los detalles insignificantes dan forma a la singularidad de nuestra vida. Y nosotros, en nuestro trabajo, buscamos la magia de estas pequeñas cosas en las cosas ordinarias que nos rodean y en las cosas que nos inspiran...

Los primeros proyectos independientes de a1architects datan del año 2003. Dos años más tarde, se funda en Praga un estudio y taller creativo. Hoy en día este estudio está construido sobre los trabajos de los arquitectos Lenka Křemenová y David Maštálka que habían estudiado juntos en la Academia de Artes, Arquitectura y Diseño de Praga.

La comunicación interdisciplinaria y la búsqueda de soluciones unicas son las principales características de nuestro estudio. Todos nuestros proyectos se resuelven de forma compleja, empezando por el concepto completo y pasando por los detalles interiores y el diseño de objetos utilitarios.

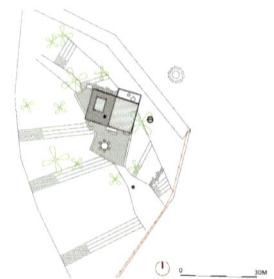

Site plan

ROBINSON HUT

60 M² // CENTRAL BOHEMIA, CZECH REPUBLIC

PHOTOS © A1ARCHITECTS – DAVID MAŠTÁLKA

There was an old hut in a marvelous hidden place called "The Island". It is a unique forested small hill in the middle of Central Bohemia country-side, with its own specific atmosphere. Which gives the feeling of isolation within secret landscape. The site is divided into very steep hill part and flat meadow beneath. The task of the project was complete rebuilding of the original structure and just its underground storage stone masonry was used and "recycled" as fundament for the new small house. The main discussion within the whole project was how to design a minimal house for the couple, who would use it as weekend house and later as their home when retired. The architecture of this tiny forest house has an ambition to be natural part of this charming place with its own magic of being a Robinson´s secret shed.

Es gab mal eine alte Hütte an einem wundervollen, versteckten Ort namens „Die Insel". Es handelt sich um einen einzigartigen, kleinen, bewaldeten Hügel inmitten der mittelböhmischen Landschaft, mit einer eigenen Atmosphäre, die das Gefühl der Abgeschiedenheit innerhalb einer geheimen Landschaft vermittelt. Der Ort liegt in einem sehr steilen Teil des Hügels und in einer flachen Wiese darunter. Die Aufgabe des Projekts war die vollständige Rekonstruktion der ursprünglichen Struktur und nur ihr Keller aus Steinmauern wurde als Fundament für das neue kleine Haus verwendet und wiederverwertet. Die größte Frage innerhalb des gesamten Projekts war, wie man ein minimalistisches Haus für das Paar entwerfen könnte, das es als Wochenendhaus und später als ihr Zuhause nutzen würde, wenn sie in Rente gehen. Die Architektur dieses kleinen Waldhauses hat den Ehrgeiz, ein natürlicher Teil dieses bezaubernden Ortes zu sein, mit seiner eigenen Magie eines geheimen Robinsonschuppens.

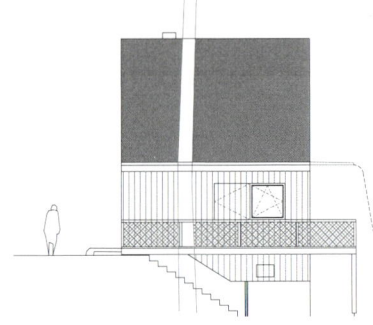

Il y avait une vieille cabane dans un merveilleux endroit caché appelé « L'île ». C'est une petite colline boisée unique au milieu de la campagne de Bohême centrale, avec son atmosphère propre, qui donne le sentiment d'être isolé dans un paysage secret. Le lieu est immergé dans une partie très escarpée de la colline et dans une prairie plate en contrebas. La tâche du projet était la reconstruction complète de la structure originale et seul son sous-sol de murs en pierre a été utilisé et « recyclé » comme fondation pour la nouvelle petite maison. Le principal débat dans le cadre de ce projet était de savoir comment concevoir une maison minimaliste pour le couple, qui l'utiliserait comme maison de week-end et plus tard comme leur maison lorsqu'ils prendraient leur retraite. L'architecture de cette petite maison forestière a l'ambition de faire partie intégrante de ce lieu charmant avec sa propre magie d'être une cabane secrète de Robinson.

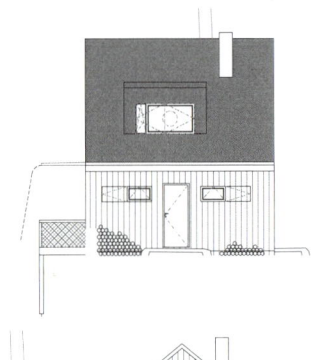

Había una vieja cabaña en un maravilloso lugar escondido llamado «La Isla». Es una pequeña colina boscosa única en medio del campo de Bohemia Central, con su propia atmósfera, lo que da la sensación de aislamiento dentro de un paisaje secreto. El lugar se sumerge en una parte muy empinada de la colina y en una pradera plana debajo. La tarea del proyecto fue la reconstrucción completa de la estructura original y solo se utilizó y «recicló» su sótano de muros de piedra como cimientos para la nueva pequeña casa. El principal debate dentro de todo el proyecto fue cómo diseñar una casa minimalista para la pareja, que la utilizaría como casa de fin de semana y más tarde como su hogar cuando se retiraran. La arquitectura de esta pequeña casa del bosque tiene la ambición de ser parte natural de este encantador lugar con su propia magia de ser una cabaña secreta de Robinson.

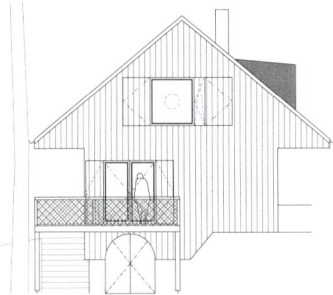

Elevations

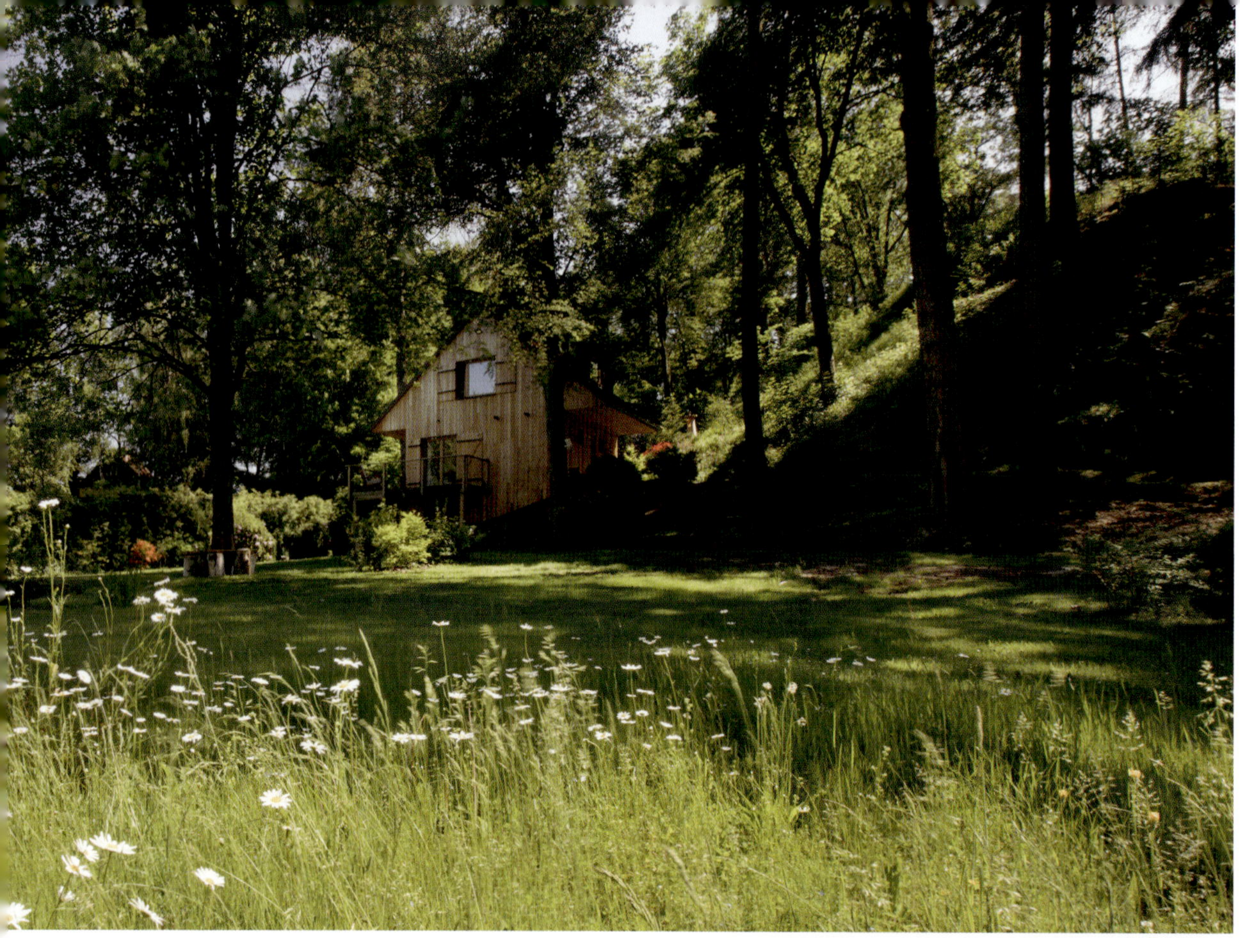

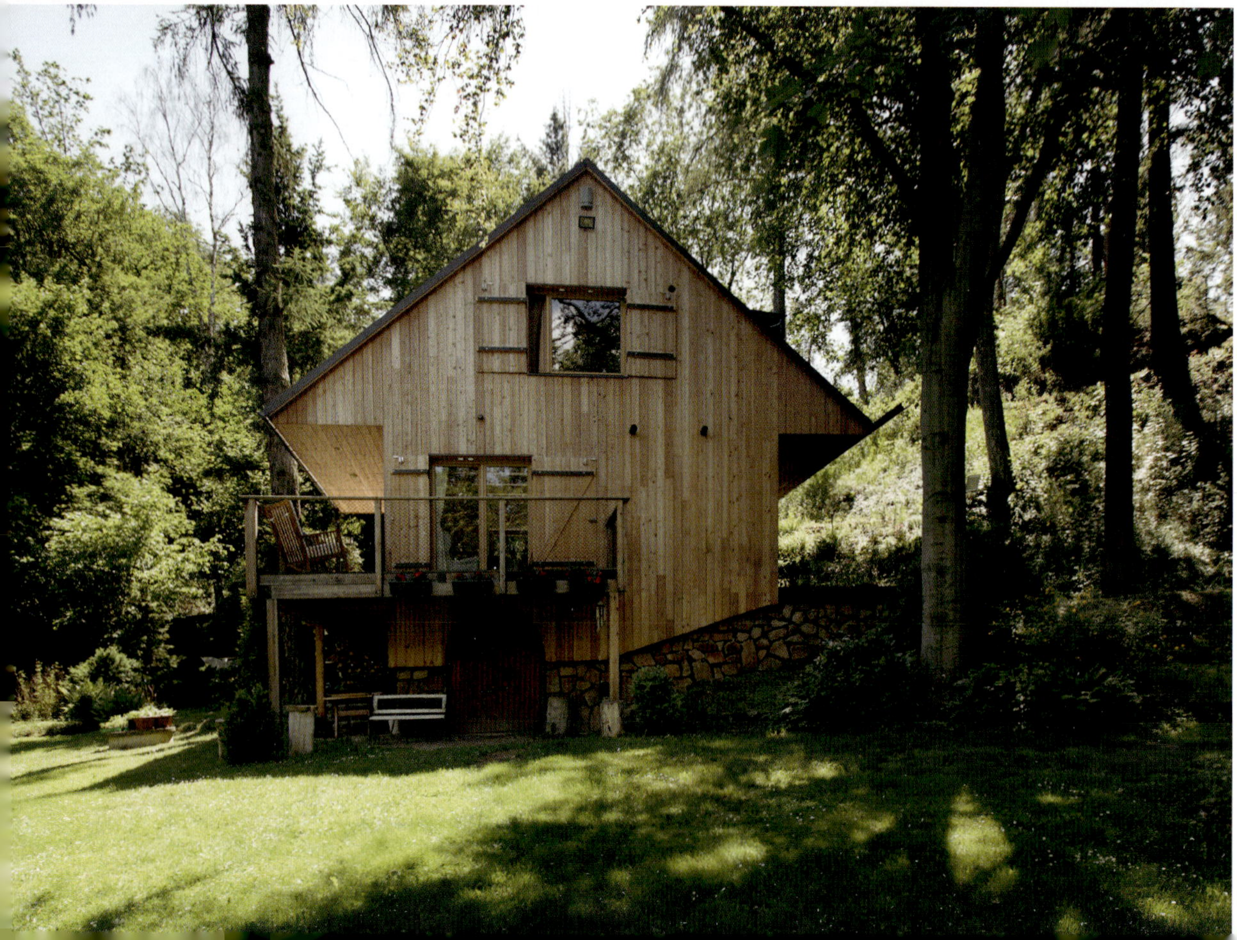

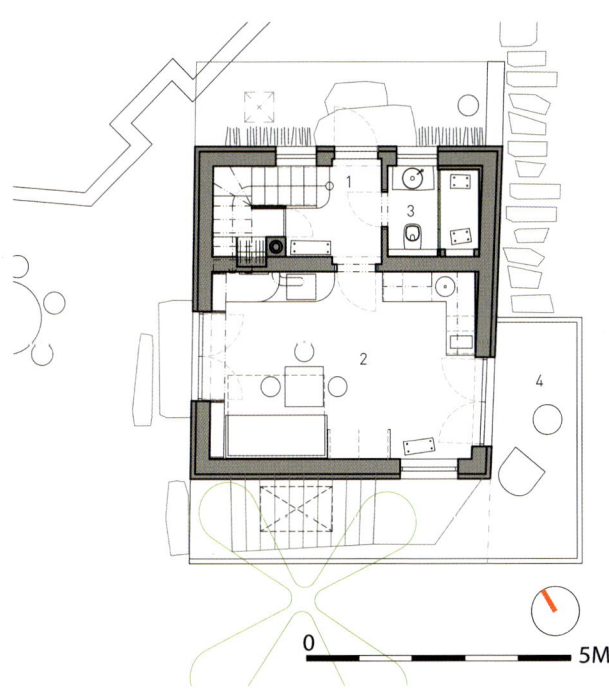

Ground floor plan

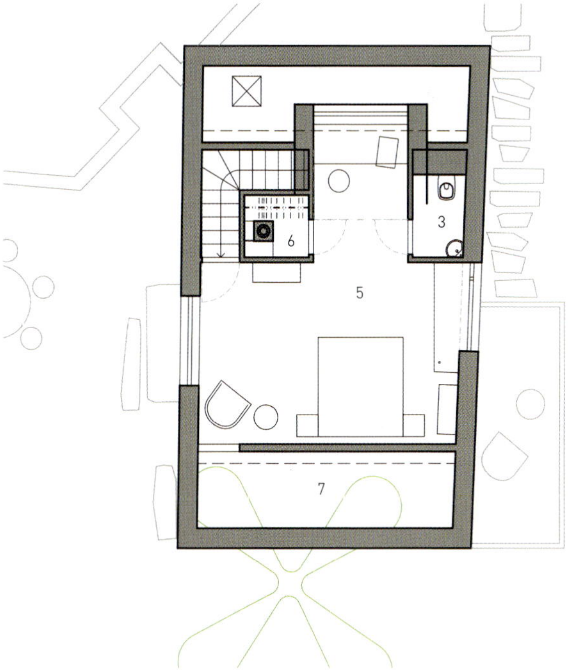

First floor plan

1. Entrance
2. Living space + kitchen
3. Toilet
4. Veranda
5. Bedroom
6. Wardrobe
7. Storage

0   5M

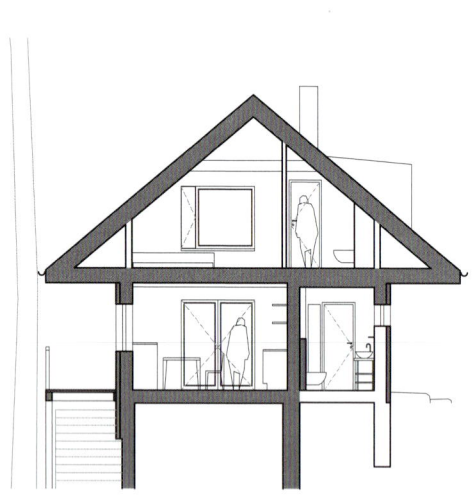

Section

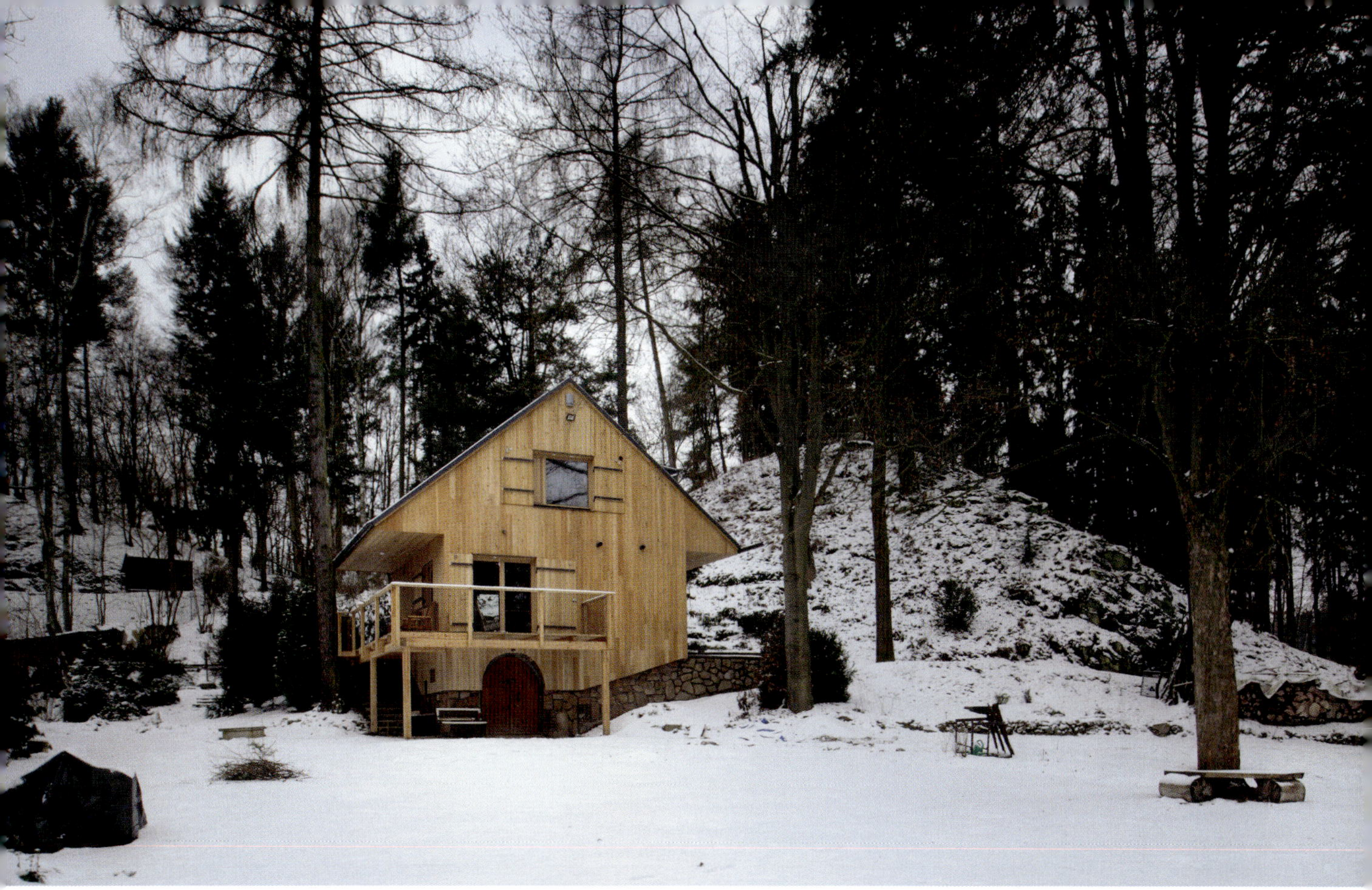

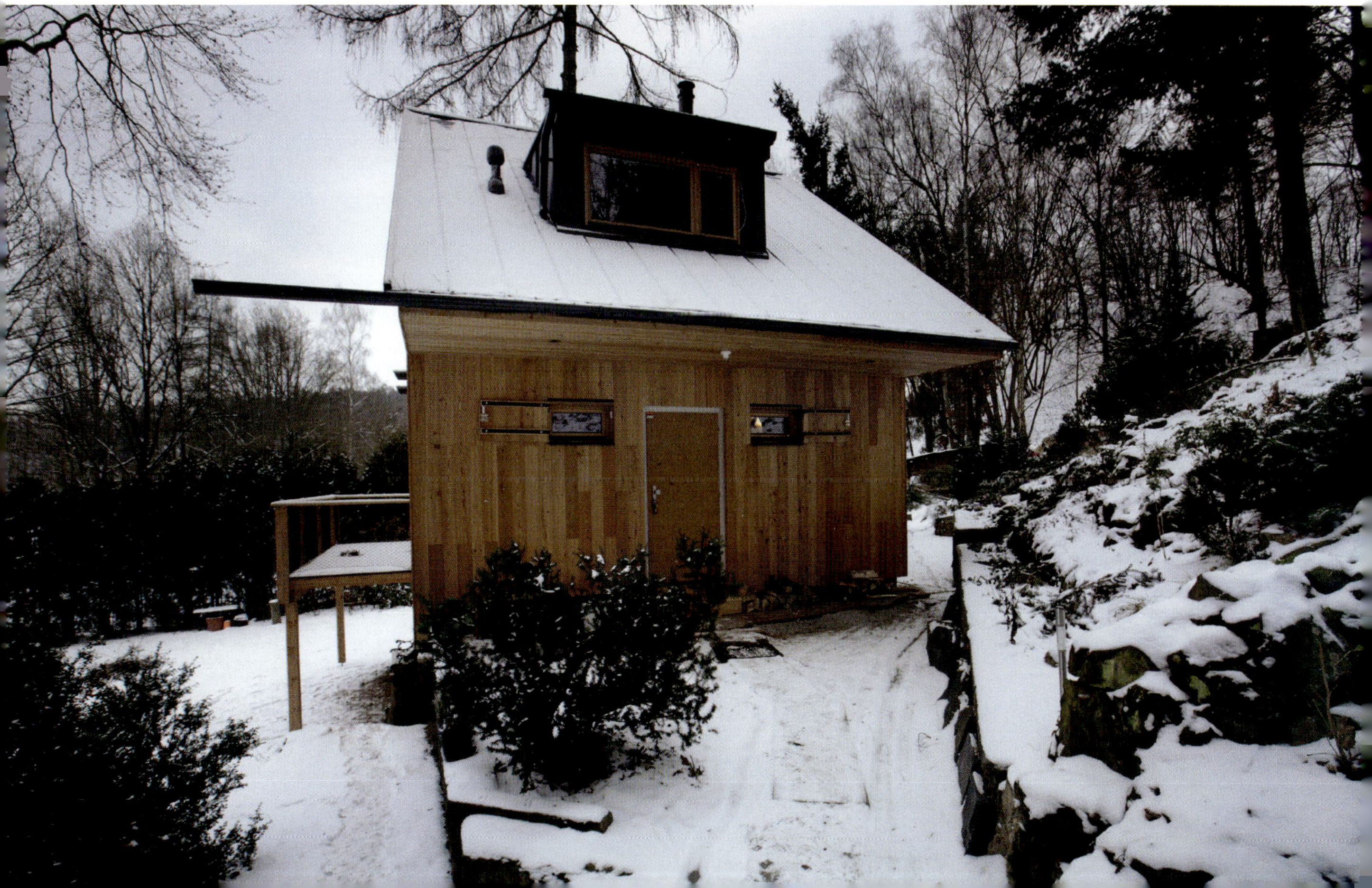

NEUBAU STADTHAUS
IN PFULLINGEN

BAMBERG ARCHITEKTUR
THOMAS BAMBERG

BAMBERG-ARCHITEKTUR.DE

Single-family houses, apartment buildings, public buildings, traffic structures and town planning. The projects are specifically adapted to the respective properties and topographies and to the urban environment.
The simple, clearly structured buildings are specifically oriented to their surroundings and nature. Generous openings let in light and create special light and ambience situations. The design work ranges from the form of the building to the interior architecture and the planning of the associated lighting and the design of the built-in furniture which, together with the reduced choice of materials, create spaces that radiate tranquillity and security.

Einfamilienhäuser, Mehrfamilienhäuser, öffentliche Gebäude, Verkehrsbauwerke und Stadtplanung. Die Projekte sind spezifisch an die jeweiligen Grundstücke und Topographien sowie an das städtische Umfeld angepasst.
Die einfachen und klar strukturierten Gebäude orientieren sich gezielt an ihrer Umgebung und der Natur. Großzügige Öffnungen lassen Licht herein und schaffen besondere Licht- und Stimmungslagen. Die Entwurfsarbeit reicht von der Form des Gebäudes über die Innenarchitektur und die Planung der zugehörigen Beleuchtung bis hin zum Design der Einbaumöbel, die zusammen mit der reduzierten Materialwahl Räume schaffen, die Ruhe und Geborgenheit ausstrahlen.

BAMBERG ARCHITEKTUR

Maisons unifamiliales, immeubles d'habitation, bâtiments publics, structures de circulation et urbanisme. Les projets sont spécifiquement adaptés aux propriétés et topographies respectives et à l'environnement urbain.

Les bâtiments simples et clairement structurés sont spécifiquement orientés vers leur environnement et leur nature. Des ouvertures généreuses laissent entrer la lumière et créent des situations particulières de lumière et d'atmosphère. Le travail de conception va de la forme du bâtiment à l'architecture intérieure, en passant par la planification de l'éclairage associé et la conception du mobilier intégré qui, avec le choix réduit de matériaux, crée des espaces qui rayonnent de tranquillité et de sécurité.

Viviendas unifamiliares, edificios de apartamentos, edificios públicos, estructuras de tráfico y urbanismo. Los proyectos se adaptan específicamente a las respectivas propiedades y topografías y al entorno urbano.

Los edificios simples y claramente estructurados están específicamente orientados a su entorno y a la naturaleza. Las generosas aberturas dejan entrar la luz y generan situaciones especiales de luz y ambiente. El trabajo de diseño abarca desde la forma del edificio hasta la arquitectura interior y la planificación de la iluminación asociada y el diseño de los muebles empotrados que junto con la elección reducida de materiales, crean espacios que irradian tranquilidad y seguridad.

NEUBAU STADTHAUS IN PFULLINGEN

192 M² // PFULLINGEN, GERMANY

PHOTOS © MARIO P. RODRIGUES

This modern detached house stands on a 7 x 20 m plot in the centre of the city. Arranged over four floors, the top floor, which has a sauna and fitness area, offers a beautiful view of the Swabian Alb over the rooftops of the city from the terrace. Due to the narrowness of the site and the hustle and bustle of the street, the entire house was built with prefabricated, thermally insulated concrete parts. The concrete surfaces were contrasted with a high-quality interior finish. Alongside the concrete, the predominance of white is absolute in both walls and furnishings, and contrasts with a rustic oak floor that gives the living areas a warm, homely atmosphere. The east- and west-facing aluminium windows allow for maximum light incidence, which is reinforced by the skylight in the attic that lets daylight fall on the central area of the house.

Auf einem Grundstück von 7 x 20 Metern, im Zentrum der Stadt, steht dieses moderne Einfamilienhaus. Auf vier Etagen verteilt, bietet die oberste Etage mit Sauna und Fitnessbereich von der Terrasse aus einen schönen Blick auf die Schwäbische Alb über die Dächer der Stadt. Aufgrund des schmalen Grundstücks und der Hektik der Straße wurde das gesamte Haus mit vorgefertigten, wärmegedämmten Betonteilen gebaut. Die Betonflächen wurden mit einem hochwertigen Innenausbau kontrastiert. Das starke Weiß der Wände, Beton und Möbel steht in Kontrast zu einem rustikalen Eichenboden, der den Wohnbereichen eine warme und gemütliche Atmosphäre verleiht. Die nach Osten und Westen ausgerichteten Aluminiumfenster ermöglichen einen maximalen Lichteinfall, der durch das Oberlicht im Dachgeschoss, das Tageslicht auf den zentralen Bereich des Hauses fallen lässt, noch verstärkt wird.

Sur un terrain de 7 x 20 mètres, au centre de la ville, se dresse cette maison individuelle moderne. Conçu sur quatre étages, le dernier dispose d'un sauna et d'un espace de remise en forme, offre depuis la terrasse une belle vue sur le Jura souabe et sur les toits de la ville. En raison de l'étroitesse du terrain et de l'agitation de la rue, toute la maison a été construite avec des éléments en béton préfabriqués et isolés thermiquement. Les surfaces en béton ont été mises en contraste avec une finition intérieure de haute qualité. À côté du béton, la prédominance du blanc est absolue, tant dans les murs que dans le mobilier, et contraste avec un parquet en chêne rustique qui donne aux pièces de vie une atmosphère chaleureuse et accueillante. Les fenêtres en aluminium orientées à l'est et à l'ouest permettent une incidence maximale de la lumière, qui est renforcée par la lucarne du grenier qui laisse la lumière du jour tomber sur la zone centrale de la maison.

En un terreno de 7 x 20 metros, en el centro de la ciudad, se levanta esta moderna vivienda unifamiliar. Organizada en cuatro plantas, en la última, que cuenta con zona de sauna y fitness, se puede disfrutar desde la terraza de preciosas vistas a la Jura de Suabia sobre los tejados de la ciudad. Debido a la estrechez del terreno y al ajetreo de la calle, toda la casa se construyó con piezas prefabricadas de hormigón con aislamiento térmico. Las superficies de hormigón se contrastaron con un acabado interior de alta calidad. Junto al hormigón, el predominio del blanco es absoluto tanto en paredes como en el mobiliario, y contrasta con un suelo de roble rústico que proporciona a las zonas de estar un ambiente cálido y hogareño. Las ventanas de aluminio orientadas hacia el este y el oeste permiten una máxima incidencia de luz, que se ve reforzada por el tragaluz del ático que deja caer la luz del día sobre la zona central de la casa.

Site plan

Front elevation

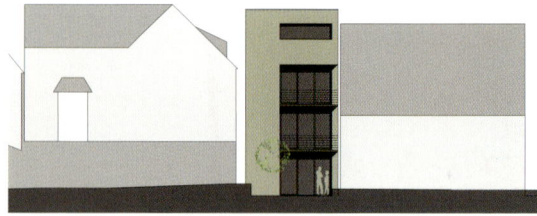

Rear elevation

Section 2-2

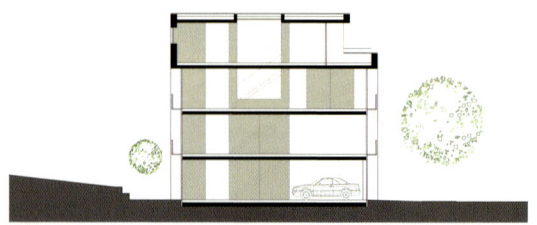

Section 1-1

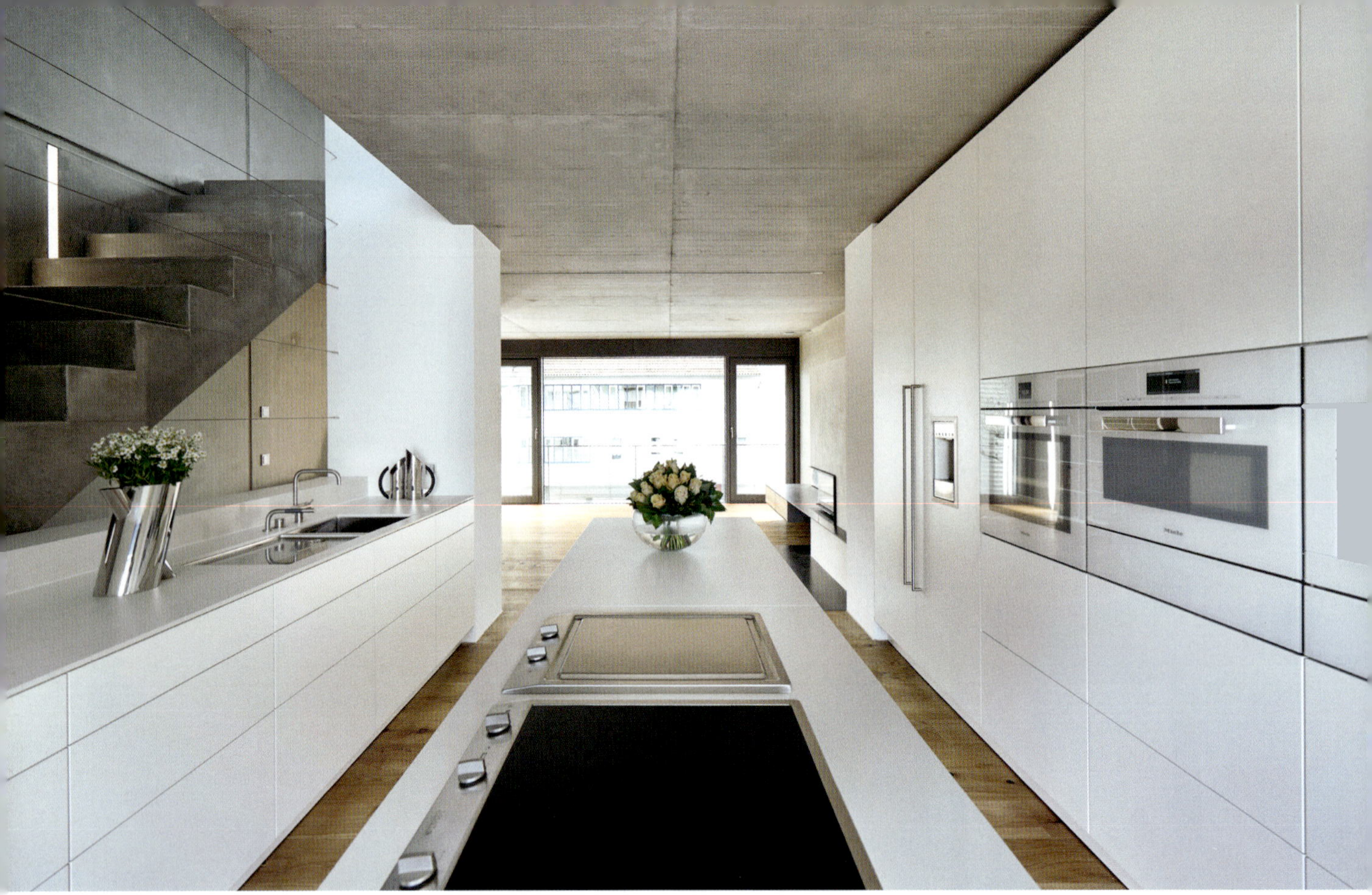

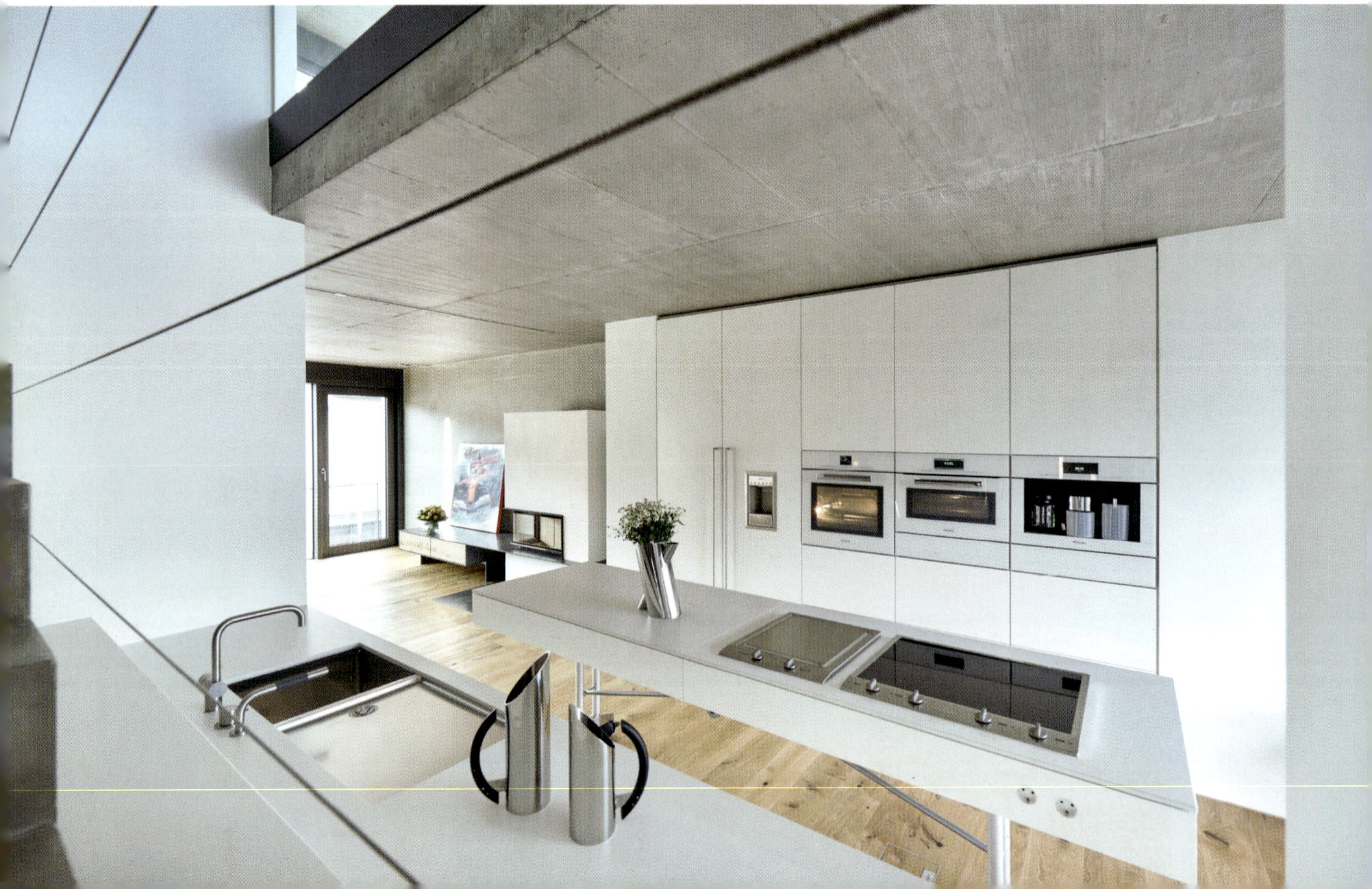

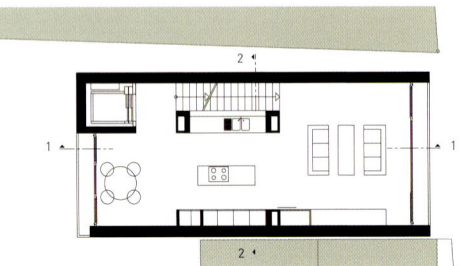

First floor plan

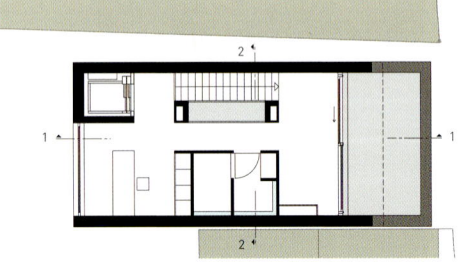

Third floor plan

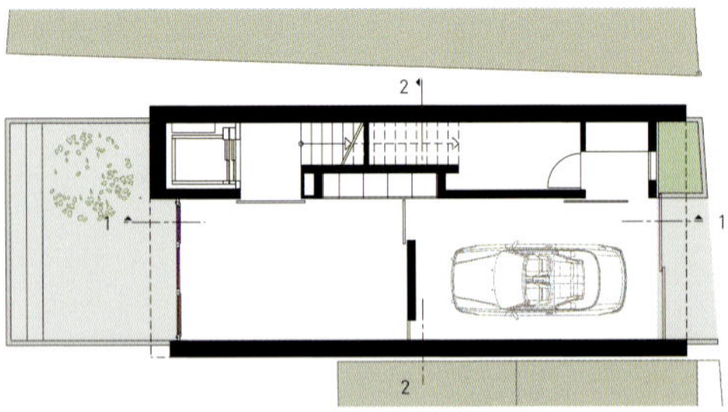

Ground floor plan

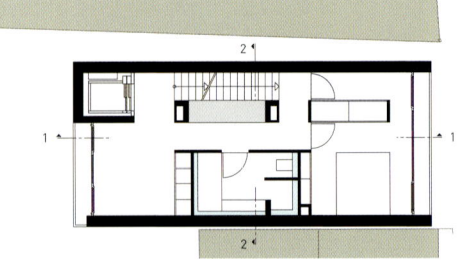

Second floor plan

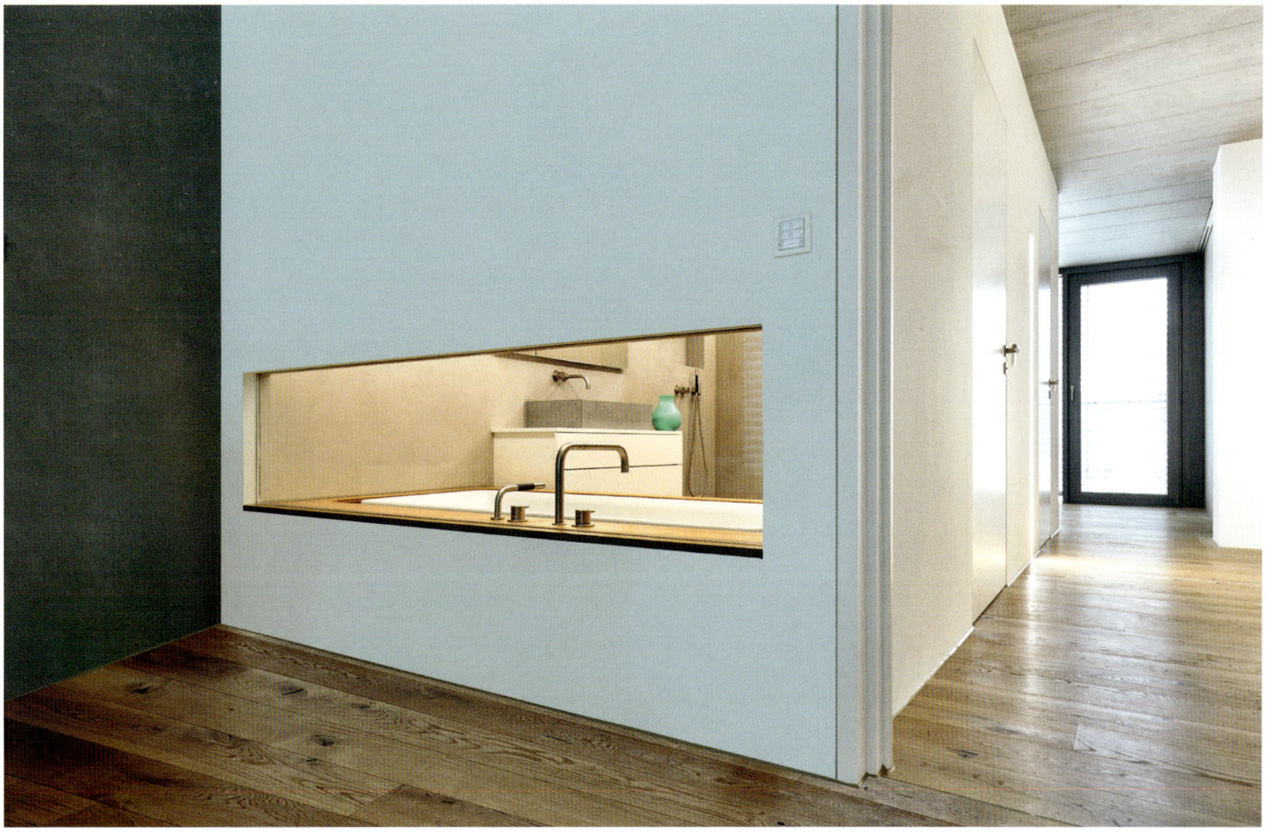

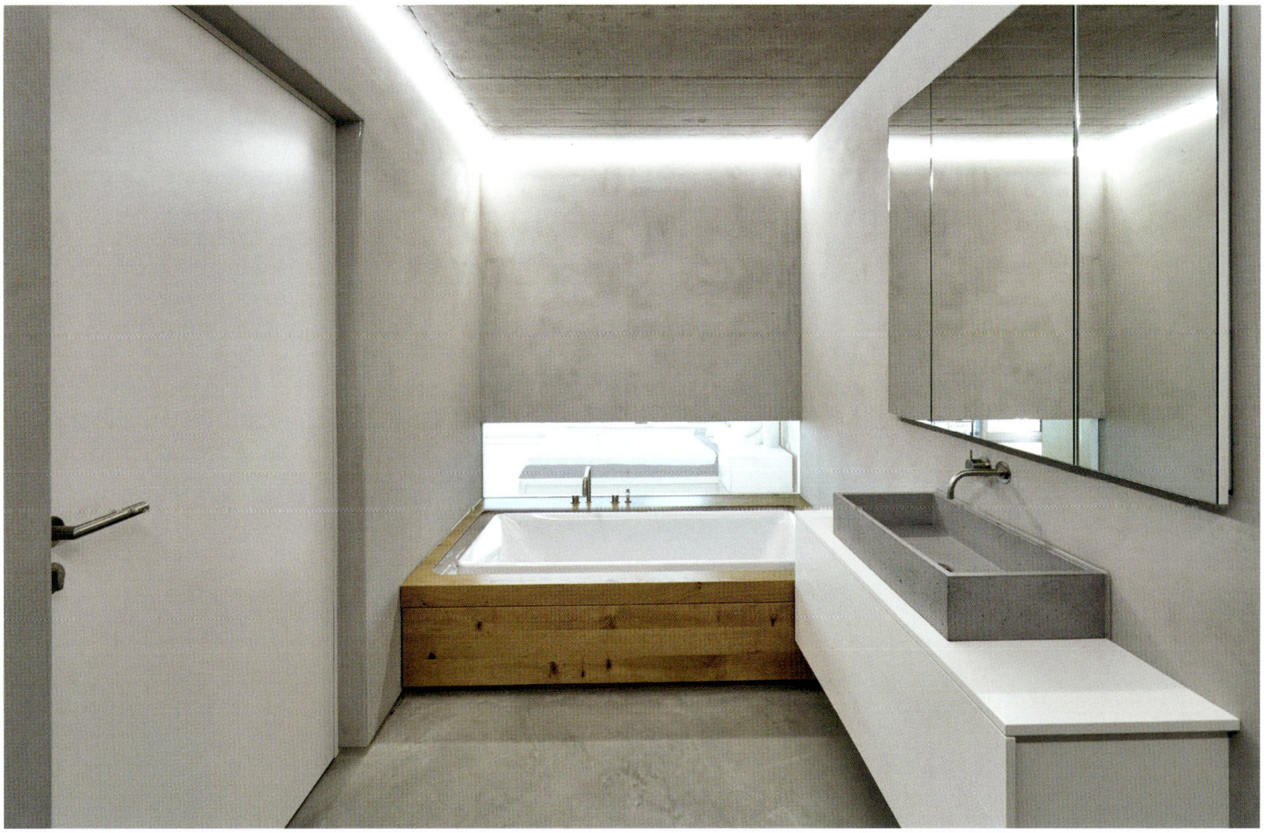

GRANNY PAD

BEST PRACTICE ARCHITECTURE
KAILIN GREGGA, IAN BUTCHER

WWW.BESTPRACTICEARCHITECTURE.COM

Best Practice is a nimble-minded, design-intensive firm located in Seattle, founded in 2011, and led by Ian Butcher and Kailin Gregga. The firm engages in a diverse range of work, from residential to large-scale office and cultural projects, taking inspiration from their clients' needs and choreographing intuitive experiences. Best Practice seeks to provide innovative solutions that explore the precarious balance between content, beauty and function. The firm received the 2019 Emerging Firm Award from the AIA Northwest and Pacific Regions, as well as an AIA Honor award and AIA Home of Distinction award for multifamily project Big Mouth House.

Best Practice ist ein flinkes, designintensives Unternehmen mit Sitz in Seattle, das 2011 gegründet wurde und von Ian Butcher und Kailin Gregga geleitet wird. Das Büro beschäftigt sich mit einem breiten Spektrum an Arbeiten, von Wohngebäuden bis hin zu großen Büro- und Kulturprojekten, wobei es sich von den Bedürfnissen seiner Kunden inspirieren lässt und intuitive Erfahrungen choreografiert. Best Practice ist bestrebt, innovative Lösungen anzubieten, die das prekäre Gleichgewicht zwischen Inhalt, Schönheit und Funktion erforschen. Das Büro erhielt den 2019 Emerging Firm Award von der AIA Northwest and Pacific Regions, sowie einen AIA Honor Award und einen AIA Home of Distinction Award für das Mehrfamilienhausprojekt Big Mouth House.

BEST PRACTICE ARCHITECTURE

Best Practice est une entreprise à l'esprit agile et au design intensif située à Seattle, fondée en 2011 et dirigée par Ian Butcher et Kailin Gregga. Le cabinet s'engage dans une gamme diversifiée de travaux, allant du résidentiel aux projets culturels et de bureaux à grande échelle, en s'inspirant des besoins de leurs clients et en chorégraphiant des expériences intuitives. Best Practice cherche à fournir des solutions innovantes qui explorent l'équilibre précaire entre le contenu, la beauté et la fonction. Le cabinet a reçu le prix du cabinet émergent 2019 des régions Nord-Ouest et Pacifique de l'AIA, ainsi qu'un prix d'honneur et un prix de distinction de l'AIA pour le projet multifamilial Big Mouth House.

Best Practice es una empresa ágil y de diseño intensivo situada en Seattle, fundada en 2011 y dirigida por Ian Butcher y Kailin Gregga. La firma se dedica a una amplia gama de trabajos, desde proyectos residenciales hasta proyectos culturales y de oficinas a gran escala, inspirándose en las necesidades de sus clientes y coreografiando experiencias intuitivas. Best Practice busca ofrecer soluciones innovadoras que exploren el precario equilibrio entre contenido, belleza y función. La firma recibió el Premio a la Firma Emergente 2019 de las Regiones del Noroeste y del Pacífico de la AIA, así como un premio de Honor de la AIA y un premio AIA Home of Distinction por el proyecto multifamiliar Big Mouth House.

GRANNY PAD

53 M² // SEATTLE, WASHINGTON, UNITED STATES
PHOTOS © ED SOZINHO

The project began when the client couldn't find appropriate housing for "Granny" in their neighborhood. With a growing family, they didn't have enough space in their house to accommodate her needs and maintain the privacy everyone in the family wanted. And with a shortage of affordable housing in Seattle, the option of moving to a larger house in the city was out of reach. Best Practice saw converting the client's existing garage (previously used as storage) as the perfect solution. Design considerations included looking at the project on both a short-term and long-term timeline. First, Best Practice needed to address the immediate needs of the client. They also considered future uses of the space as a possible rental unit, studio, office, or other income-generating projects for the family.

Das Projekt begann, als der Bauherr in seiner eigenen Nachbarschaft keine geeignete Wohnung für „Einliegerwohnung" finden konnte. Mit einer wachsenden Familie hatten sie zu Hause nicht genug Platz, um ihre Bedürfnisse zu erfüllen und die Privatsphäre zu wahren, die alle Familienmitglieder benötigten. Und angesichts des Mangels an erschwinglichem Wohnraum in Seattle war die Option, in ein größeres Haus in der Stadt zu ziehen, außer Reichweite. Best Practice war der Meinung, dass der Umbau der Garage des Hauses, die zuvor als Lagerraum genutzt wurde, die perfekte Lösung war. Zu den Designüberlegungen gehörte die Betrachtung des Projekts sowohl auf kurze als auch auf lange Sicht. Also musste Best Practice zunächst auf die unmittelbaren Bedürfnisse des Kunden reagieren. Und dann die zukünftige Nutzung des Raumes als mögliche Mieteinheit, Studio oder andere Projekte, die ein Einkommen für die Familie generieren könnten, in Betracht zu ziehen.

Le projet a débuté lorsque le client n'a pas pu trouver de logement approprié pour « maison de grand-mère » dans son propre quartier. Avec une famille qui s'agrandit, ils n'avaient pas assez d'espace à la maison pour répondre à leurs besoins et préserver l'intimité dont tous les membres de la famille avaient besoin. Et avec la pénurie de logements abordables à Seattle, l'option de déménager dans une maison plus grande dans la ville était hors de portée. Best Practice a estimé que la conversion du garage de la maison, qui servait auparavant de lieu de stockage, était la solution idéale. Les considérations relatives à la conception comprenaient l'examen du projet à court et à long terme. La meilleure pratique devait donc d'abord répondre aux besoins immédiats du client. Et ensuite d'envisager les utilisations futures de l'espace comme une éventuelle unité de location, un studio ou d'autres projets qui pourraient générer des revenus pour la famille.

El proyecto comenzó cuando el cliente no pudo encontrar una vivienda adecuada para su «abuelita» en su mismo barrio. Con una familia en crecimiento, no tenían suficiente espacio en casa para cubrir sus necesidades y mantener la privacidad que todos los miembros de la familia requerían. Y con la escasez de viviendas asequibles en Seattle, la opción de mudarse a una casa más grande en la ciudad estaba fuera de su alcance. Best Practice consideró que la conversión del garaje de la vivienda, que hasta entonces se utilizaba como almacén, era la solución perfecta. Las consideraciones de diseño incluían estudiar el proyecto tanto a corto como a largo plazo. Así pues, en primer lugar Best Practice tenía que responder a las necesidades inmediatas del cliente. Y, después, considerar los usos futuros del espacio como posible unidad de alquiler, estudio u otros proyectos que pudieran generar ingresos para la familia.

Site plan

South elevation

West elevation

East elevation

North elevation

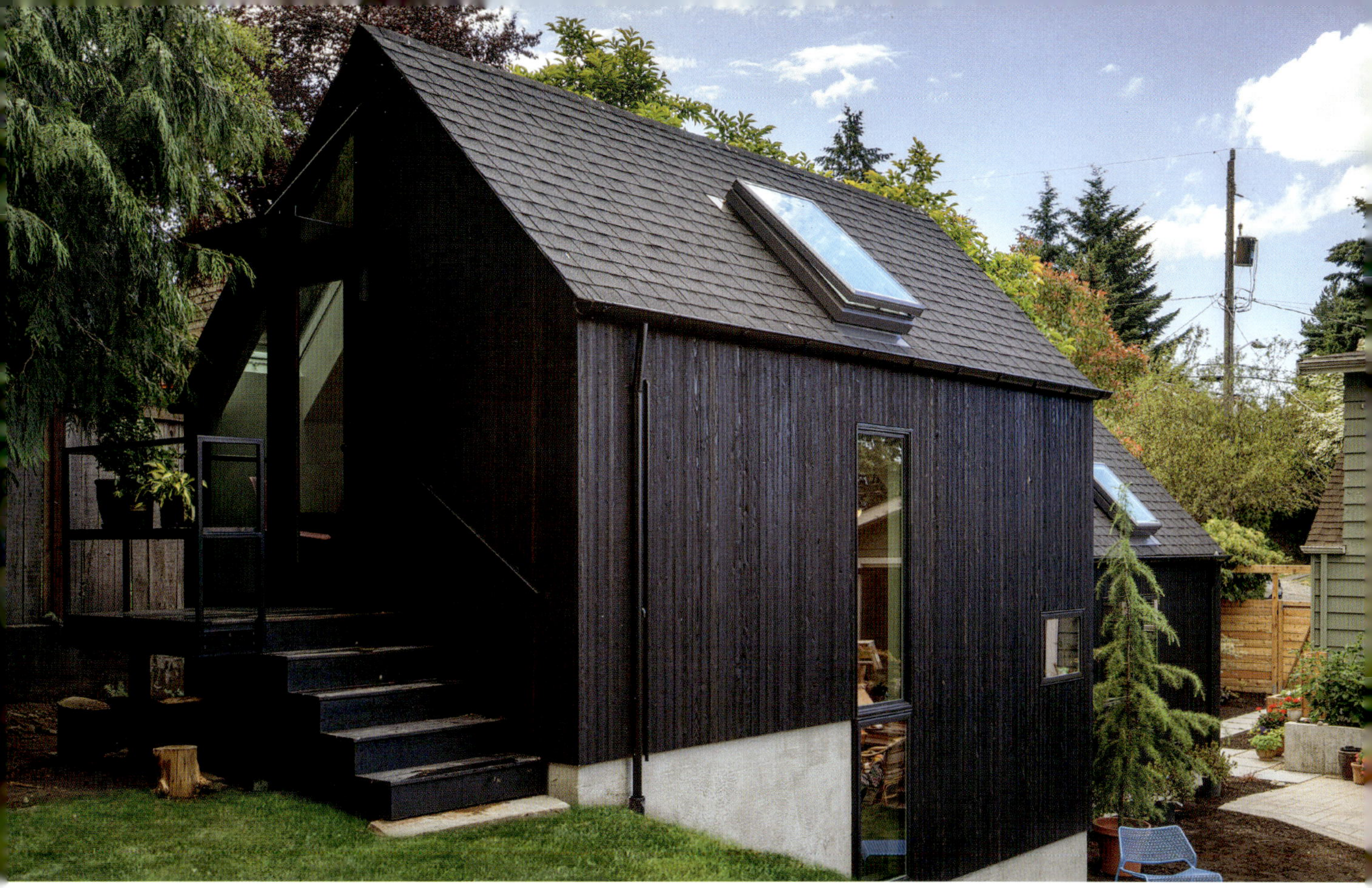

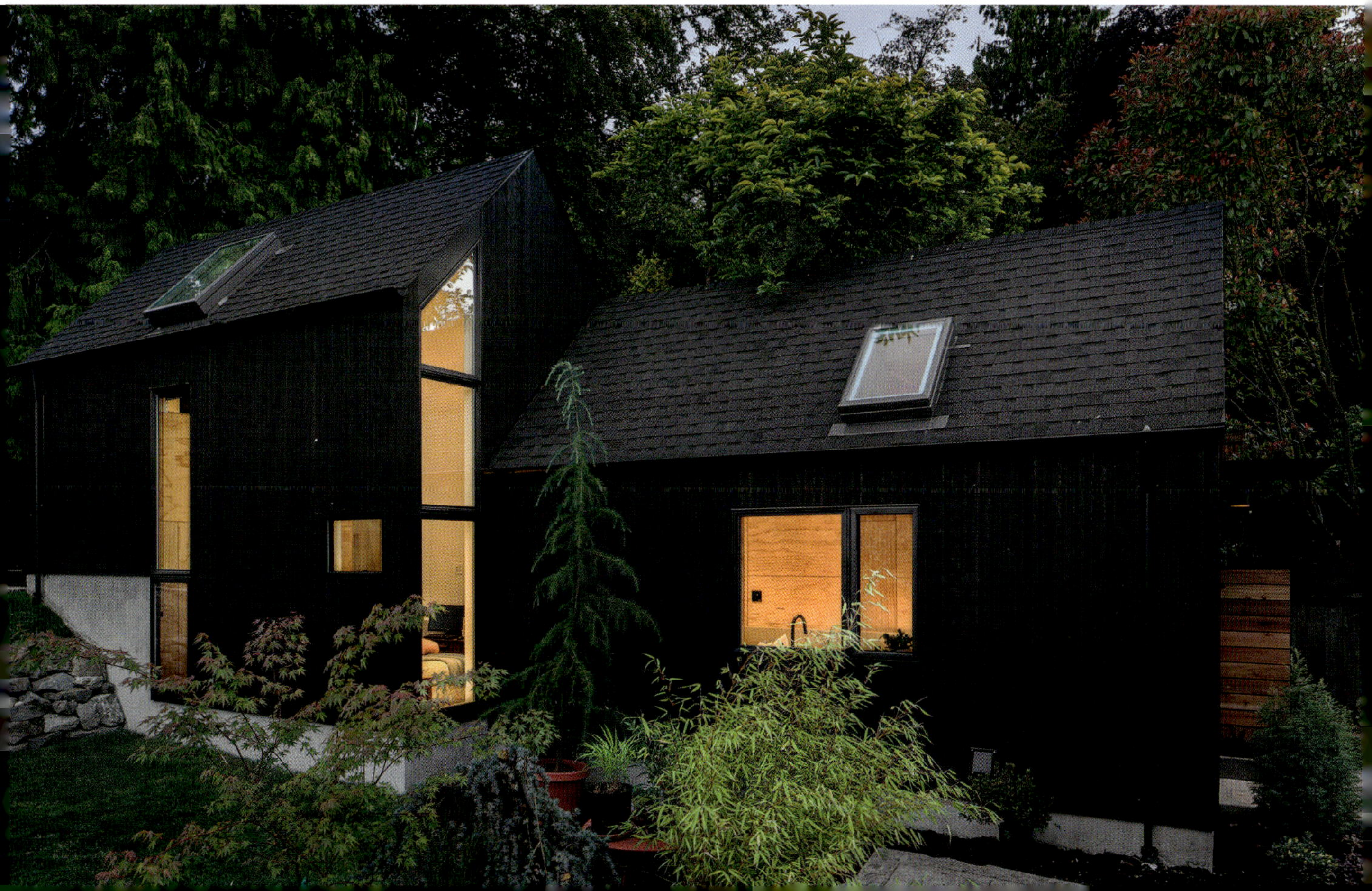

Section perspective

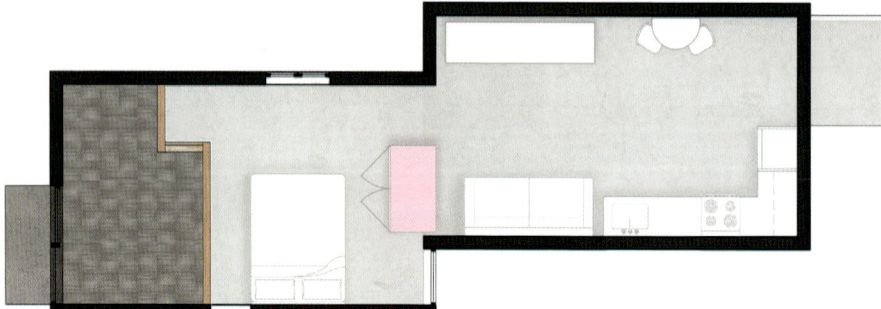

Loft level plan

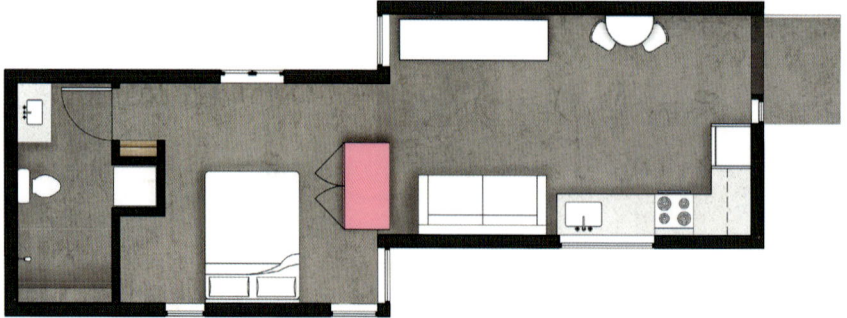

Main level plan

DENGSHIKOU HUTONG RESIDENCE

B.L.U.E. ARCHITECTURE STUDIO
SHUHEI AOYAMA

WWW.B-L-U-E.NET

Founded in 2014, B.L.U.E. Architecture Studio was established in Beijing by Japanese architects Yoko Fujii and Shuhei Aoyama. B.L.U.E. is the abbreviation of Beijing Laboratory for Urban Environment, and is also the core design philosophy of the studio.
B.L.U.E. Architecture Studio has a wide range of project practices, ranging from small buildings, new type retail spaces, micro-renovation of the old city, urban renewal, and experimental studies of lifestyles. Among them, the L-shaped house at Dengshikou Hutong in Dongcheng District, Beijing was widely favored by many professional medias as soon as it was published. The UMASSIF/WITH Bakery of Huamao center in Beijing CBD fully suffered the high praise because of its unique design style. In the Qing Dynasty, the 2500 m² Suzhou ancient house was remodeled and transformed into a shared new urban space. B.L.U.E. Architecture Studio has been rated as "100 Top Architecture and Design Talents in China" by AD.

Das 2014 gegründete B.L.U.E. Architecture Studio wurde von den japanischen Architekten Yoko Fujii und Shuhei Aoyama in Peking ins Leben gerufen. B.L.U.E. ist die Abkürzung für Beijing Laboratory for Urban Environment und zugleich die zentrale Entwurfsphilosophie des Studios.
B.L.U.E. Architecture Studio hat ein breites Spektrum an Projektpraktiken, die von kleinen Gebäuden, neuartigen Einzelhandelsflächen, Mikrorenovierung der Altstadt, Stadterneuerung und experimentellen Studien von Lebensstilen reichen. Unter ihnen wurde das L-förmige Haus in der Dengshikou Hutong im Dongcheng Distrikt in Peking von vielen Fachmedien sofort nach der Veröffentlichung favorisiert. Die UMASSIF/WITH-Bäckerei im Huamao-Zentrum im Pekinger CBD wurde wegen ihres einzigartigen Designstils hoch gelobt. In der Qing-Dynastie wurde das 2.500 m² große alte Haus in Suzhou umgebaut und in einen neuen gemeinsamen Stadtraum verwandelt. B.L.U.E. Architecture Studio wurde von AD als „100 Top Architecture and Design Talents in China" bewertet.

B.L.U.E. ARCHITECTURE STUDIO

Fondé en 2014, B.L.U.E. Architecture Studio a été créé à Pékin par les architectes japonais Yoko Fujii et Shuhei Aoyama. B.L.U.E. est l'abréviation de Beijing Laboratory for Urban Environment, et constitue également la philosophie de conception centrale du studio.

Le studio d'architecture B.L.U.E. a un large éventail de projets, allant des petits bâtiments aux espaces commerciaux d'un nouveau type, en passant par la microrénovation de la vieille ville, la rénovation urbaine et les études expérimentales sur les modes de vie. Parmi eux, la maison en forme de L de Dengshikou Hutong dans le district de Dongcheng, à Pékin, a été largement plébiscitée par de nombreux médias professionnels dès sa publication. La boulangerie UMASSIF/WITH du centre Huamao, dans le centre des affaires de Pékin, a reçu de nombreux éloges pour son style unique. Dans la dynastie Qing, la maison ancienne de Suzhou, d'une superficie de 2 500 m², a été remodelée et transformée en un nouvel espace urbain partagé. B.L.U.E. Architecture Studio a été classé parmi les « 100 Top Architecture and Design Talents in China » par AD.

Fundado en 2014, el estudio de arquitectura B.L.U.E. fue creado en Pekín por los arquitectos japoneses Yoko Fujii y Shuhei Aoyama. B.L.U.E. es la abreviatura de Beijing Laboratory for Urban Environment (Laboratorio de Pekín para el Medio Ambiente Urbano), y es también la filosofía de diseño central del estudio.

El estudio de arquitectura B.L.U.E. cuenta con una amplia gama de proyectos, que van desde pequeños edificios, espacios comerciales de nuevo tipo, microrrenovación de la ciudad antigua, renovación urbana y estudios experimentales de estilos de vida. Entre ellos, la casa en forma de L de Dengshikou Hutong, en el distrito de Dongcheng, en Pekín, recibió el favor de muchos medios profesionales en cuanto se publicó. La panadería UMASSIF/WITH del centro de Huamao, en el CBD de Pekín, fue elogiada por su estilo de diseño único. En la dinastía Qing, la antigua casa de Suzhou, de 2500 m², fue remodelada y transformada en un nuevo espacio urbano compartido. El estudio de arquitectura B.L.U.E. ha sido calificado como «100 Top Architecture and Design Talents in China» por AD.

DENGSHIKOU HUTONG RESIDENCE

43 M² // BEIJING, CHINA
PHOTOS © RUIJING PHOTO

Located on a street near the historic city centre, the L-shaped house is sandwiched between an old brick street wall and a two-storey building. The aim of the renovation was to transform the former residence into a modern and functional space for a family of six. The design is a feat that showcases exceptional planning and space-saving solutions to accommodate the needs of the occupants as a family and as individuals. Taking advantage of the ceiling height, a timber structure houses all domestic functions such as eating, cooking, sleeping and bathing. Occupying only half the height of the space, the upper part of the structure serves as additional usable space. Natural light, which enters the house through several skylights, is a key element of the design, contributing to the creation of an interior space that appears larger than it is.

Das L-förmige Haus liegt an einer Straße in der Nähe des historischen Stadtzentrums und ist zwischen einer alten Backstein-Straßenmauer und einem zweistöckigen Gebäude eingezwängt. Das Ziel der Renovierung war es, das ehemalige Wohnhaus in einen modernen, funktionalen Raum für eine sechsköpfige Familie zu verwandeln. Das Design ist ein Kunststück, das außergewöhnliche Planung und platzsparende Lösungen zeigt, um den Bedürfnissen der Bewohner als Familie und als Einzelpersonen gerecht zu werden. Die Deckenhöhe ausnutzend, beherbergt eine Holzkonstruktion alle häuslichen Funktionen wie Essen, Kochen, Schlafen und Baden. Nur die Hälfte der Raumhöhe einnehmend, dient der obere Teil des Aufbaus als zusätzliche Nutzfläche. Das natürliche Licht, das durch mehrere Oberlichter in das Haus fällt, ist ein Schlüsselelement des Entwurfs und trägt dazu bei, dass der Innenraum größer erscheint als er ist.

Située dans une rue proche du centre historique de la ville, la maison en forme de L est prise en sandwich entre un vieux mur de rue en briques et un bâtiment de deux étages. L'objectif de la rénovation était de transformer l'ancienne résidence en un espace moderne et fonctionnel pour une famille de six personnes. La conception est un exploit qui met en avant une planification exceptionnelle et des solutions d'économie d'espace pour répondre aux besoins des occupants en tant que famille et en tant qu'individus. Profitant de la hauteur du plafond, une structure en bois abrite toutes les fonctions domestiques telles que manger, cuisiner, dormir et se laver. Occupant seulement la moitié de la hauteur de l'espace, la partie supérieure de la structure sert d'espace utilisable supplémentaire. La lumière naturelle, qui pénètre dans la maison par plusieurs puits de lumière, est un élément clé de la conception, contribuant à la création d'un espace intérieur qui semble plus grand qu'il ne l'est.

Situada en una calle cerca del centro histórico de la ciudad, la casa, con forma de L, se encuentra encajada entre un muro antiguo de ladrillo de la calle y un edificio de dos plantas. El objetivo de la renovación era transformar la antigua residencia en un espacio moderno y funcional para una familia de seis personas. El diseño es una proeza que muestra una planificación excepcional y soluciones de ahorro de espacio para acomodar las necesidades de los ocupantes como familia y como individuos. Aprovechando la altura del techo, una estructura de madera alberga todas las funciones domésticas, como comer, cocinar, dormir y bañarse. Al ocupar solo la mitad de la altura del espacio, la parte superior de la estructura sirve como espacio útil adicional. La luz natural, que entra en la casa a través de varias claraboyas, es un elemento fundamental del diseño, ya que contribuye a la creación de un espacio interior que parece más grande de lo que es.

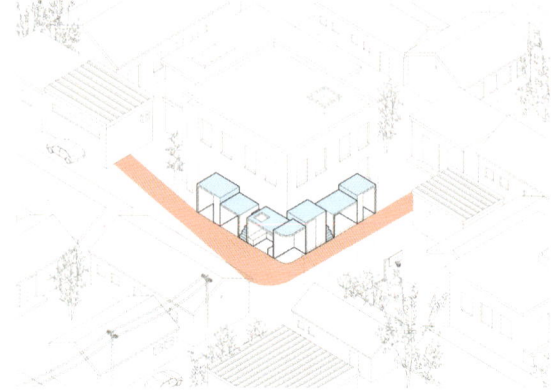

Conceptual diagram

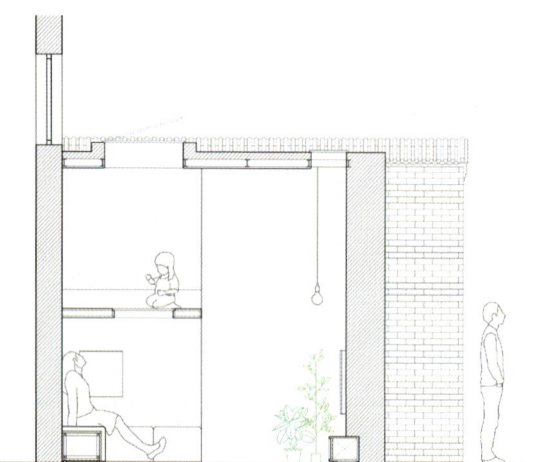

Building sections

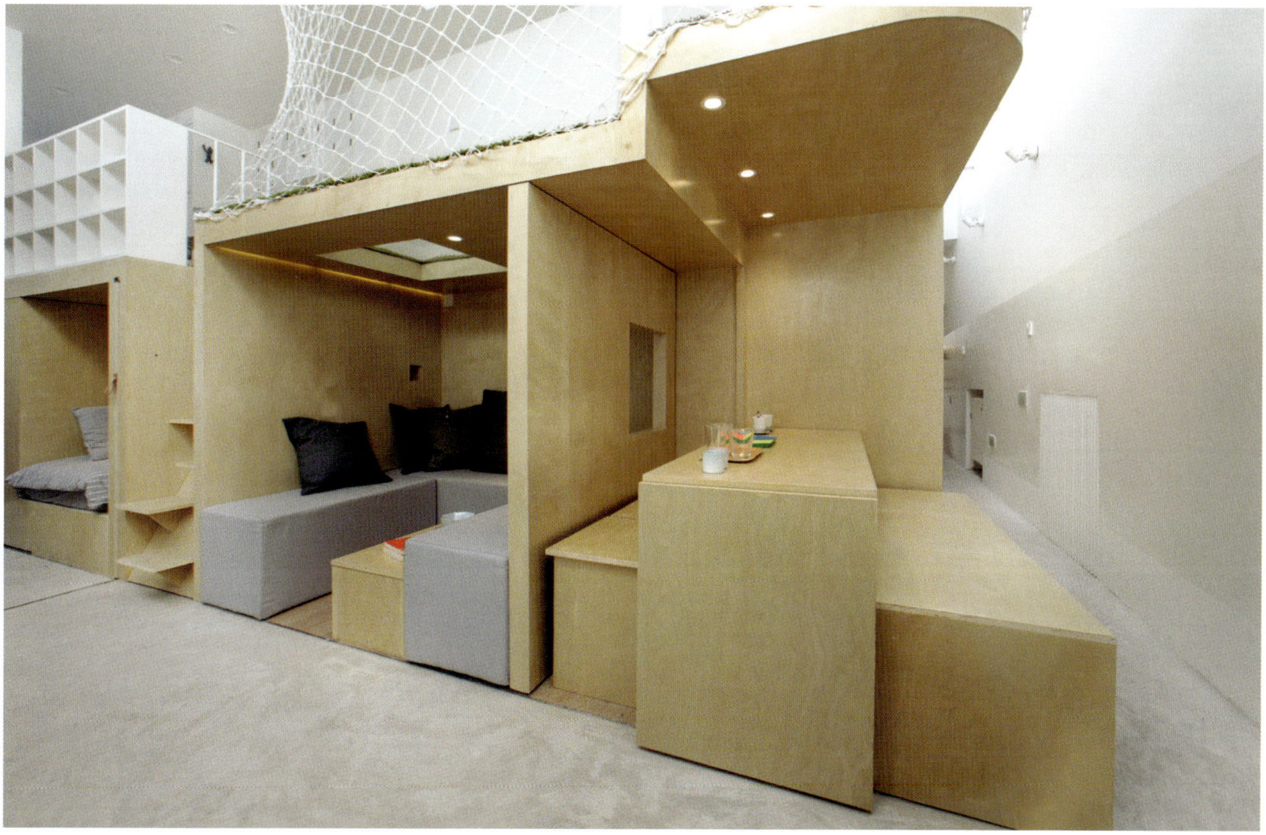

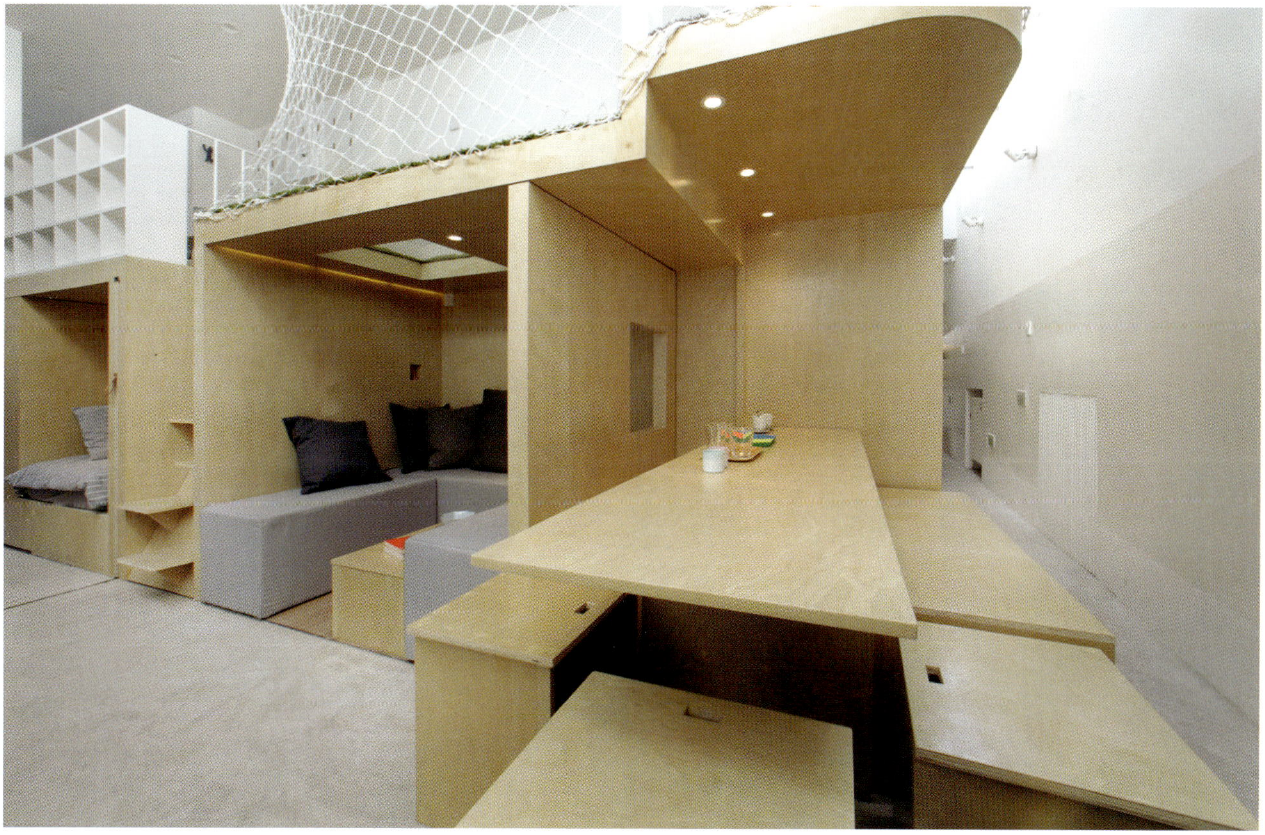

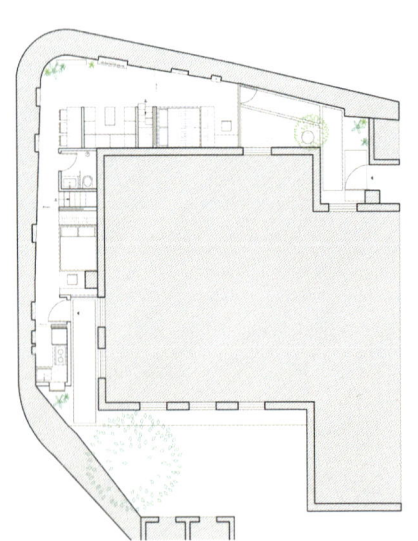

Ground floor plan

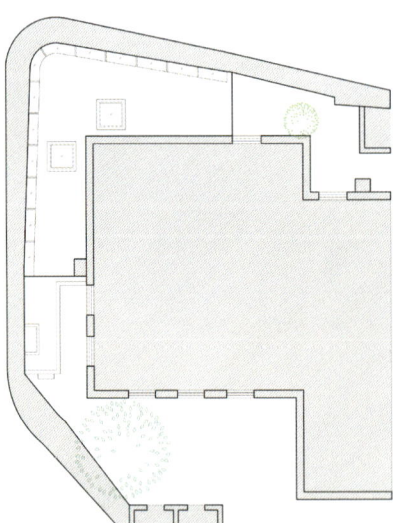

First floor plan

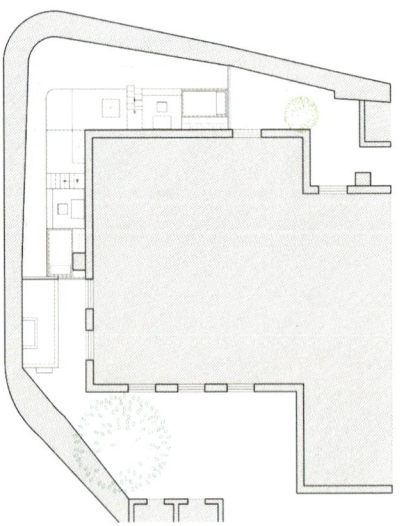

Roof plan

HOUSE E

BUERGER KATSOTA ARCHITECTS
STEPHAN BUERGER & DEMETRA KATSOTA

WWW.BUERGER-KATSOTA.COM

Buerger Katsota Architects was founded in 2005 by Stephan Buerger and Demetra Katsota. The collaborative architectural practice operates internationally within the field of architecture, urbanism, place making and research delivering projects from master planning to urban design, housing to private residences and interiors, exhibitions, and publications. They are engaged with a variety of architectural and urban design projects as well as academic and editorial research.

The practice's work is direct, poetic, and pragmatic. Informed by the physical, cultural, and socio-political context of each project, the continuous questioning of the given generates a process of abstraction leading to subtle yet innovative visions for new realities. Working together with clients, end users, consultants, and contractors from the initial concept through planning and realisation, high quality design, detailing and construction are achieved.

Buerger Katsota Architekten wurde im Jahr 2005 von Stephan Buerger und Demetra Katsota gegründet. Das Studio ist international in den Bereichen Architektur, Stadtplanung, Placemaking und Forschung tätig. Die Projekte reichen von der Masterplanung bis zum Städtebau, vom Wohnungsbau bis zu Privatwohnungen und Innenräumen, Ausstellungen und Publikationen. Sie beschäftigen sich mit einer Vielzahl von architektonischen und städtebaulichen Projekten sowie mit akademischer und redaktioneller Forschung.

Die Arbeit des Studios ist direkt, poetisch und pragmatisch. Informiert durch den physischen, kulturellen und sozio-politischen Kontext eines jeden Projekts, erzeugt die Hinterfragung des Gegebenen einen Prozess der Abstraktion, der zu subtilen und dennoch innovativen Visionen für neue Realitäten führt. Durch die Zusammenarbeit mit Kunden, Beratern und Auftragnehmern vom ersten Konzept über die Planung bis hin zur Realisierung wird eine hohe Qualität in Design, Detaillierung und Konstruktion erreicht.

BUERGER KATSOTA ARCHITECTS

Buerger Katsota Architects a été fondé en 2005 par Stephan Buerger et Demetra Katsota. Le studio opère au niveau international dans le domaine de l'architecture, de l'urbanisme, de la création de lieux et de la recherche. Avec des projets d'expositions et de publications qui vont du master planning, au design urbain et du logement résidenciel privées. Ils participent à divers projets d'architecture et d'urbanisme, ainsi qu'à des recherches universitaires et éditorialistes.

Le travail du studio est direct, poétique et pragmatique. Informée par le contexte physique, culturel et socio-politique de chaque projet, la remise en question génère un processus d'abstraction qui conduit à des visions subtiles mais innovantes de nouvelles réalités. La collaboration avec les clients, les consultants et les entrepreneurs, depuis le concept initial jusqu'à la planification et la réalisation, permet d'obtenir une conception, des détails et une construction de haute qualité.

Buerger Katsota Architects fue fundada en 2005 por Stephan Buerger y Demetra Katsota. El estudio opera internacionalmente en el campo de la arquitectura, el urbanismo, la creación de lugares y la investigación, con proyectos que van desde la planificación maestra hasta el diseño urbano, desde viviendas hasta residencias privadas e interiores, exposiciones y publicaciones. Se dedican a una variedad de proyectos de diseño arquitectónico y urbano, así como a la investigación académica y editorial.

El trabajo del estudio es directo, poético y pragmático. Informado por el contexto físico, cultural y sociopolítico de cada proyecto, el cuestionamiento de lo dado genera un proceso de abstracción que conduce a visiones sutiles pero innovadoras para nuevas realidades. Trabajando conjuntamente con clientes, consultores y contratistas desde el concepto inicial hasta la planificación y la realización, se logra un diseño, un detalle y una construcción de alta calidad.

HOUSE E

65 M² // ARTEMIDA, ATTICA, GREECE
PHOTOS © YIORGIS YEROLYMBOS

The dwelling aims to redefine the "ephemeral" and flexible nature of living near the coast, achieving comfortable and high quality indoor and outdoor spaces, revealing selected sea views and protecting the privacy of its residents. On a concrete base, clad in terrazzo, the volume is divided into two parts - with different volume and materials - placed at right angles to each other. The white, seemingly floating volume outlines with its cantilevers a generous open-plan ground floor space for easy indoor and outdoor living within a garden enclosure, and houses The upper volume houses two high-ceilinged bedrooms and a bathroom organised around a staircase and a study. In terms of construction, the building is a composite construction with a minimal footprint on the small plot.

Dieses Objekt versucht, die „flüchtige" und flexible Natur des Wohnens in Küstennähe neu zu definieren, komfortable und qualitativ hochwertige Innen- und Außenräume zu schaffen, ausgewählte Meerblicke zu enthüllen und die Privatsphäre der Bewohner zu schützen. Auf einem Betonsockel, der mit Terrazzo verkleidet ist, entstanden zwei Gebäudeteile - mit unterschiedlichen Größen und Materialien - die im rechten Winkel zueinander stehen. Das weiße, scheinbar schwebende Haus begrenzt mit seinen Auskragungen einen großzügigen, offenen Raum im Erdgeschoss, was ein bequemes Leben im Innen- und Außenbereich innerhalb einer Gartenanlage ermöglicht. Im oberen Gebäudeteil befinden sich zwei hohe Schlafzimmer und ein Bad, die um eine Treppe und ein Arbeitszimmer angeordnet sind. Konstruktiv ist das Gebäude eine Verbundkonstruktion mit minimaler Grundfläche auf einem kleinen Grundstück.

Le logement vise à redéfinir la nature « éphémère » et flexible de la vie près de la côte, en réalisant des espaces intérieurs et extérieurs confortables et de haute qualité, en révélant des vues orientées sur la mer et en protégeant l'intimité de ses résidents. Sur un socle en béton, revêtu de terrazzo, le volume est divisé en deux parties - de volumétrie et de matériaux différents - placées à angle droit l'une par rapport à l'autre. Le volume blanc, apparemment flottant, délimite avec ses porte-à-faux un généreux espace ouvert au rez-de-chaussée pour faciliter la vie à l'intérieur et à l'extérieur dans une enceinte de jardin. Le volume supérieur abrite deux chambres à haut plafond et une salle de bains situées autour d'un escalier et d'un bureau. En termes de construction, le bâtiment est un ouvrage composite avec une empreinte minimale sur la petite parcelle.

La vivienda tiene como objetivo redefinir la naturaleza «efímera» y flexible de la vida cerca de la costa, logrando espacios interiores y exteriores cómodos y de alta calidad, revelando vistas seleccionadas al mar y protegiendo la privacidad de sus residentes. Sobre una base de hormigón, revestida de terrazo, el volumen se divide en dos partes —con volumetría y materiales diferentes— colocadas en ángulo recto entre sí. El volumen blanco, aparentemente flotante, delinea con sus voladizos un generoso espacio de planta baja de plano abierto para vivir fácilmente en el interior y exterior dentro de un recinto de jardín. El volumen superior alberga dos dormitorios de techo alto y un baño organizado alrededor de una escalera y un estudio. En términos de construcción, el edificio es una construcción compuesta con una mínima huella en la pequeña parcela.

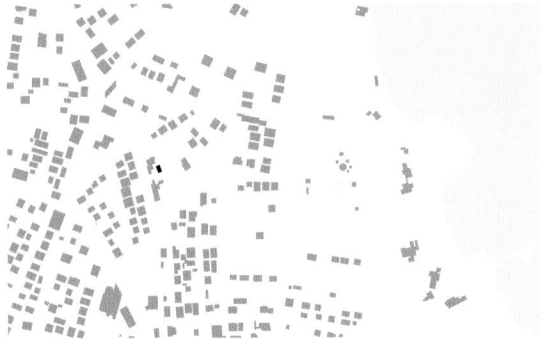

Site plan

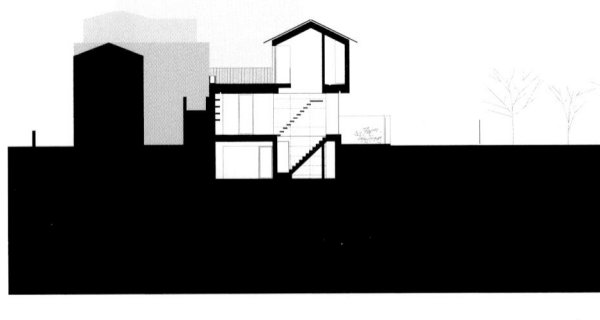

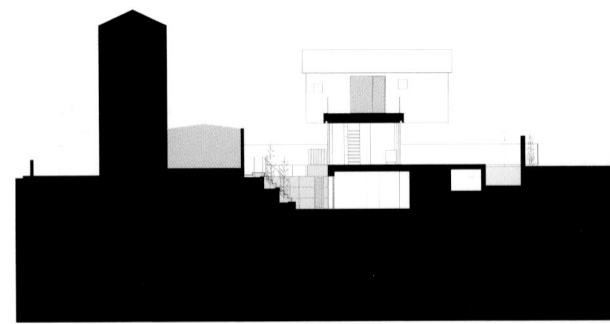

Sections

Basement plan

Ground floor plan

First floor plan

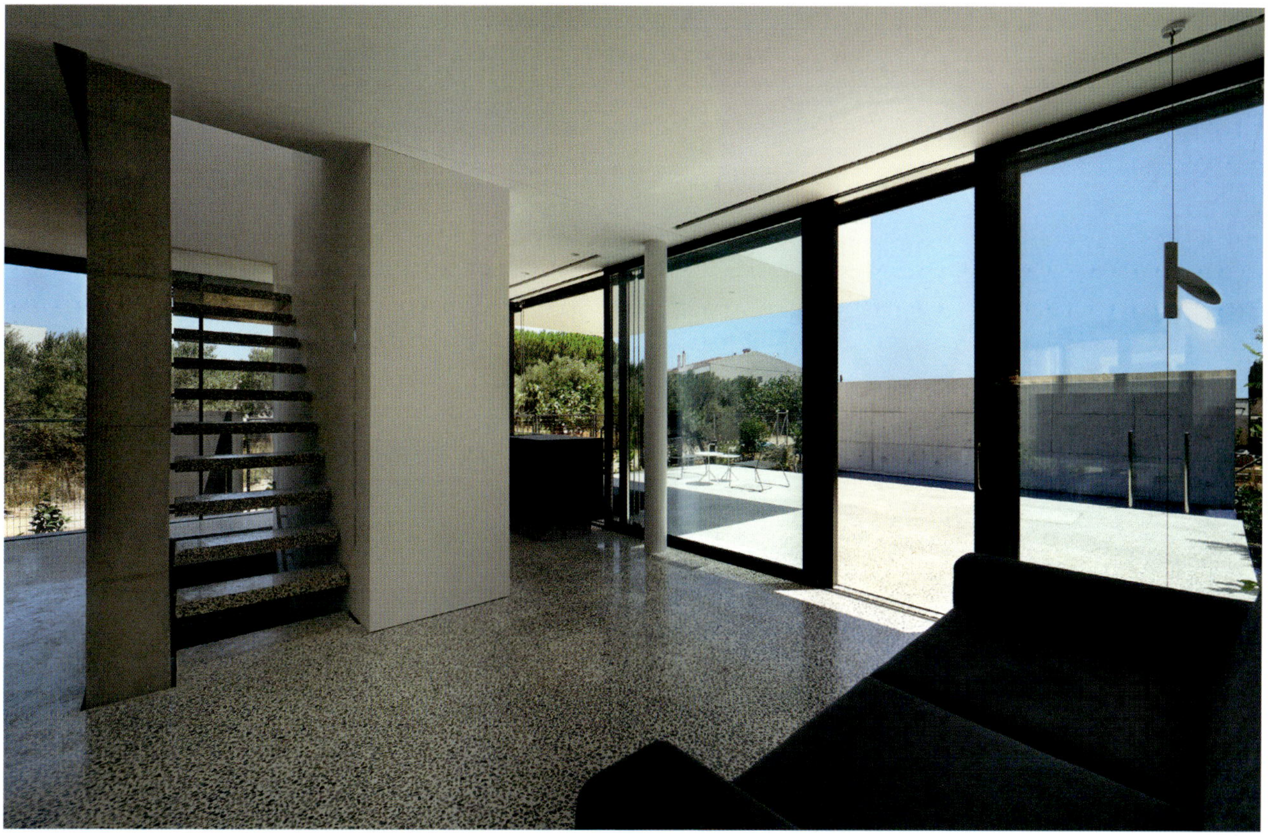

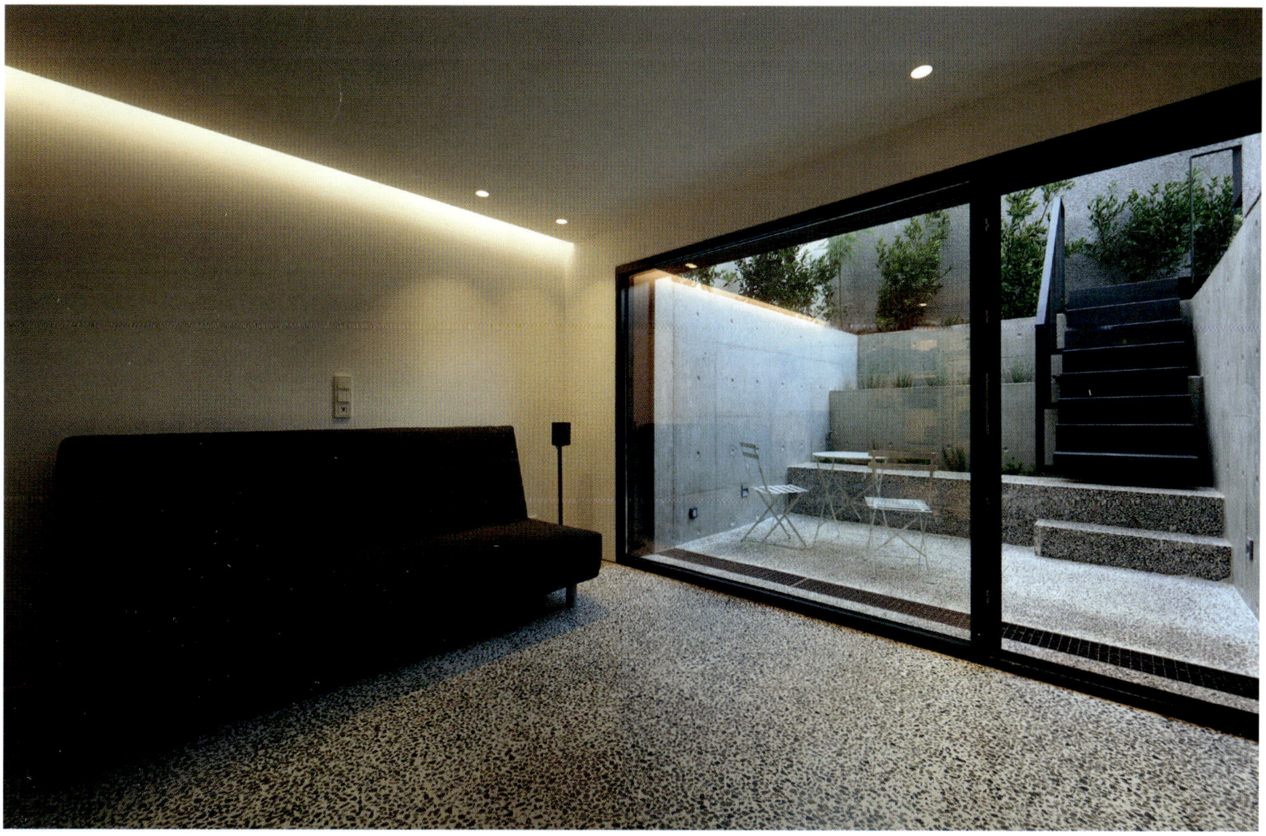

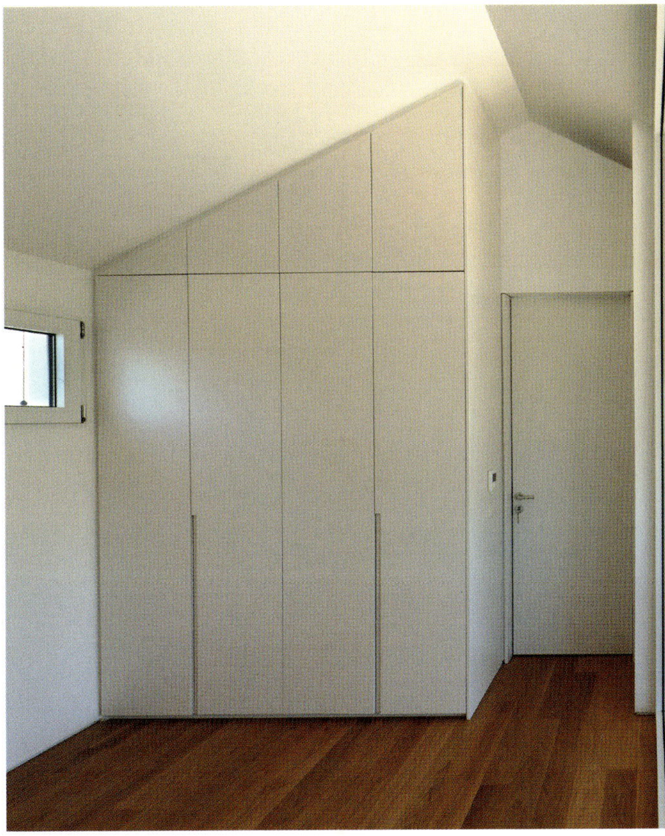

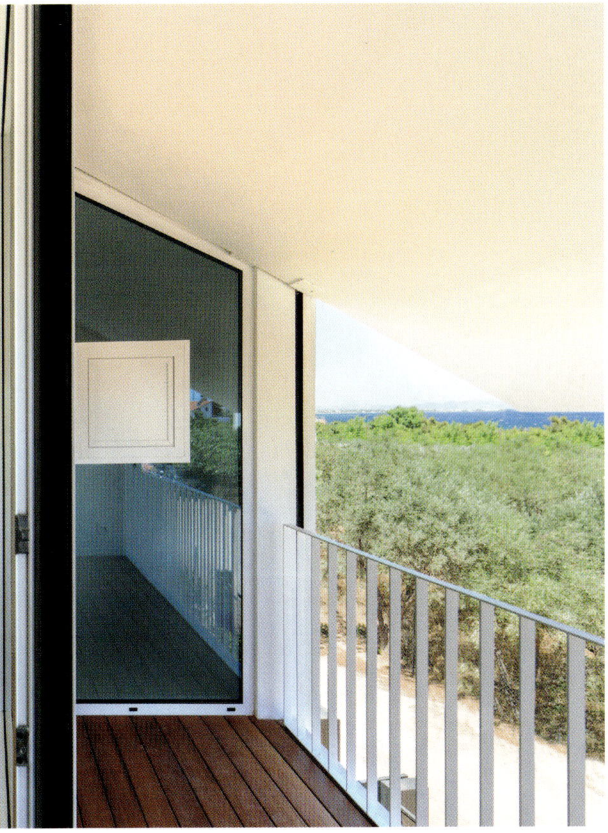

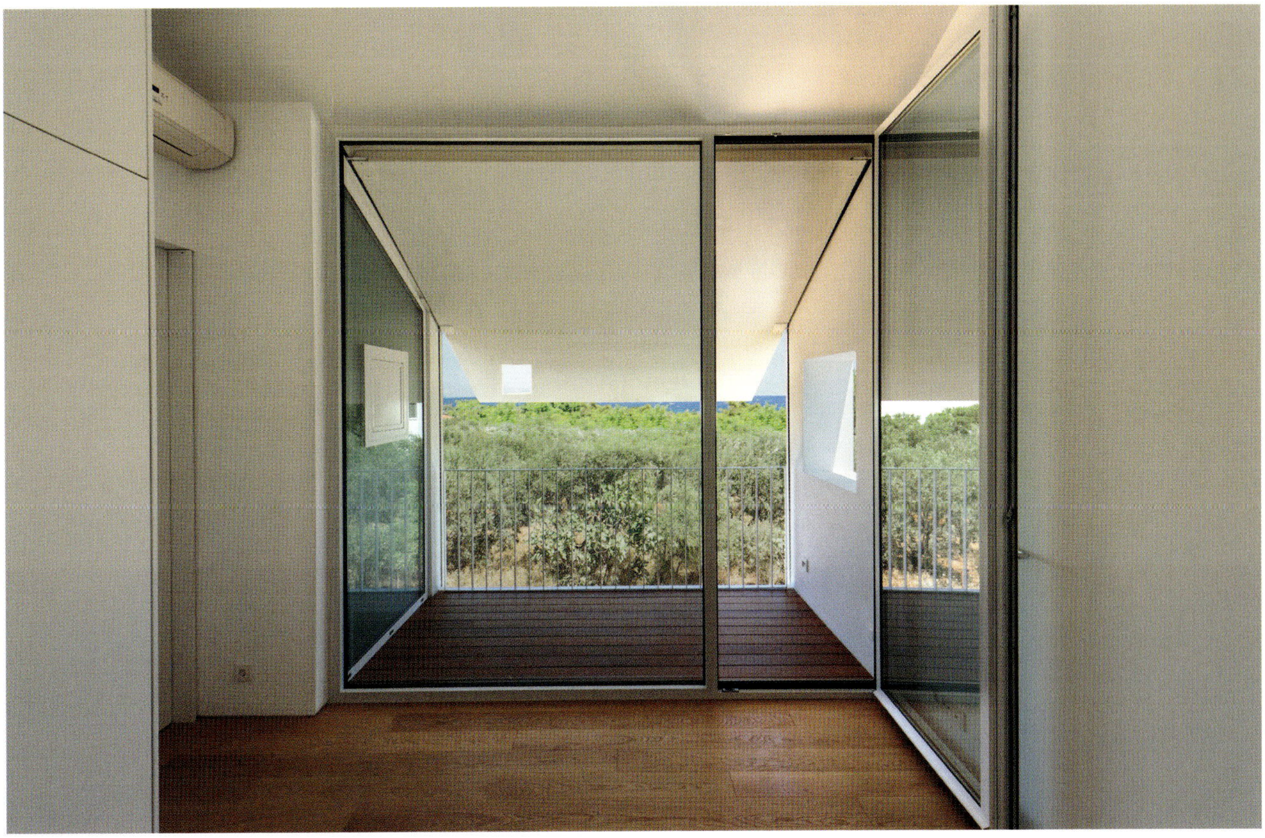

SOOKE 01 HOUSE

CAMPOS STUDIO

JAVIER CAMPOS, CZARINA RAY, ALIX DEMONTROND

WWW.CAMPOS.STUDIO

Based in Vancouver, Canada, Campos Studio works primarily along the west coast of North America, from Baja California, Mexico, to Haida Gwaii, British Columbia. Emerging from the critical regionalist tradition of the Pacific Northwest, the studio explores the relationship between geography, climate and cultural traditions, and employs vernacular strategies and local building technologies as a means to generate modern architectural responses that are nested within their context. Its aim is to create sensitive contemporary projects that cannot be divorced from their surroundings.

Since its initial project, Campos Studio has shown a commitment to integrating passive design into architecture to the point where it becomes integral, essential and invisible.

At its core is the belief that architecture can have a positive impact on our lives and expand our interactions with the environment and our communities.

Mit Sitz in Vancouver, Kanada, arbeitet Campos Studio hauptsächlich entlang der Westküste Nordamerikas, von Baja California, Mexiko, bis Haida Gwaii, British Columbia. Entstanden aus der kritischen regionalistischen Tradition des pazifischen Nordwestens, erforscht das Studio die Beziehung zwischen Geographie, Klima und kulturellen Traditionen und nutzt landestypische Strategien und lokale Bautechnologien als Mittel, um moderne architektonische Antworten zu generieren, die in ihrem Kontext eingebettet sind. Ihr Ziel ist es, sensible zeitgenössische Projekte zu schaffen, die sich nicht von ihrer Umgebung trennen lassen.

Seit seinem ersten Projekt hat Campos Studio sein Engagement für die Integration von passivem Design in die Architektur bis zu dem Punkt gezeigt, an dem es integral, essentiell und unsichtbar wird.

Im Kern steht die Überzeugung, dass Architektur einen positiven Einfluss auf unser Leben haben und unsere Interaktionen mit der Umwelt und unseren Gemeinden erweitern kann.

CAMPOS STUDIO

Basé à Vancouver, au Canada, Campos Studio travaille principalement le long de la côte ouest de l'Amérique du Nord, de la Basse-Californie, au Mexique, à Haida Gwaii, en Colombie-Britannique. Issu de la tradition régionaliste critique du nord-ouest du Pacifique, le studio explore la relation entre la géographie, le climat et les traditions culturelles, et utilise des stratégies vernaculaires et des technologies de construction locales comme moyen de générer des réponses architecturales modernes qui sont imbriquées dans leur contexte. Son but est de créer des projets contemporains sensibles qui ne peuvent être dissociés de leur environnement.

Depuis son projet initial, Campos Studio s'est engagé à intégrer la conception passive dans l'architecture au point qu'elle devienne intégrale, essentielle et invisible.

L'architecture peut avoir un impact positif sur nos vies et élargir nos interactions avec l'environnement et nos communautés.

Con base en Vancouver, Canadá, Campos Studio trabaja principalmente a lo largo de la costa oeste de Norteamérica, desde Baja California, México, hasta Haida Gwaii, Columbia Británica. Emergiendo de la tradición regionalista crítica del noroeste del Pacífico, el estudio explora la relación entre geografía, clima y tradiciones culturales, y emplea estrategias vernáculas y tecnologías de construcción locales como un medio para generar respuestas arquitectónicas modernas que se anidan en su contexto. Su objetivo es crear proyectos contemporáneos sensibles que no se puedan separar de su entorno.

Desde su proyecto inicial, Campos Studio ha mostrado un compromiso con la integración del diseño pasivo en la arquitectura hasta el punto en que se vuelve integral, esencial e invisible.

En su núcleo se encuentra la creencia de que la arquitectura puede tener un impacto positivo en nuestras vidas y ampliar nuestras interacciones con el medio ambiente y nuestras comunidades.

SOOKE 01 HOUSE

135 M² // VANCOUVER ISLAND, BRITISH COLUMBIA, CANADA
PHOTOS © EMA PETER

The aim of the house was to embrace the natural environment and integrate the experience of being in the forest into the everyday experiences of home life. The tectonics of the house were inspired by the surrounding Douglas fir, Sitka spruce and cedar logs. The structure was organised around a concrete column that rises from the ground and mimics the tree trunks in size and scale, with the aim of integrating the house with the rhythm of the forest. The experience of the forest inspired the organisation of the spaces in the house. Each space is organised around a different abstract view of the landscape, presenting a series of diverse views of the forest as one moves through the house. These different experiences of the site, tree trunks, tree canopies, coastline, ocean and mountains, can be reconstructed to understand the site as a whole that can never be seen.

Das Ziel dieses Hauses war es, die natürliche Umgebung zu integrieren und die Erfahrung, im Wald zu sein, in die alltäglichen Erfahrungen des Hauslebens zu integrieren. Die Tektonik des Hauses wurde von den umliegenden Douglasien, Sitka-Fichten und Zedernstämmen inspiriert. Die Struktur wurde um eine Betonsäule herum organisiert, die aus dem Boden ragt und die Baumstämme in Größe und Maßstab nachahmt, mit dem Ziel, das Haus in die Waldumgebung zu integrieren. Die Erfahrung des Waldes inspirierte die Organisation der Räume des Hauses. Jeder Raum ist um eine andere abstrakte Ansicht der Landschaft herum organisiert und präsentiert verschiedene Aussichten auf den Wald, während man sich durch das Haus bewegt. Diese verschiedenen Erfahrungen des Ortes, Baumstämme, Baumkronen, Küstenlinie, Meer und Berge, können rekonstruiert werden, um den Ort als ein Ganzes zu verstehen, das nie vollständig gesehen werden kann.

Le but de la maison était d'embrasser l'environnement naturel et d'intégrer la forêt dans les expériences quotidiennes de la vie à la maison. La tectonique de la maison a été inspirée par le sapin de Douglas, l'épicéa de Sitka et les rondins de cèdre qui l'entourent. La structure s'est organisée autour d'une colonne en béton qui s'élève du sol et imite les troncs d'arbres par sa taille et son échelle, dans le but d'intégrer la maison au rythme de la forêt. La nature de la forêt a inspiré l'organisation des espaces de la maison. Chaque lieu est organisé autour d'une vision abstraite, différente du paysage, présentant une série de vues diverses de la forêt, au fur et à mesure que l'on se déplace dans la maison. Les différents éléments du site , les troncs d'arbres, les auvents, le littoral, l'océan et les montagnes, peuvent être reconstitués pour comprendre le lieu qui ne peut jamais être vu dans son ensemble.

El objeto de la casa era abrazar el entorno natural e integrar la experiencia de estar en el bosque en las experiencias cotidianas de la vida hogareña. La tectónica de la casa se inspiró en los troncos de abeto Douglas, abeto Sitka y cedro que la rodean. Se organizó la estructura alrededor de una columna de hormigón que se eleva del suelo y que imita los troncos de los árboles en tamaño y escala, con el objetivo de integrar la casa con el ritmo del bosque. La experiencia del bosque inspiró la organización de los espacios de la casa. Cada espacio se organiza alrededor de una vista abstracta diferente del paisaje, presentando una serie de diversas vistas del bosque a medida que uno se mueve por la casa. Estas diferentes experiencias del sitio, troncos de árboles, doseles de árboles, costa, océano y montañas, pueden ser reconstruidas para entender el sitio como un todo que nunca puede ser visto.

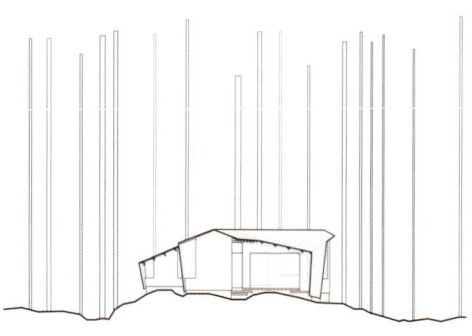

East elevation

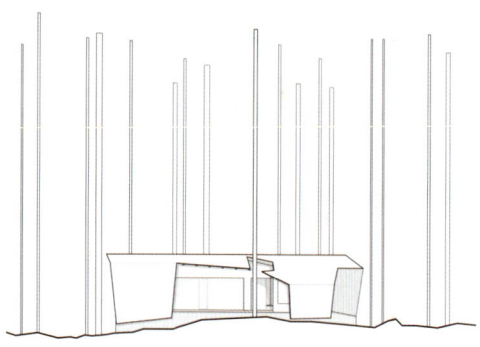

North elevation

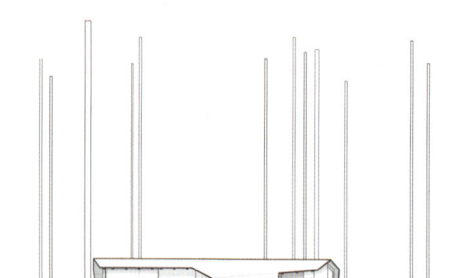

South elevation

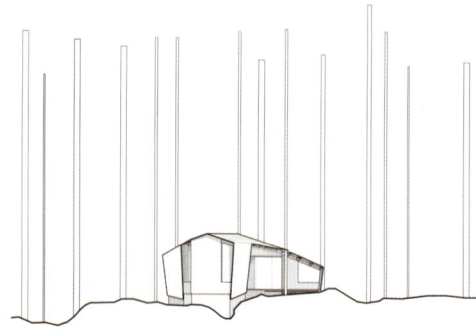

West elevation

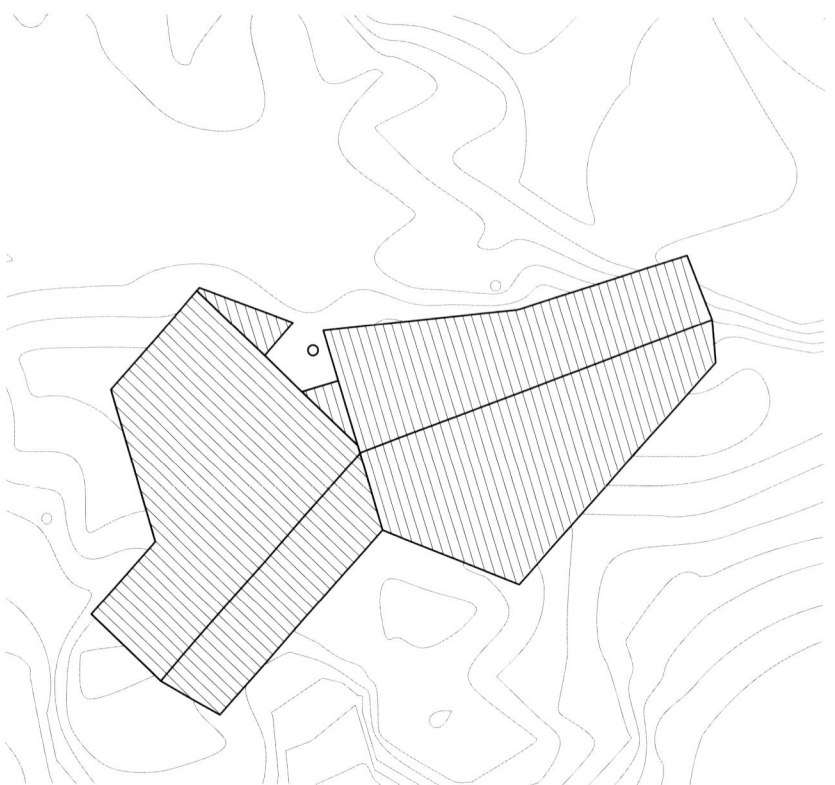

Roof plan

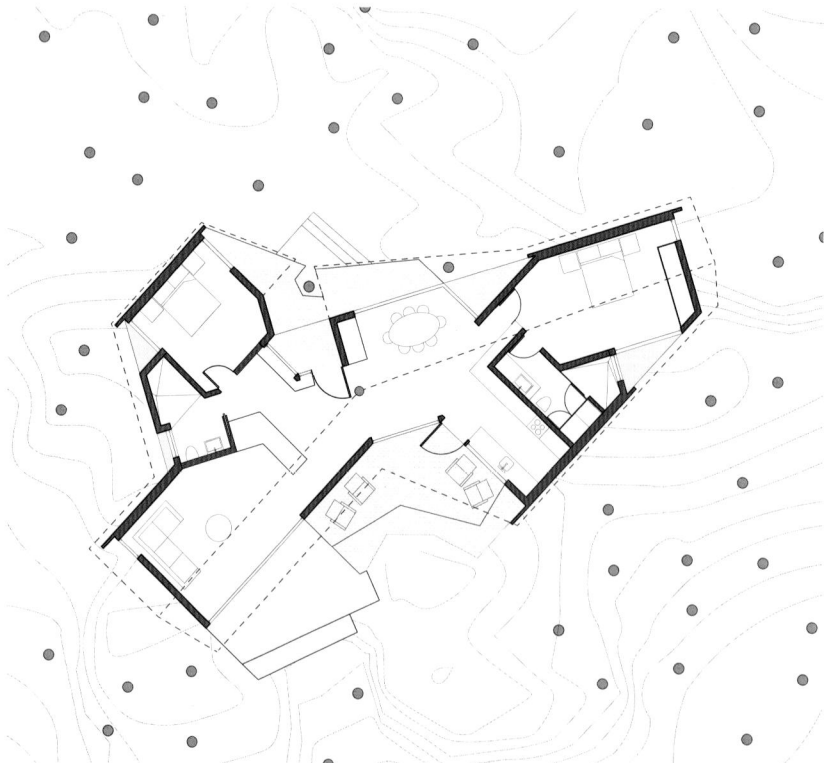

Floor plan

FLAT 8

DESIGN EIGHT FIVE TWO
NORMAN UNG

WWW.DESIGNEIGHTFIVETWO.COM

Founded in 2014, DEFT is a young, diverse, interdisciplinary design studio with a passion for design at multiple scales and across various media, encompassing architecture, interiors, branding and identities.DEFT exists to create quietly brilliant projects— spaces and brands with longevity and adaptability that deliver daily value to the people who use them. Rather than operating within a defined aesthetic, DEFT nurtures a diverse mix of styles and skills to provide thoughtful and innovative design solutions that evolve with the needs of each project. As a proudly diverse and close-knit team of designers, makers, and professionals from various backgrounds, DEFT is led by two partners, Norman Ung and Peter Lampard, who met while attending the University of Hong Kong in 2010.

DEFT wurde 2014 gegründet und ist ein junges, vielseitiges, interdisziplinäres Designstudio mit einer Leidenschaft für Design in verschiedenen Maßstäben und Medien, das Architektur, Inneneinrichtung, Branding und Identitäten umfasst.DEFT existiert, um leise brillante Projekte, Räume und Marken mit Langlebigkeit und Anpassungsfähigkeit zu schaffen, die den Menschen, die sie nutzen, täglich einen Mehrwert bieten. Anstatt innerhalb einer definierten Ästhetik zu arbeiten, pflegt DEFT eine vielfältige Mischung von Stilen und Fähigkeiten, um durchdachte und innovative Designlösungen zu bieten, die sich mit den Anforderungen jedes Projekts weiterentwickeln. DEFT wird von den beiden Partnern Norman Ung und Peter Lampard geleitet, die sich 2010 während ihres Studiums an der Universität Hongkong kennengelernt haben. Sie sind stolz darauf, ein vielfältiges und eng verbundenes Team von Designern, Herstellern und Fachleuten mit unterschiedlichem Hintergrund zu sein.

DESIGN EIGHT FIVE TWO

Fondé en 2014, DEFT est un jeune studio de design interdisciplinaire et diversifié, passionné par le design à plusieurs échelles et sur différents supports, englobant l'architecture, les intérieurs, le branding et les identités. DEFT existe pour créer tranquillement des projets, des espaces et des marques brillants, avec une longévité et une adaptabilité qui apportent une valeur quotidienne aux personnes qui les utilisent. Plutôt que d'opérer dans le cadre d'une esthétique définie, DEFT nourrit un mélange diversifié de styles et de compétences pour fournir des solutions de conception réfléchies et innovantes qui évoluent avec les besoins de chaque projet. DEFT est dirigée par deux associés, Norman Ung et Peter Lampard, qui se sont rencontrés lors de leurs études à l'université de Hong Kong en 2010.

Fundado en 2014, DEFT es un estudio de diseño joven, diverso e interdisciplinario con una pasión por el diseño a múltiples escalas y a través de varios medios, abarcando la arquitectura, los interiores, la marca y las identidades. DEFT existe para crear proyectos, espacios y marcas silenciosamente brillantes con longevidad y adaptabilidad que ofrecen valor diario a las personas que los utilizan. En lugar de operar dentro de una estética definida, DEFT cultiva una mezcla diversa de estilos y habilidades para proporcionar soluciones de diseño reflexivas e innovadoras que evolucionan con las necesidades de cada proyecto. DEFT es un equipo diverso y unido de diseñadores, creadores y profesionales de diversos orígenes, y está dirigido por dos socios, Norman Ung y Peter Lampard, que se conocieron cuando cursaban sus estudios en la Universidad de Hong Kong en 2010.

FLAT 8

51 M² // HONG KONG, SAR CHINA

PHOTOS © HAZEL YUEN FUN

The client's brief for this flat was simple: to create a home as spacious as space and function would allow. With these premises in mind, the design focused on optimising natural lighting to create a sense of openness and ventilation and on providing generous and functional storage. The design solution to optimise the use of space is a flexible layout. The flat includes a living area and a bedroom. They can be seamlessly connected to create a large, light-filled open space or they can be separated from each other to meet privacy needs.

The palette and details are sober and have been chosen with materiality in mind: an ash wood finish throughout, with subtle nuances that differentiate each space and its use.

Das Briefing des Kunden für diese Wohnung war einfach: ein Zuhause zu schaffen, das so geräumig ist, wie es Platz und Funktion erlauben. Vor diesem Hintergrund konzentrierte sich der Entwurf auf die Optimierung der natürlichen Beleuchtung, um ein Gefühl von Offenheit und Belüftung zu schaffen, und auf die Bereitstellung von großzügigem und funktionellem Stauraum. Die Designlösung zur Optimierung der Raumnutzung ist ein flexibles Layout. Die Wohnung umfasst einen Wohn- und einen Schlafraum, die sich nahtlos zu einem großen, lichtdurchfluteten offenen Raum verbinden lassen. Unabhängig davon erfüllen sie die Bedürfnisse der Privatsphäre.

Die Farbpalette und die Details sind nüchtern und wurden mit Blick auf die Materialität gewählt: ein Eschenholz-Finish in der gesamten Wohnung, mit subtilen Nuancen, die jeden Raum und seine Nutzung differenzieren.

Le briefing du client pour cet appartement était simple : créer une maison aussi spacieuse que l'espace et la fonction le permettent. Dans cette optique, la conception s'est concentrée sur l'optimisation de l'éclairage naturel afin de créer une sensation d'ouverture et de ventilation et d'offrir un rangement généreux et fonctionnel. La solution pour optimiser l'utilisation de l'espace est une disposition flexible. L'appartement comprend un espace de vie et une chambre à coucher qui peuvent être reliés sans problème pour créer un grand espace ouvert et lumineux. Séparément, ils répondent aux besoins de protection de la vie privée.

La palette et les détails sont sobres et ont été choisis dans un souci de matérialité : une finition en frêne dans tout l'appartement, avec des nuances subtiles qui différencient chaque espace et son utilisation.

Para este apartamento el encargo del cliente era sencillo: crear una vivienda tan amplia como el espacio y las funciones lo permitieran. Partiendo de estas premisas, el diseño se centró en optimizar la iluminación natural para crear una sensación de apertura y ventilación y en proporcionar un almacenamiento generoso y funcional. La solución de diseño para optimizar el uso del espacio consiste en una distribución flexible. El apartamento incluye una zona de estar y un dormitorio que pueden estar perfectamente conectados para crear un amplio espacio abierto lleno de luz. Por separado, satisfacen las necesidades de privacidad.

La paleta y los detalles son sobrios y se han elegido teniendo en cuenta la materialidad: un acabado de madera de fresno en todo la vivienda, con sutiles matices que diferencian cada espacio y su uso.

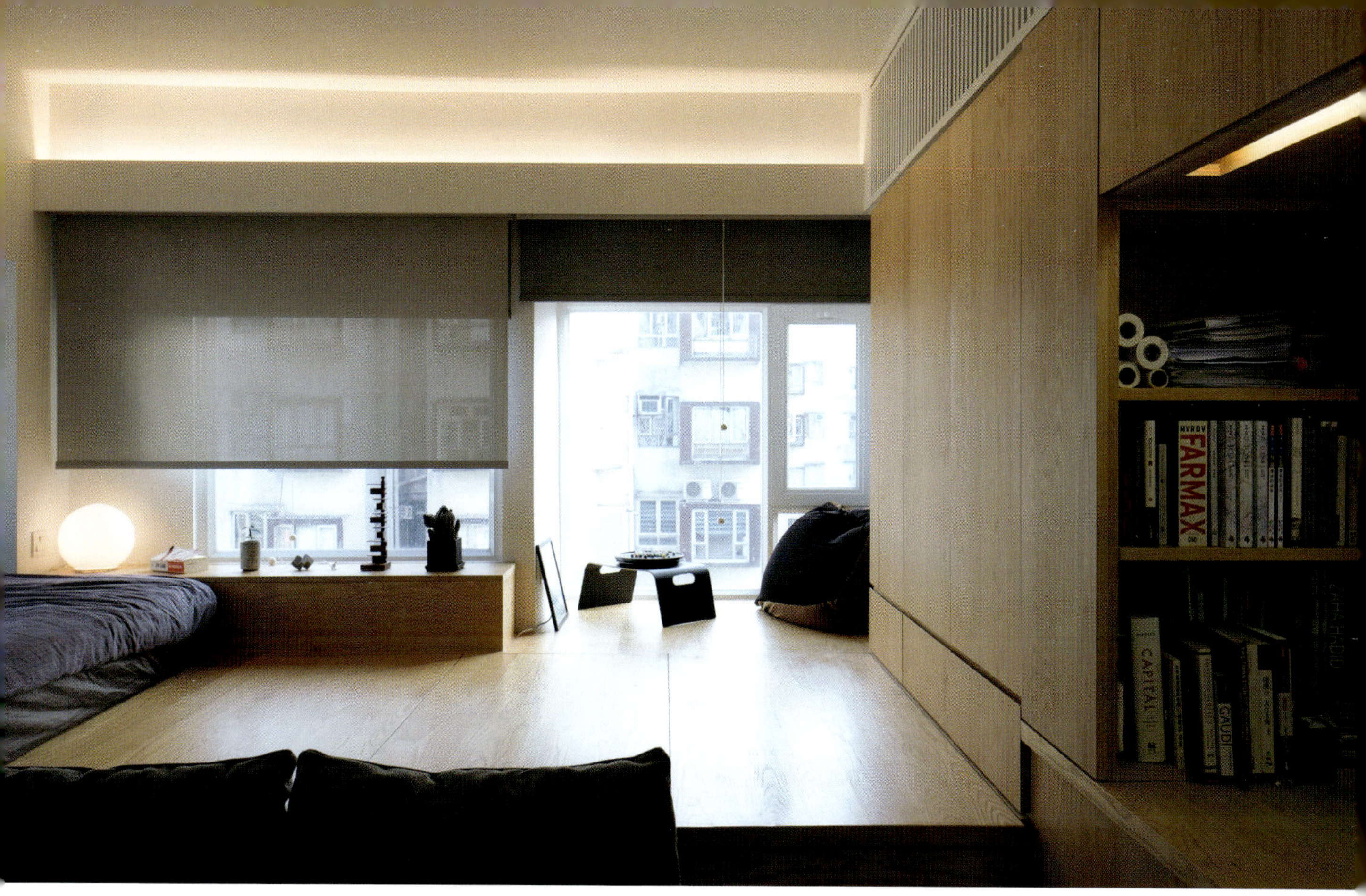

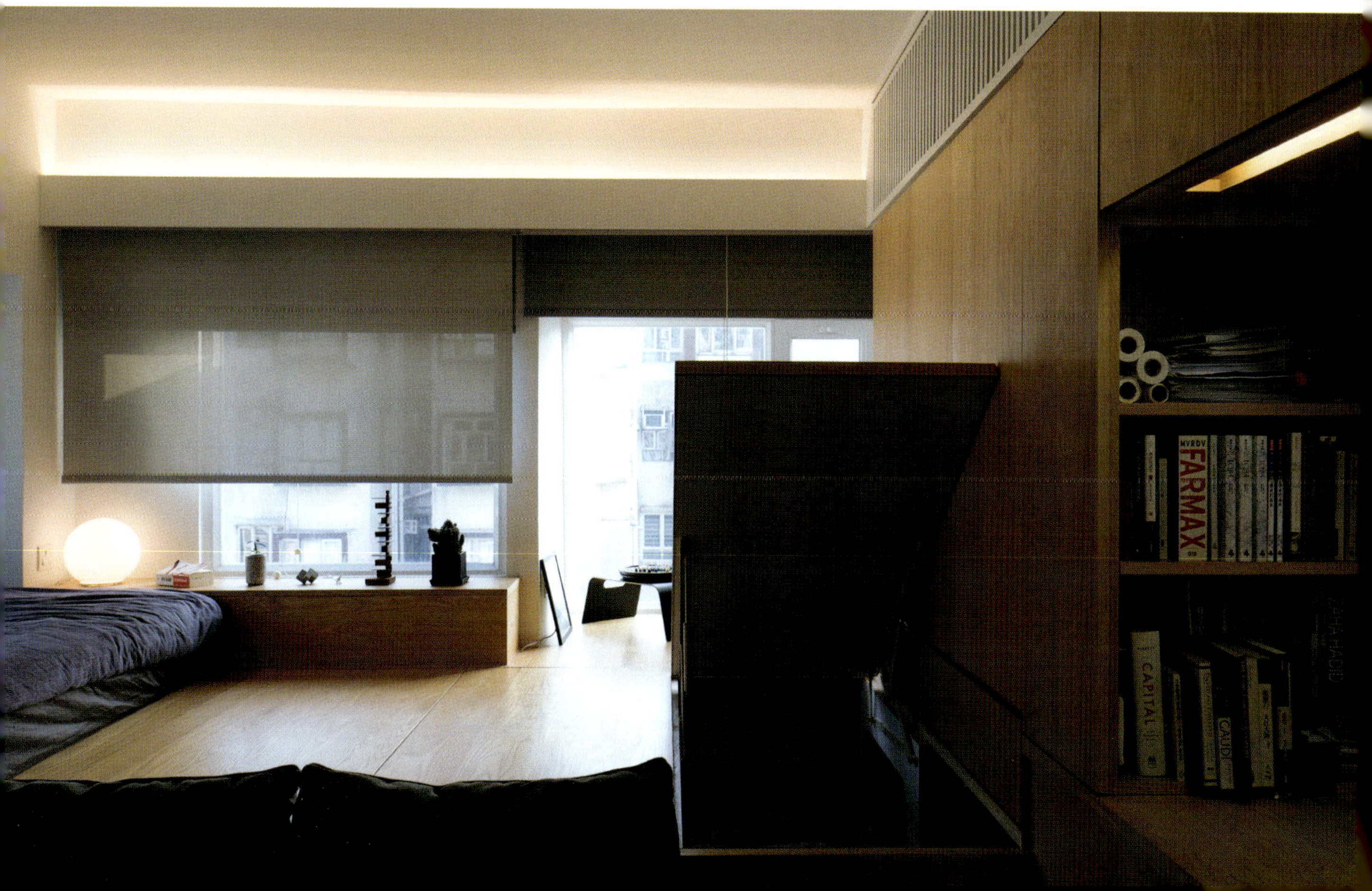

Conceptual design sketch

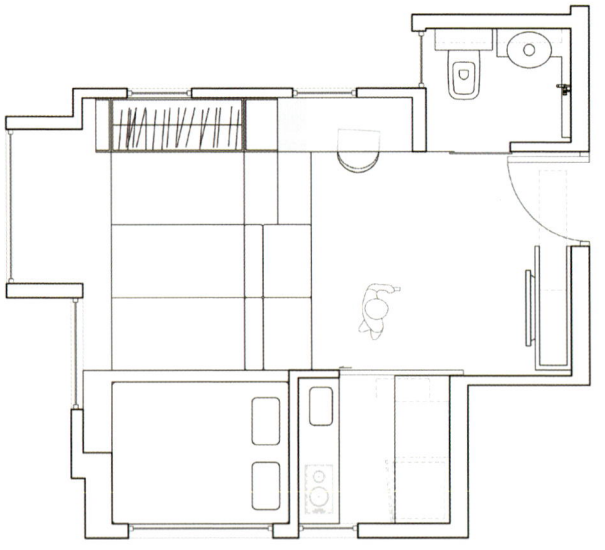

Floor plan

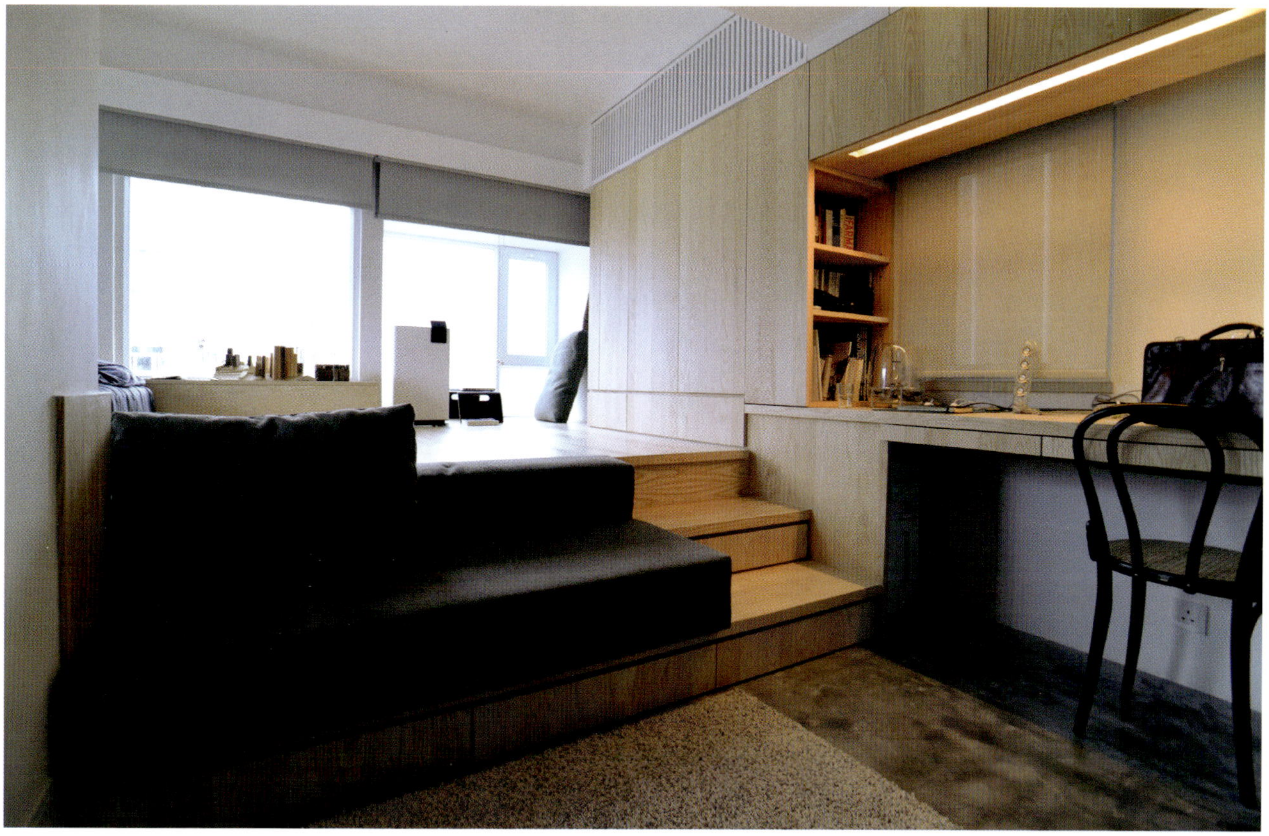

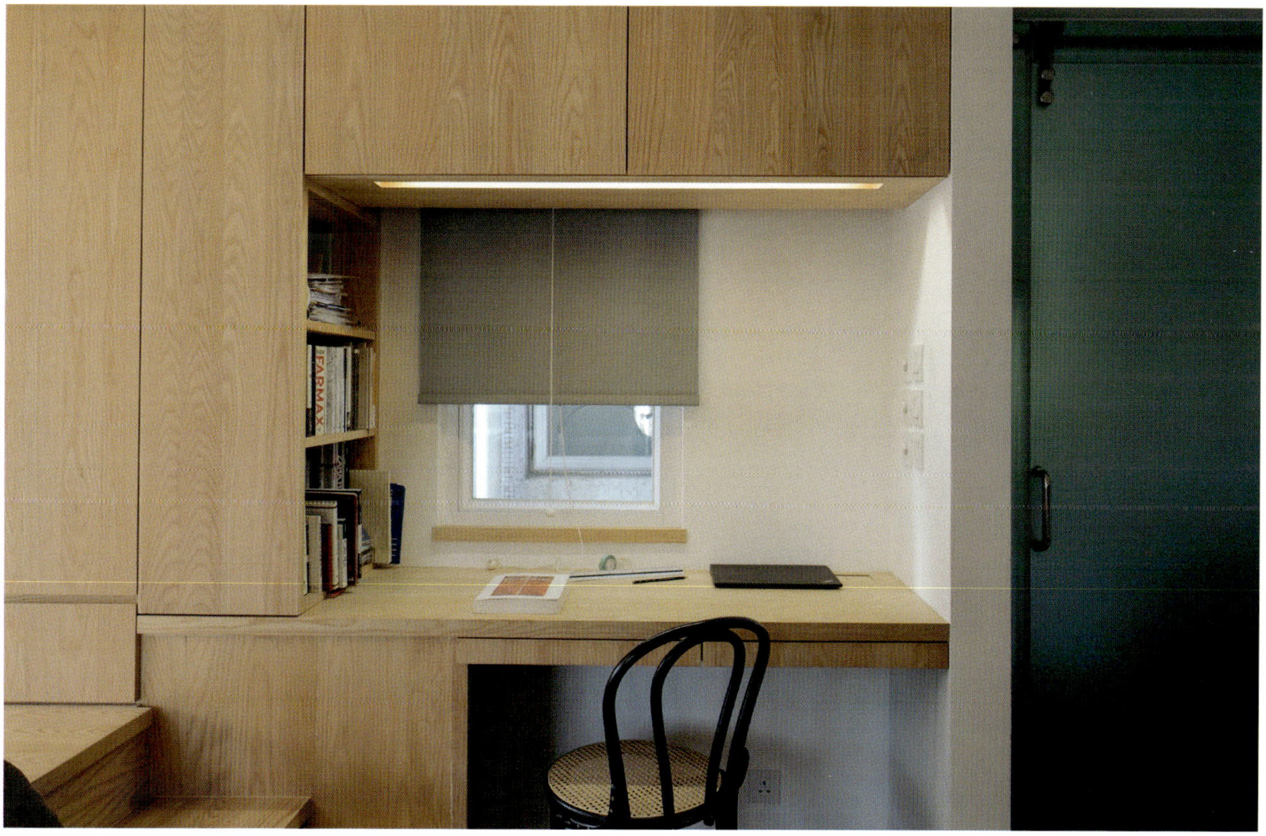

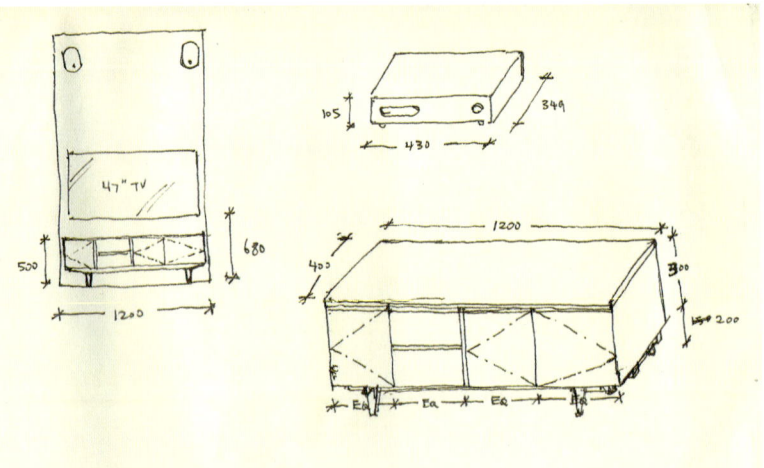

Wall unit design sketches

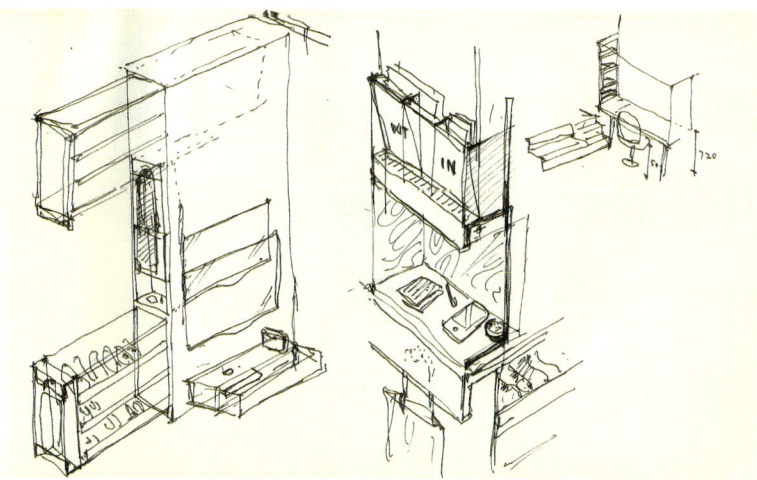

Pull out drawers design sketches

CASA BRASILITO

DINAMO STUDIO
ERICK LEDEZMA FERNÁNDEZ

DINAMOSTUDIO.COM

Construction Technician from the University of Costa Rica, 1992 and Bachelor of Architecture from the Central University, 2004, Erik Ledezma worked from 1992 to 2008 for the companies ZITRO Sistemas Prefabricados and EKSTROM. In 2008 he created Dinamo Studio together with Architect Marco Ávila, which functions as a platform for the publication of projects by both architects on social networks. He has participated in the Biennials of Architecture organized by the College of Architects of Costa Rica, receiving Honorable Mention of the Metalco Grand Prize in 2006. His projects have been published in local magazines such as "Su Casa" and "Estilos y Casas", and in the Costa Rican television programme "Habitat Soluciones". His main objective when designing is that the sum of practical architecture and constructive efficiency result in a functional, stable, aesthetic and sustainable project, capable of adapting to the expectations of the inhabitant and his environment.

Als Bautechniker der Universität von Costa Rica (1992) und Bachelor of Architecture der Zentraluniversität (2004) arbeitete Erik Ledezma von 1992 bis 2008 für die Unternehmen ZITRO Sistemas Prefabricados und EKST-ROM. Im Jahr 2008 gründete er zusammen mit dem Architekten Marco Avila das Dinamo Studio, das als Plattform für die Veröffentlichung von Projekten der beiden Architekten in sozialen Netzwerken fungiert. Er hat an der Architekturbiennale teilgenommen, die vom College of Architects of Costa Rica organisiert wurde, und erhielt 2006 eine ehrenvolle Erwähnung des Metalco Grand Prize. Seine Projekte wurden in lokalen Magazinen wie Su Casa und Estilos y Casas sowie in der costa-ricanischen Fernsehsendung Habitat Soluciones veröffentlicht. Sein Hauptziel beim Entwerfen ist, dass das Zusammenspiel aus praktischer Architektur und konstruktiver Effizienz ein funktionales, stabiles, ästhetisches und nachhaltiges Projekt ergibt, das in der Lage ist, sich an die Erwartungen der Bewohners und der Umgebung anzupassen.

DINAMO STUDIO

Technicien en construction de l'Université du Costa Rica, 1992 et licencié en architecture de l'Université centrale, 2004, Erik Ledezma a travaillé de 1992 à 2008 pour les entreprises ZITRO Sistemas Prefabricados et EKSTROM. En 2008, il a créé Dinamo Studio avec l'architecte Marco Avila, qui fonctionne comme une plateforme pour la publication des projets des deux architectes dans les réseaux sociaux. Il a participé à la Biennale d'architecture organisée par le Collège des architectes du Costa Rica, recevant la mention honorable du Grand prix Metalco en 2006. Ses projets ont été publiés dans des magazines locaux tels que Su Casa et Estilos y Casas, ainsi que dans le programme de télévision costaricain Habitat Soluciones. Son principal objectif en matière de conception est que la somme d'une architecture pratique et d'une efficacité constructive aboutisse à un projet fonctionnel, stable, esthétique et durable, capable de s'adapter aux attentes de l'habitant et de son environnement.

Técnico en Construcción por la Universidad de Costa Rica, 1992 y Licenciado en Arquitectura por la Universidad Central, 2004, Erik Ledezma trabajó de 1992 al 2008 para la empresas ZITRO Sistemas Prefabricados y EKSTROM. En 2008 crea Dinamo Studio en conjunto con el Arquitecto Marco Ávila, que funciona como una plataforma para la publicación de proyectos de ambos arquitectos en redes sociales. Ha participado en la Bienales de Arquitectura organizadas por el Colegio de Arquitectos de Costa Rica, recibiendo Mención de Honor del Gran Premio Metalco, en el año 2006. Sus proyectos han sido publicados en revistas locales como Su Casa y Estilos y Casas, y en el programa televisivo costarricense Habitat Soluciones. Su principal objetivo al diseñar es que la suma de una arquitectura práctica más una eficiencia constructiva den como resultado un proyecto funcional, estable, estético y sostenible, capaz de adecuarse a las expectativas del habitante y a su entorno.

CASA BRASILITO

115 M² // PLAYA BRASILITO, GUANACASTE, COSTA RICA
PHOTOS © ROBERTO D'AMBROSIO

Located very close to the beach, the goal was to design a house as compact as possible but with comfortable spaces, with a contemporary tropical architecture, with an adequate management of sunlight, natural ventilation and using light materials. The house coexists with many natural elements, the existence of runoffs on the site coming from the mountain and from the land in the highest part of the housing development where it is located, was the reason for proposing that the ground level of the project be elevated from the terrain. The house is located in a clearing on the property where trees were not cut down and their shade is used as shelter for the project. Its linear design both in plan and roof allows very easy growth with lateral extensions.

In unmittelbarer Nähe zum Strand gelegen, war das Hauptziel, ein möglichst kompaktes Haus mit komfortablen Räumen zu entwerfen. Das Objekt besticht mit einer zeitgenössischen Architektur im tropischen Stil, einem adäquaten Management des Sonnenlichts, natürlicher Belüftung und verwendet leichte Materialien. Das Haus lebt im Zusammenspiel mit vielen natürlichen Elementen, die vom Berg und von den Ländereien kommen, die sich im höchsten Teil der Wohnsiedlung befinden. Aufgrund dieser Lage wurde das Bodenniveau des Projekts vom Gelände angehoben wurde. Das Haus befindet sich in einer Lichtung, in der es vermieden wurde, Bäume zu fällen und deren Schatten als Schutz für das Projekt genutzt werden. Das geradlinige Design, sowohl im Grundriss als auch im Dach, ermöglichen ein einfaches Wachstum mit seitlichen Anbauten.

Situé tout près de la plage, l'objectif principal était de concevoir une maison aussi compacte que possible mais avec des espaces confortables, avec une architecture tropicale contemporaine, avec une gestion adéquate de la lumière du soleil, une ventilation naturelle et l'utilisation de matériaux légers. La maison coexiste avec de nombreux éléments naturels, l'existence de ruissellements dans le site provenant de la montagne et des terrains qui se trouvent dans la partie la plus élevée du lotissement où elle est située, a été la raison pour laquelle on a proposé que le niveau du sol du projet soit surélevé par rapport au terrain. La maison était située dans une clairière de la propriété où l'on évitait d'abattre des arbres et où leur ombre servait d'abri au projet. Sa conception linéaire, tant en plan qu'en toiture, permet une croissance facile avec des extensions latérales.

Ubicada muy cerca de la playa, el principal objetivo fue diseñar una vivienda lo más compacta posible pero con espacios cómodos, de una arquitectura contemporánea de corte tropical, con un manejo adecuado del asoleamiento, de la ventilación natural y usando materiales livianos. La casa convive con muchos elementos naturales, la existencia de escorrentías en el sitio provenientes de la montaña y de los terrenos que se encuentran en la parte más alta del desarrollo habitacional donde se ubica, fue el motivo para proponer que el nivel del piso del proyecto estuviera elevado del terreno. La casa se ubicó en un claro de la propiedad donde se evitó talar árboles y se aprovecha la sombra de ellos como cobijo del proyecto. Su diseño lineal tanto en planta como en cubierta permite de forma muy fácil el crecimiento con ampliaciones laterales.

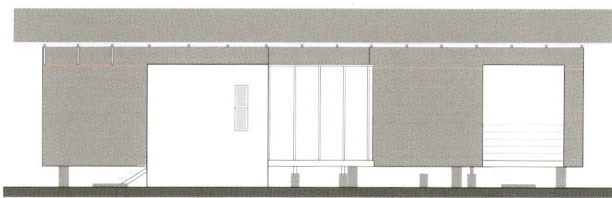

East elevation

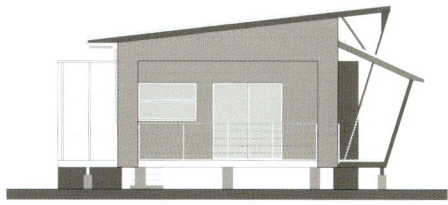

North elevation

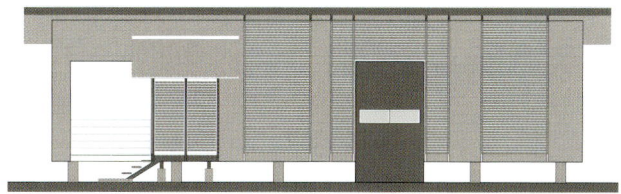

West elevation

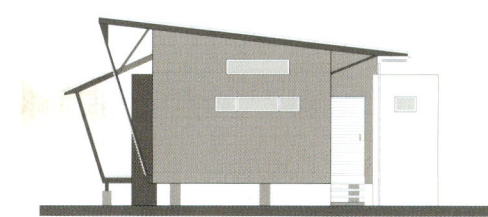

South elevation

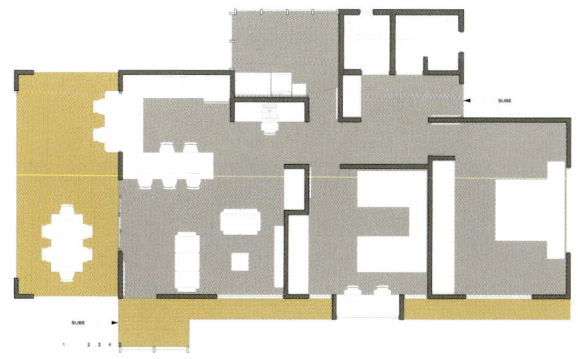

Floor plan

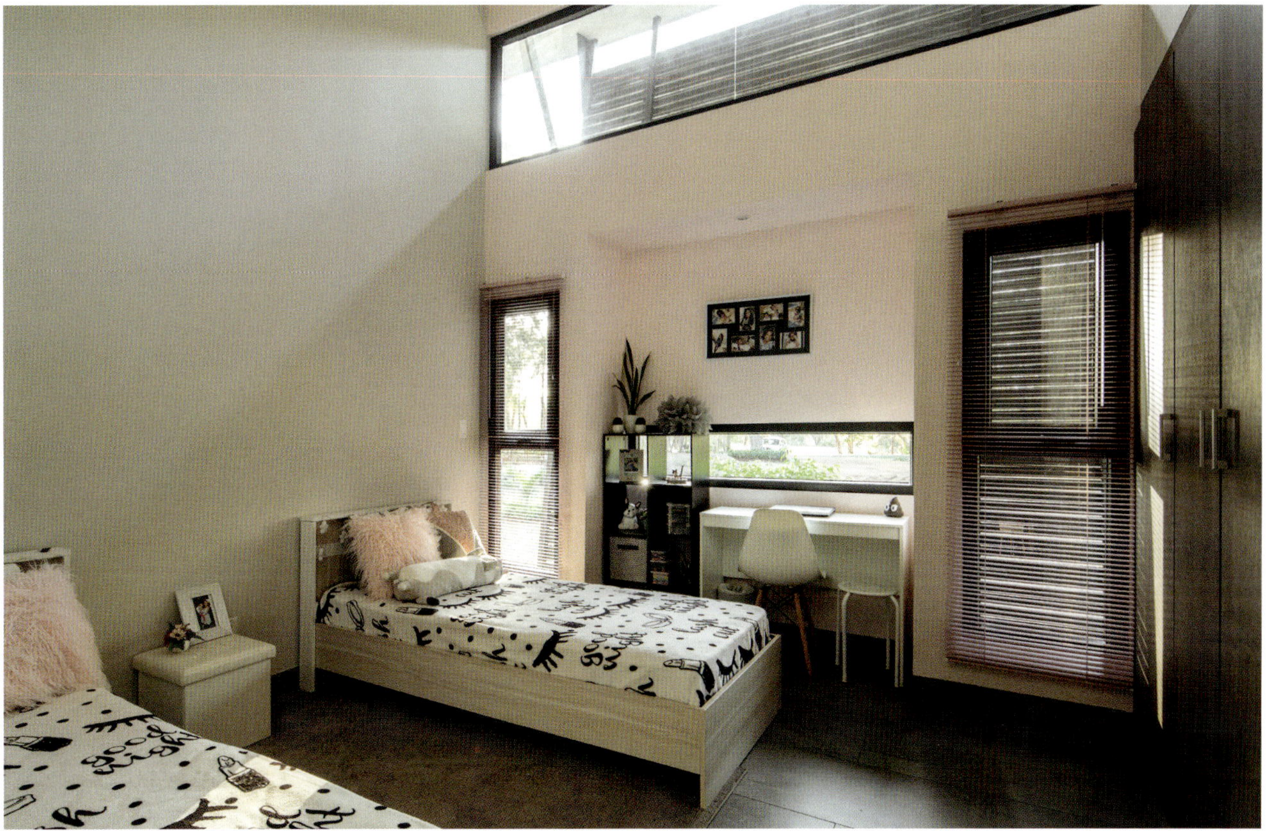

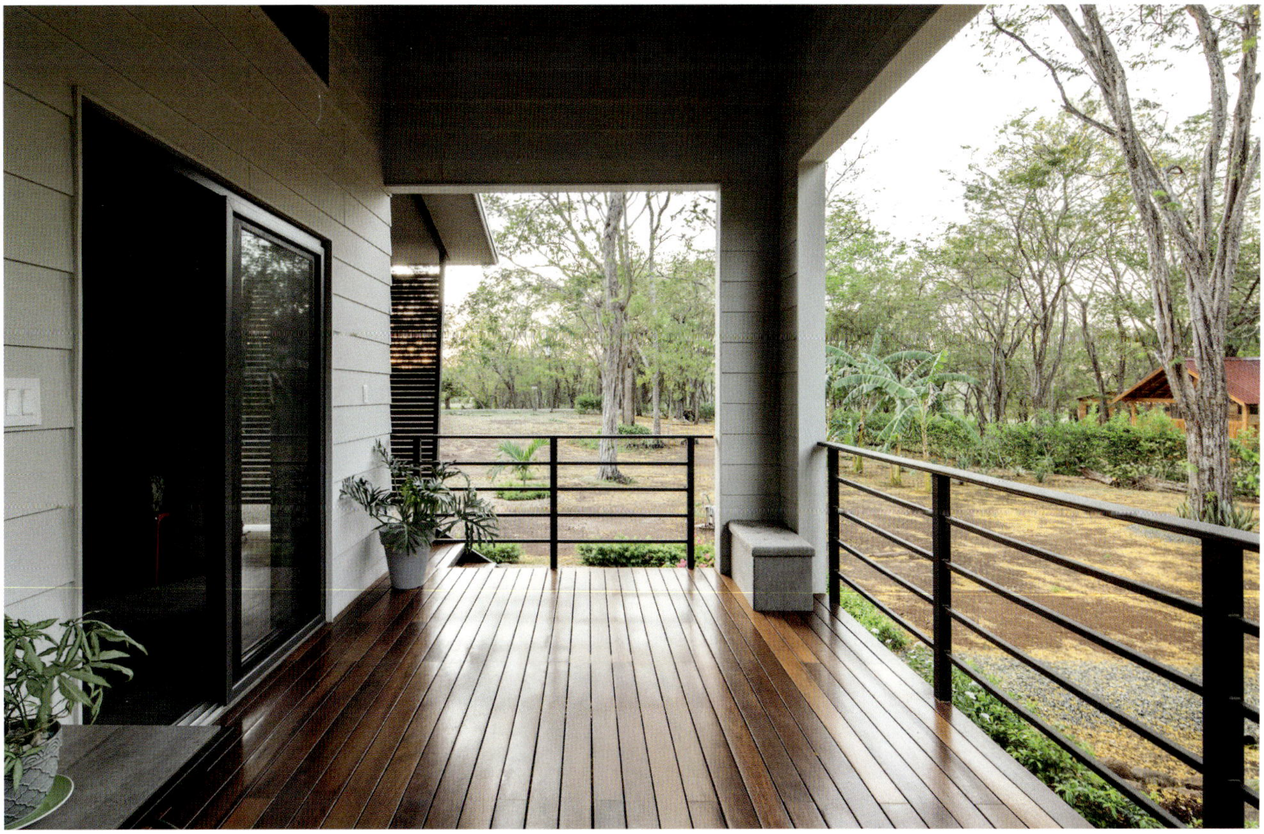

HOUSE H

dmvA

DAVID DRIESEN, TOM VERSCHUEREN

WWW.DMVA-ARCHITECTEN.BE

David Driesen and Tom Verschueren passion for architecture led to dmvA, 'door middel van Architectuur' ('by means of Architecture'). A noble goal to provide a critical answer using architecture to respond to social, economic and collective matters. The creative process doesn't follow a manifesto, but it is expressed through experimenting in architecture: A research on form, material and sustainability... Architecture that always starts with a question, a context and a budget. The work of dmvA can be described as expressive and meticulous, achieving maximalism through minimalism. It also entails dedication to refined details and materiality. By claiming to have no defined style, the entire range of styles is in fact appropriated. This attitude eliminates all conformity restrictions and at the same time makes a statement that timeless architecture doesn't exist.

Aus der Leidenschaft von David Driesen und Tom Verschueren für Architektur entstand dmvA, „door middel van Architectuur" („durch Architektur"). Sie haben sich als Ziel gesetzt, eine kritische Antwort zu geben, indem die Architektur genutzt wird, um auf soziale, wirtschaftliche und kollektive Probleme zu reagieren. Der kreative Prozess drückt sich durch das Experimentieren in der Architektur aus: Es werden Untersuchung von Form, Material und Nachhaltigkeit durchgeführt – eine Architektur, die immer mit einer Frage, einem Kontext und einem Budget beginnt. Die Arbeit von dmvA kann als ausdrucksstark und akribisch beschrieben werden, wobei Maximalismus durch Minimalismus erreicht wird. Dazu gehört auch die Hingabe zu raffinierten Details und Materialität. Durch die Vorgabe, dass sie keinen klaren Stil haben, ist in der Tat die gesamte Bandbreite an Stilen vorhanden. Diese Haltung hebt alle Beschränkungen der Konformität auf und trifft gleichzeitig die Aussage, dass es keine zeitlose Architektur gibt.

dmvA

La passion de David Driesen et Tom Verschueren pour l'architecture a donné naissance à la dmvA, « door middel van Architectuur » (« par l'architecture »). Un noble objectif qui consiste à donner une réponse critique en utilisant l'architecture pour répondre à des questions sociales, économiques et collectives. Le processus créatif s'exprime à travers l'expérimentation en architecture . une recherche sur la forme, le matériau et la durabilité. Une architecture qui commence toujours par une question, un contexte et un budget. Le travail de la dmvA peut être décrit comme expressif et méticuleux, atteignant le maximalisme par le minimalisme. Elle implique également un dévouement aux détails raffinés et à la matérialité. En affirmant qu'elle n'a pas de style défini, la gamme complète des styles est en fait appropriée. Cette attitude supprime toutes les restrictions de conformité et affirme en même temps que l'architecture intemporelle n'existe pas.

La pasión de David Driesen y Tom Verschueren por la arquitectura dio lugar a dmvA, «door middel van Architectuur» («por medio de la arquitectura»). Un noble objetivo de dar una respuesta crítica usando la arquitectura para responder a los asuntos sociales, económicos y colectivos. El proceso creativo se expresa a través de la experimentación en la arquitectura: una investigación sobre la forma, el material y la sostenibilidad... Una arquitectura que siempre empieza con una pregunta, un contexto y un presupuesto. El trabajo del dmvA puede describirse como expresivo y meticuloso, logrando el maximalismo a través del minimalismo. También implica la dedicación a los detalles refinados y la materialidad. Al afirmar que no tiene un estilo definido, toda la gama de estilos es, de hecho, apropiada. Esta actitud elimina todas las restricciones de conformidad y al mismo tiempo hace una declaración de que la arquitectura atemporal no existe.

HOUSE H

110 M² // HOUTHULST, BELGIUM
PHOTOS © SERGIO PIRRONE

For the design of House H, there were different factors dmvA had to take into account: The plot was surrounded by apartment buildings and its orientation wasn't great. There was also a limited budget and the house had to have a low ecological footprint. dmvA followed the concept of the nine-square grid, with in the middle a patio with an adjacent covered terrace. In the bathroom and seating area are skylights.This resulted in a house where light and air can naturally flow. Along each side of the house hang large sliding gates, inspired by rural barn gates, that provide privacy and serve as sun blinds. Through the patio you can see the crowns of the trees, which are a legacy of the former monastery which the plot was part of.

Für den Entwurf von Haus H gab es verschiedene Faktoren, die dmvA berücksichtigen musste: Das Grundstück war von Mehrfamilienhäusern umgeben und seine Ausrichtung war nicht sehr gut. Außerdem gab es ein begrenztes Budget und das Haus musste einen geringen ökologischen Fußabdruck haben. Das dmvA-Studio folgte dem Konzept des Neun-Quadrat-Rasters, mit einem Innenhof in der Mitte und einer angrenzenden überdachten Terrasse. Im Bad und im Wohnbereich befinden sich Oberlichter. Das Ergebnis ist ein Haus, in dem Licht und Luft natürlich fließen können. Entlang jeder Seite des Hauses bieten große Schiebetüren, inspiriert von ländlichen Scheunentoren, Privatsphäre und Schutz vor der Sonne. Durch den Hof kann man die Baumkronen sehen, die ein Erbe des ehemaligen Klosters sind, zu dem das Grundstück gehörte.

Pour la conception de la maison H, la dmvA a dû tenir compte de différents facteurs : le terrain était entouré d'immeubles d'habitation et son orientation n'était pas très bonne. Le budget était également limité et la maison devait avoir une faible empreinte écologique. Le studio dmvA a suivi le concept de la grille à neuf carrés, avec une cour au milieu et une terrasse couverte adjacente. Dans la salle de bains et le salon, il y a des puits de lumière. Cela a donné naissance à une maison où la lumière et l'air peuvent circuler naturellement. De chaque côté de la maison, de grandes portes coulissantes, inspirées des portes des granges rurales, assurent l'intimité et la protection contre le soleil. A travers la cour, vous pouvez voir les cimes des arbres, qui sont un héritage de l'ancien monastère dont la parcelle faisait partie.

Para el diseño de la Casa H, hubo diferentes factores que dmvA tuvo que tener en cuenta: la parcela estaba rodeada de edificios de apartamentos y su orientación no era muy buena. También había un presupuesto limitado y la casa tenía que tener una baja huella ecológica. El estudio dmvA siguió el concepto de la cuadrícula de nueve cuadrados, con un patio en el medio y una terraza cubierta adyacente. En el baño y en la zona de estar hay tragaluces. Esto dio como resultado una casa donde la luz y el aire pueden fluir naturalmente. A lo largo de cada lado de la casa grandes puertas correderas, inspiradas en las puertas de los graneros rurales, proporcionan privacidad y protección para el sol. A través del patio se pueden ver las copas de los árboles, que son un legado del antiguo monasterio del que formaba parte la parcela.

Site plan

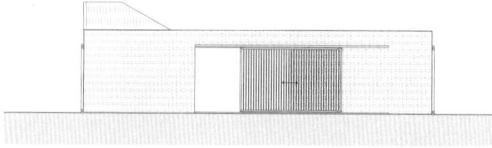

North elevation

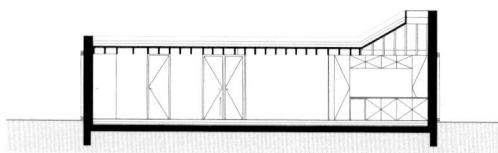

Section

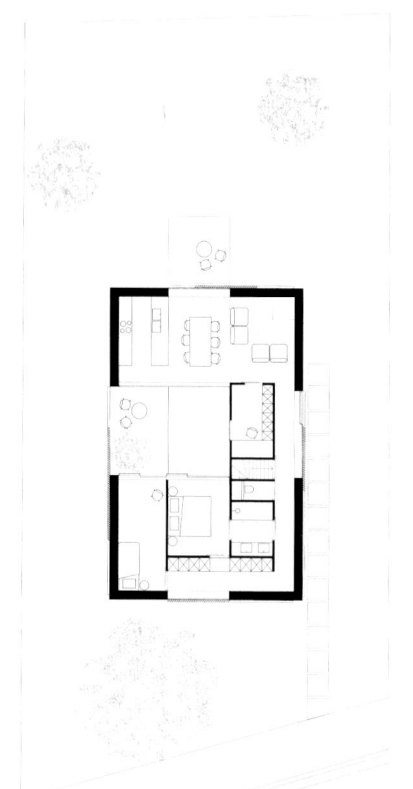

Floor plan

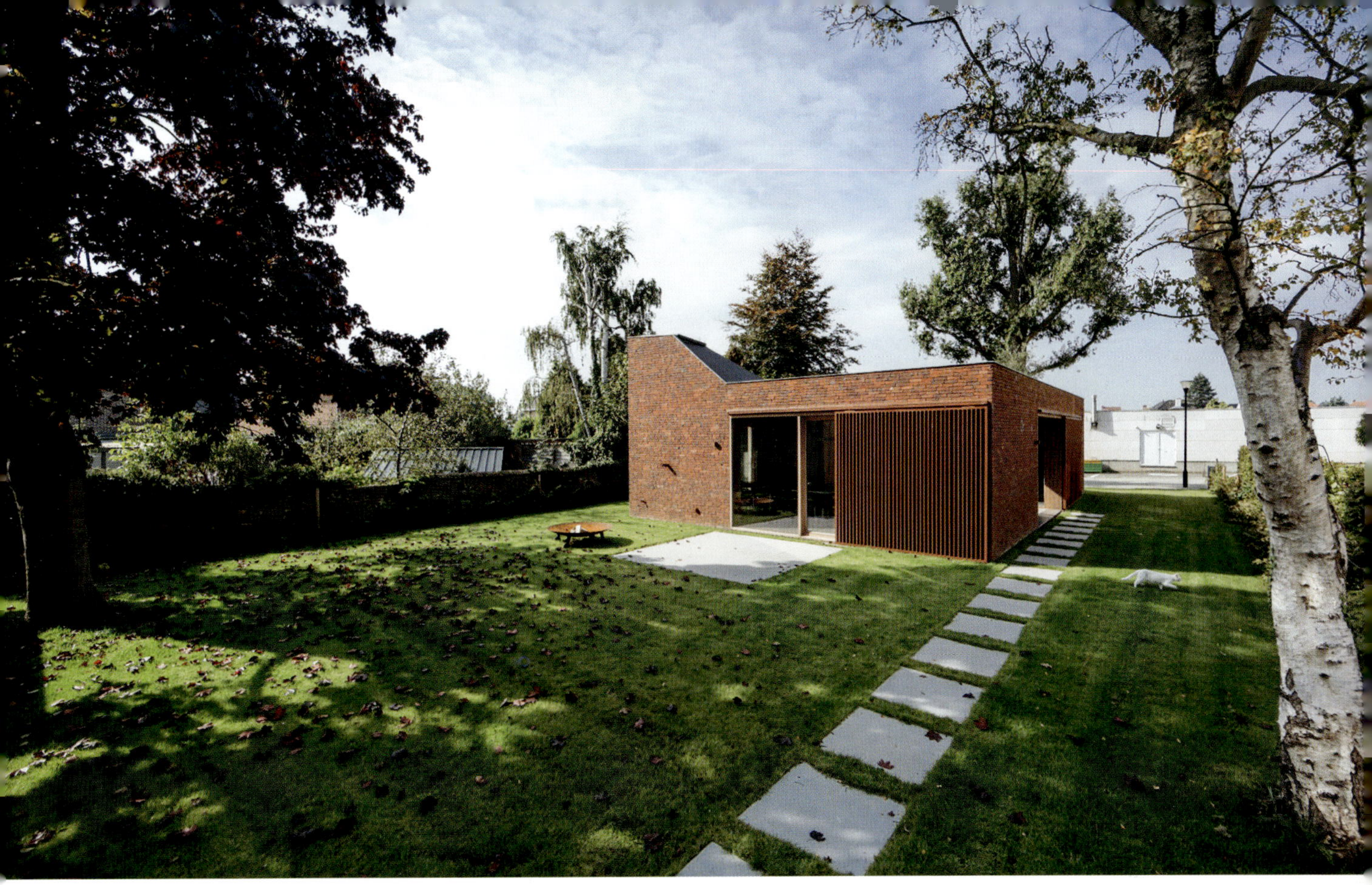

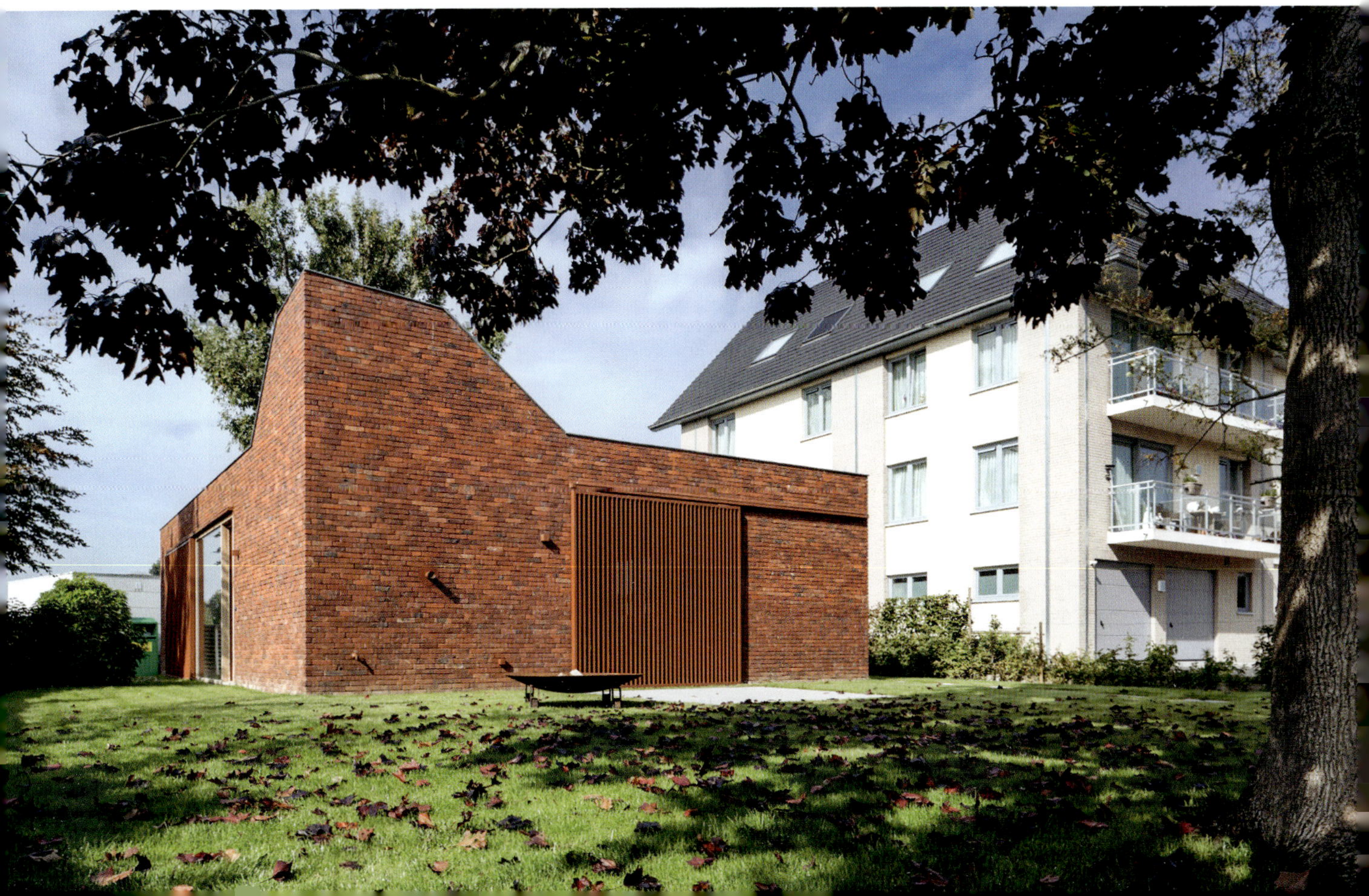

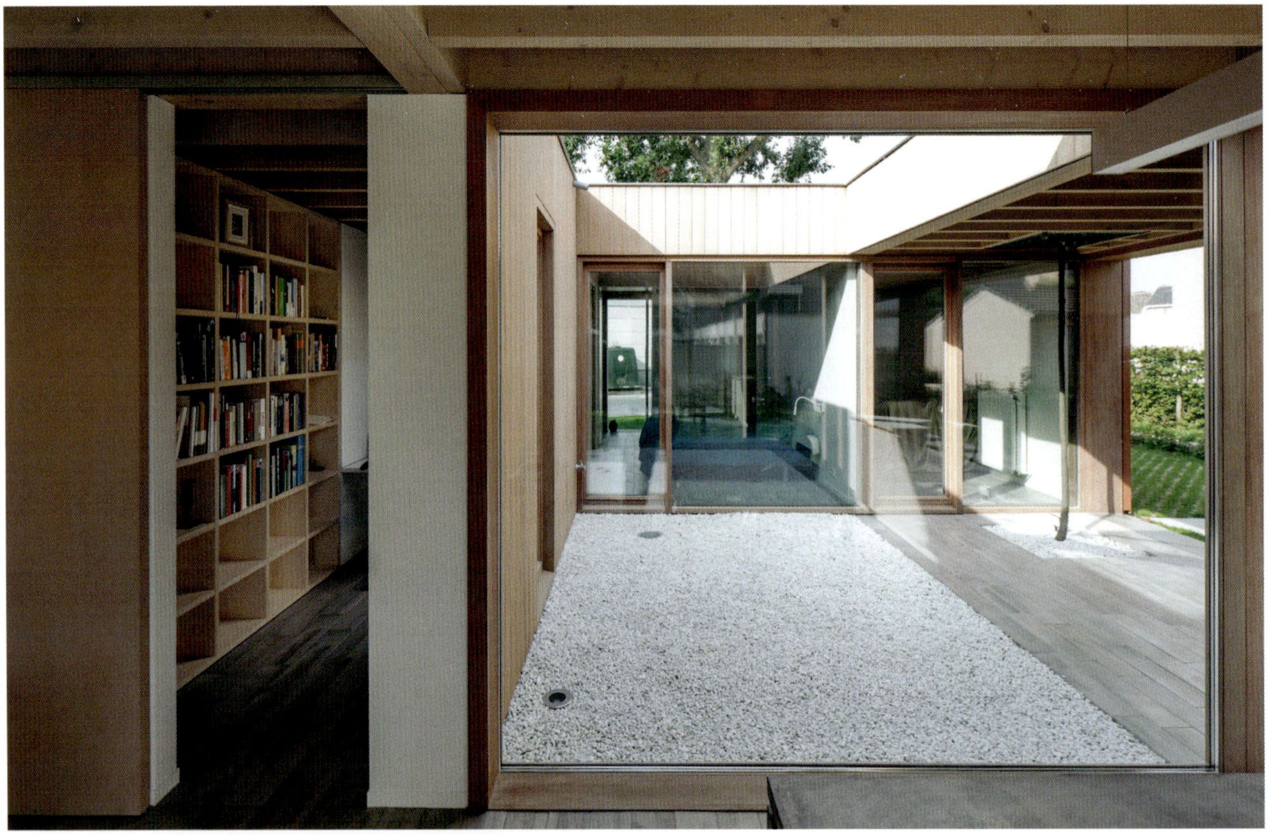

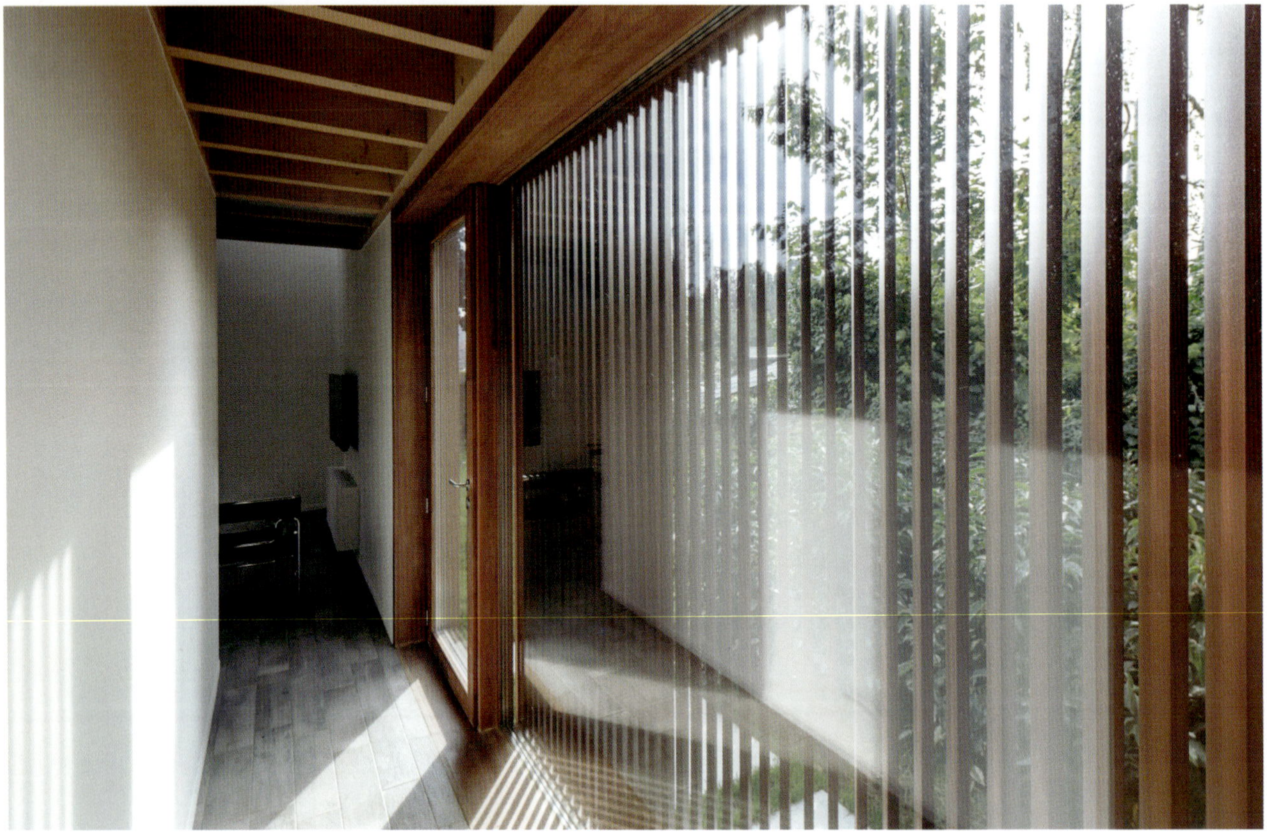

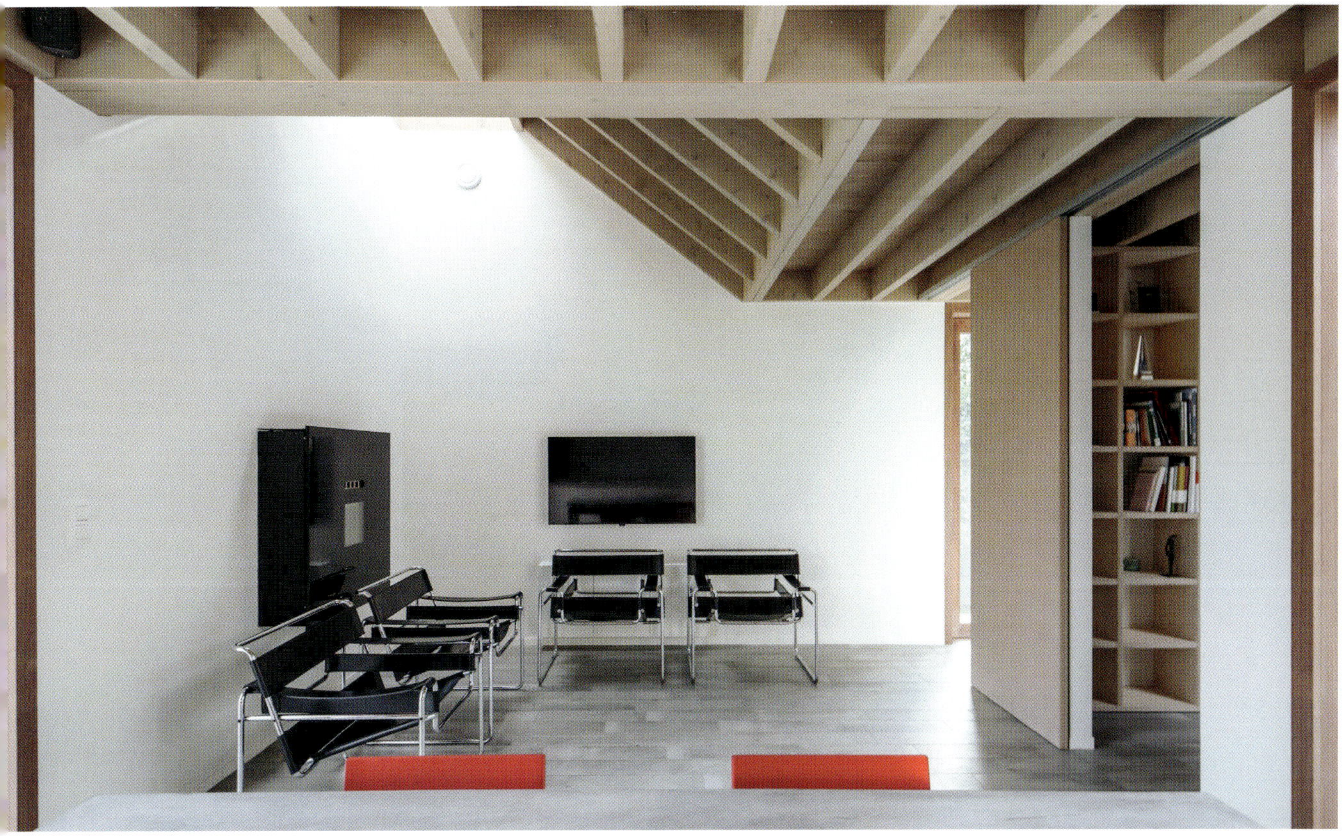

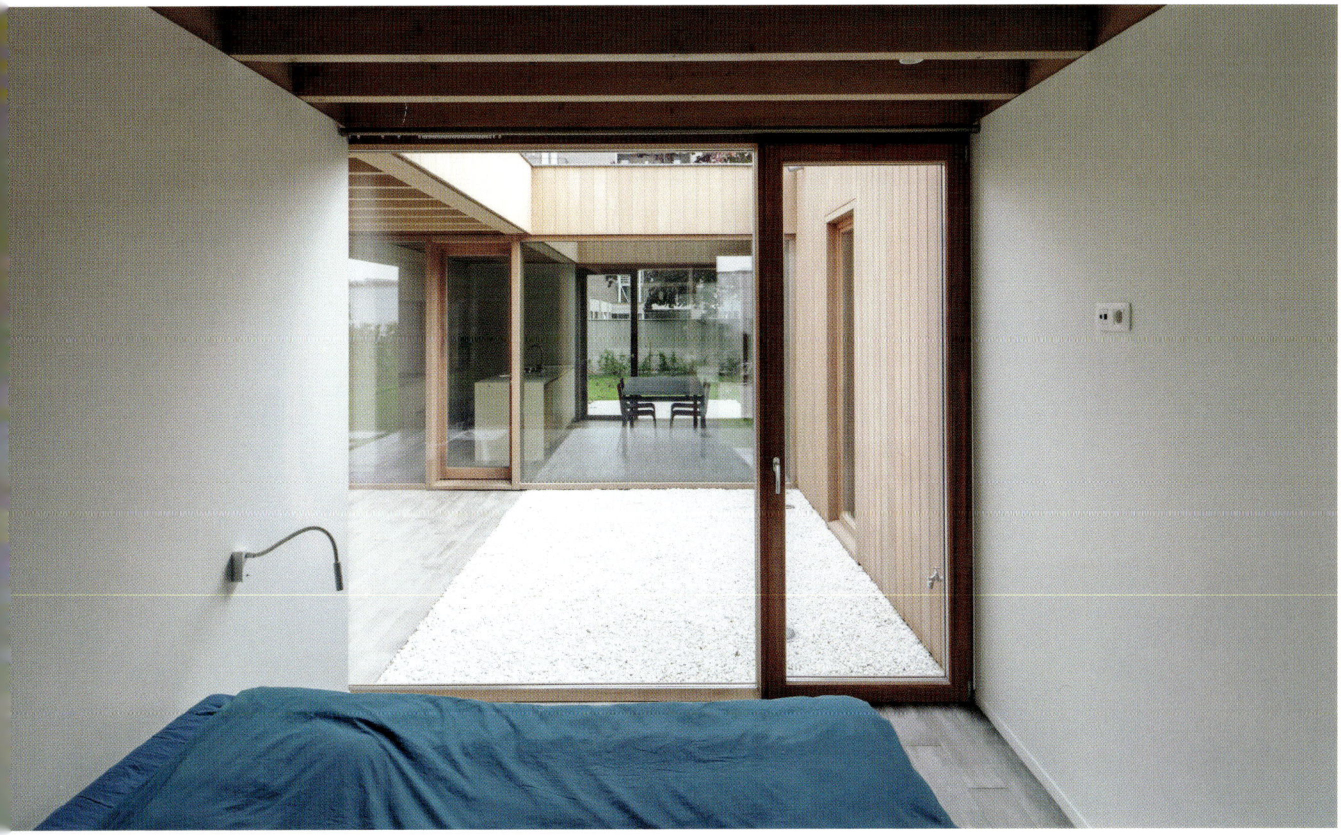

CRADOCK ST

DORRINGTON ATCHESON ARCHITECTS
TIM DORRINGTON AND SAM ATCHESON

DAA.CO.NZ

Twenty years of experience coupled with a spirit of youthful enthusiasm is the yin-yang balance that makes Dorrington Atcheson Architects (DAA) a team whose projects have won many awards. While each project requires a fresh eye and innovative approach, principals Tim Dorrington and Sam Atcheson also draw on their considerable experience in the New Zealand market. Specialising in residential design, but with a proven track record in retail and office design, the studio has won several NZIA awards. Their methodology is highly collaborative, always committed to the requirements of homeowners and clients. Responding to site, budget and idiosyncrasies is key to their work. This honest approach is reflected in the materiality of their buildings where natural products are celebrated. Functional, with measured proportions and a simple structure, the spaces designed by DAA never fail to surprise.

Zwanzig Jahre Erfahrung gepaart mit jugendlichem Enthusiasmus ist die ideale Balance, die Dorrington Atcheson Architects (DAA) zu einem Team macht, dessen Projekte vielfach ausgezeichnet wurden. Während jedes Projekt einen frischen Blick und eine innovative Herangehensweise erfordert, greifen die Geschäftsführer Tim Dorrington und Sam Atcheson auch auf ihre beträchtliche Erfahrung auf dem neuseeländischen Markt zurück. Mit einer Spezialisierung im Wohndesign sowie einer Erfolgsbilanz im Einzelhandels- und Bürodesign, hat dieses Studio mehrere NZIA-Preise gewonnen. Ihre Methodik ist hochgradig kooperativ und stets den Anforderungen von Hausbesitzern und Kunden verpflichtet. Das Integrieren von Standort, Budget und Eigenheiten ist der Schlüssel ihrer Arbeit. Diese ehrliche Herangehensweise spiegelt sich in der Materialität ihrer Gebäude wider, in denen natürliche Produkte die Stars sind. Funktional, mit gemessenen Proportionen und einer einfachen Struktur, überraschen die von DAA entworfenen Häuser immer wieder aufs Neue.

DORRINGTON ATCHESON ARCHITECTS

Vingt ans d'expérience alliés à un esprit d'enthousiasme juvénile, voilà l'équilibre yin-yang qui fait de Dorrington Atcheson Architects (DAA) une équipe dont les projets ont remporté de nombreux prix. Si chaque projet nécessite un regard neuf et une approche innovante, les directeurs Tim Dorrington et Sam Atcheson s'appuient également sur leur expérience considérable du marché néo-zélandais. Spécialisé dans le design résidentiel, mais ayant fait ses preuves dans l'aménagement de commerces et de bureaux, ce studio a remporté plusieurs prix NZIA. Leur méthodologie est très collaborative, toujours en accord avec les exigences des propriétaires et des clients. Leur travail consiste essentiellement à tenir compte du site, du budget et des particularités. Cette approche honnête se reflète dans la matérialité de leurs bâtiments où les produits naturels sont célébrés. Fonctionnels, aux proportions mesurées et à la structure simple, les espaces conçus par le DAA ne cessent d'étonner.

Veinte años de experiencia junto con un espíritu de entusiasmo juvenil es el equilibrio yin-yang que hace de Dorrington Atcheson Architects (DAA) un equipo cuyos proyectos han sido muchas veces premiados. Si bien cada proyecto requiere una mirada fresca y un enfoque innovador, los directores Tim Dorrington y Sam Atcheson también recurren a su considerable experiencia en el mercado neozelandés. Especializado en el diseño residencial, pero con un historial probado en diseño de locales comerciales y de oficinas, este estudio ha ganado varios premios NZIA. Su metodología es muy colaborativa, siempre comprometida con los requisitos de los propietarios de viviendas y los clientes. Responder al sitio, al presupuesto y a las idiosincrasias es la clave de su trabajo. Este enfoque honesto se refleja en la materialidad de sus edificios donde se celebran los productos naturales. Funcionales, con proporciones medidas y una estructura simple, los espacios diseñados por DAA nunca dejan de sorprender.

CRADOCK ST

100 M² // AVONDALE, AUCKLAND, NEW ZEALAND

PHOTOS © EMMA-JANE HETHERINGTON

This small house is the first stage of a two-part project for a couple who saw the new construction as their opportunity to create a hidden oasis in the woods and showcase a collection of mid-century furniture, art and objects collected over the years. Low-rise and surrounded by a garden that provides privacy, its modest entrance is an opening in the ribbed fibre cement coal facade. A corridor from the front door leads directly into the living area where ceilings supported by a regular rhythm of exposed plywood beams provide an industrial tone, reinforced by the dark plywood cabinets in the kitchen.
Hints of yellow, orange and lime green on the front door and window jambs brighten the ambience of this house which becomes a jewel box for modernist pieces.

Dieses kleine Haus ist die erste Etappe eines zweiteiligen Projekts für ein Ehepaar, das den Neubau als Chance sah, eine versteckte Oase im Wald zu schaffen und eine Sammlung von Möbeln, Kunst und Objekten aus der Mitte des Jahrhunderts zu präsentieren, die sie im Laufe der Jahre gesammelt haben. Das Haus ist niedrig und von einem Garten umgeben, der Privatsphäre bietet und besitzt einen unscheinbaren Eingang in Form einer Öffnung in der gerippten Faserzement-Kohlefassade. Von der Haustür führt ein Flur direkt in den Wohnbereich, wo die von freiliegender Sperrholzbalken getragenen Decken einen industriellen Charme erzeugen, der durch die dunklen Sperrholzschränke in der Küche noch verstärkt wird.
Akzente von Gelb, Orange und Limonengrün an der Haustür und den Fensterlaibungen erhellen das Ambiente dieses Hauses, das zu einem Schmuckkästchen für modernistische Stücke wird.

Cette petite maison est la première étape d'un projet en deux parties pour un couple qui a vu dans cette nouvelle construction l'occasion de créer une oasis cachée dans les bois et de mettre en valeur une collection de meubles, d'œuvres d'art et d'objets du milieu du siècle, accumulés au fil des ans. De faible hauteur et entouré d'un jardin qui lui assure une certaine intimité, son entrée modeste est une ouverture dans la façade en fibre-ciment et charbon nervuré. Un couloir partant de la porte d'entrée mène directement à la zone de séjour où les plafonds soutenus par un rythme régulier de poutres apparentes en contreplaqué donnent un ton industriel, renforcé par les armoires en contreplaqué sombre de la cuisine.
Des touches de jaune, d'orange et de vert citron sur la porte d'entrée et les montants des fenêtres égayent l'ambiance de cette maison qui devient un écrin pour les pièces modernistes.

Esta pequeña casa es la primera etapa de un proyecto de dos partes para una pareja que vio la nueva construcción como su oportunidad de crear un oasis escondido en el bosque y mostrar una colección de muebles de mediados de siglo, arte y objetos coleccionados a lo largo de los años. De baja altura y rodeada de un jardín que le proporciona privacidad, su modesta entrada es una abertura en la fachada de carbón de fibrocemento acanalado. Un pasillo desde la puerta principal lleva directamente a la zona de estar donde los techos sostenidos por un ritmo regular de vigas de madera laminada expuesta proporcionan un tono industrial, reforzado por los oscuros armarios de madera contrachapada de la cocina.
Notas de amarillo, naranja y verde lima en la puerta principal y en las jambas de las ventanas iluminan el ambiente de esta casa que deviene un joyero para piezas modernistas.

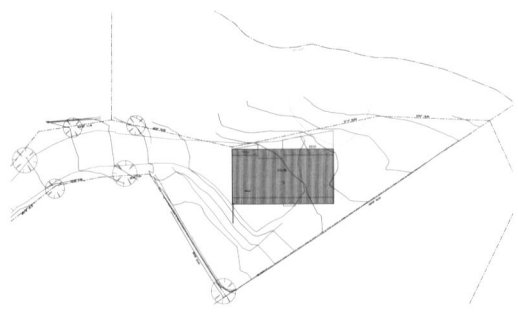

Site plan

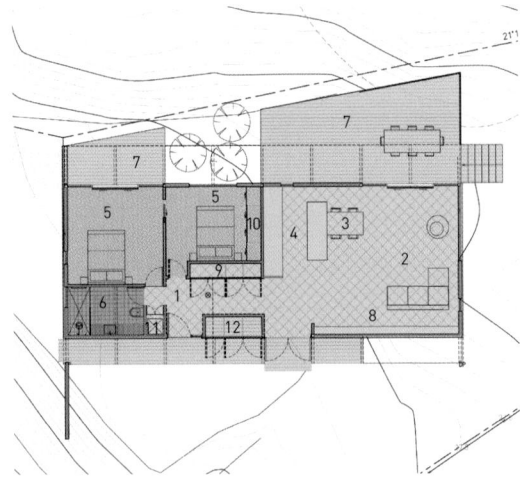

Floor plan

1. Entry	8. Study and
2. Living room	bookshelves
3. Dining room	9. Storage
4. Kitchen	10. Wardrobe
5. Bedroom	11. Laundry
6. Bathroom	12. Tools/storage
7. Deck	

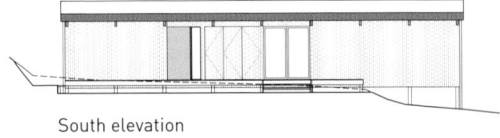

South elevation

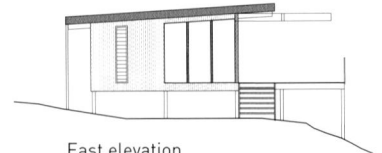

East elevation

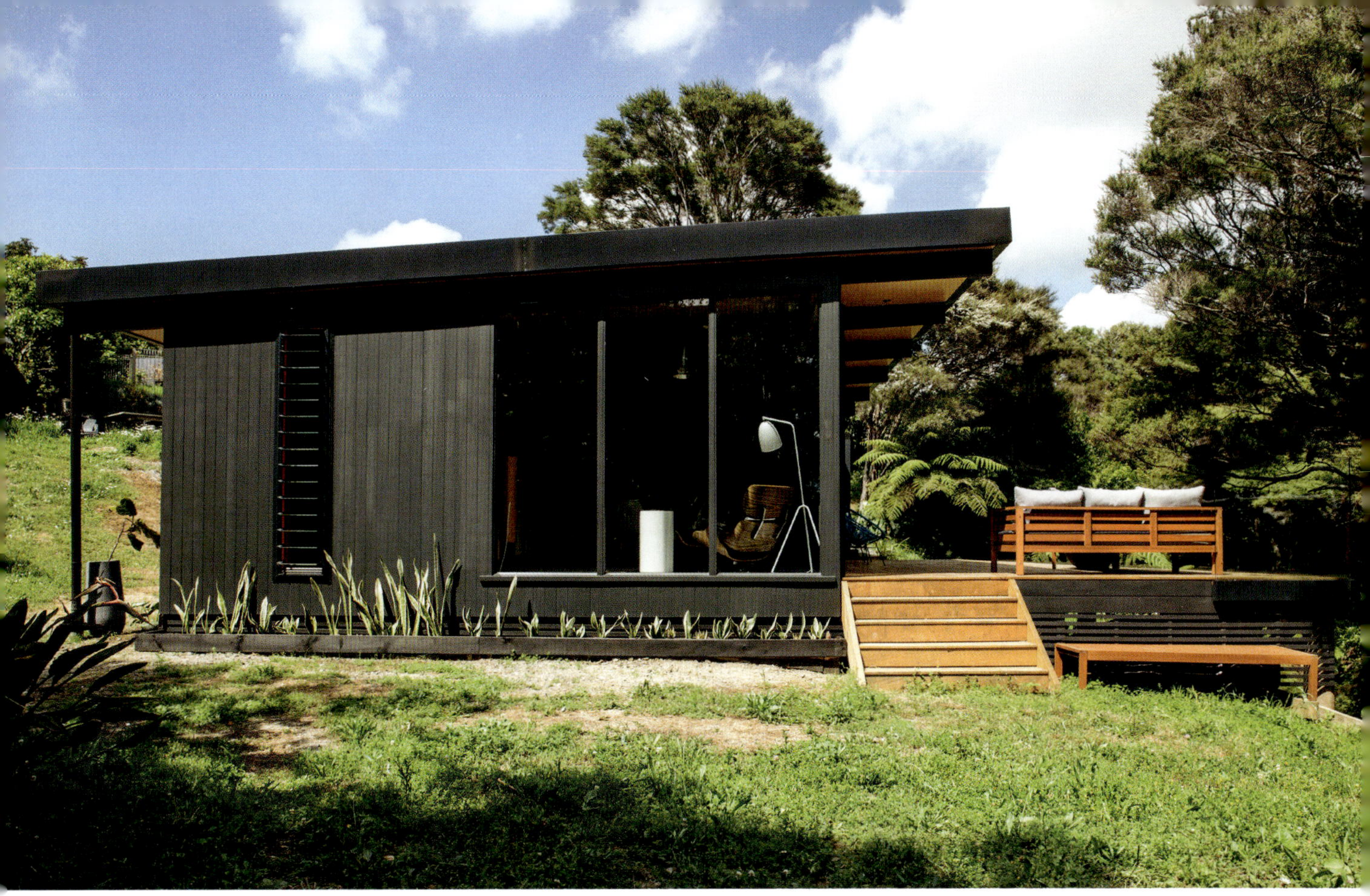

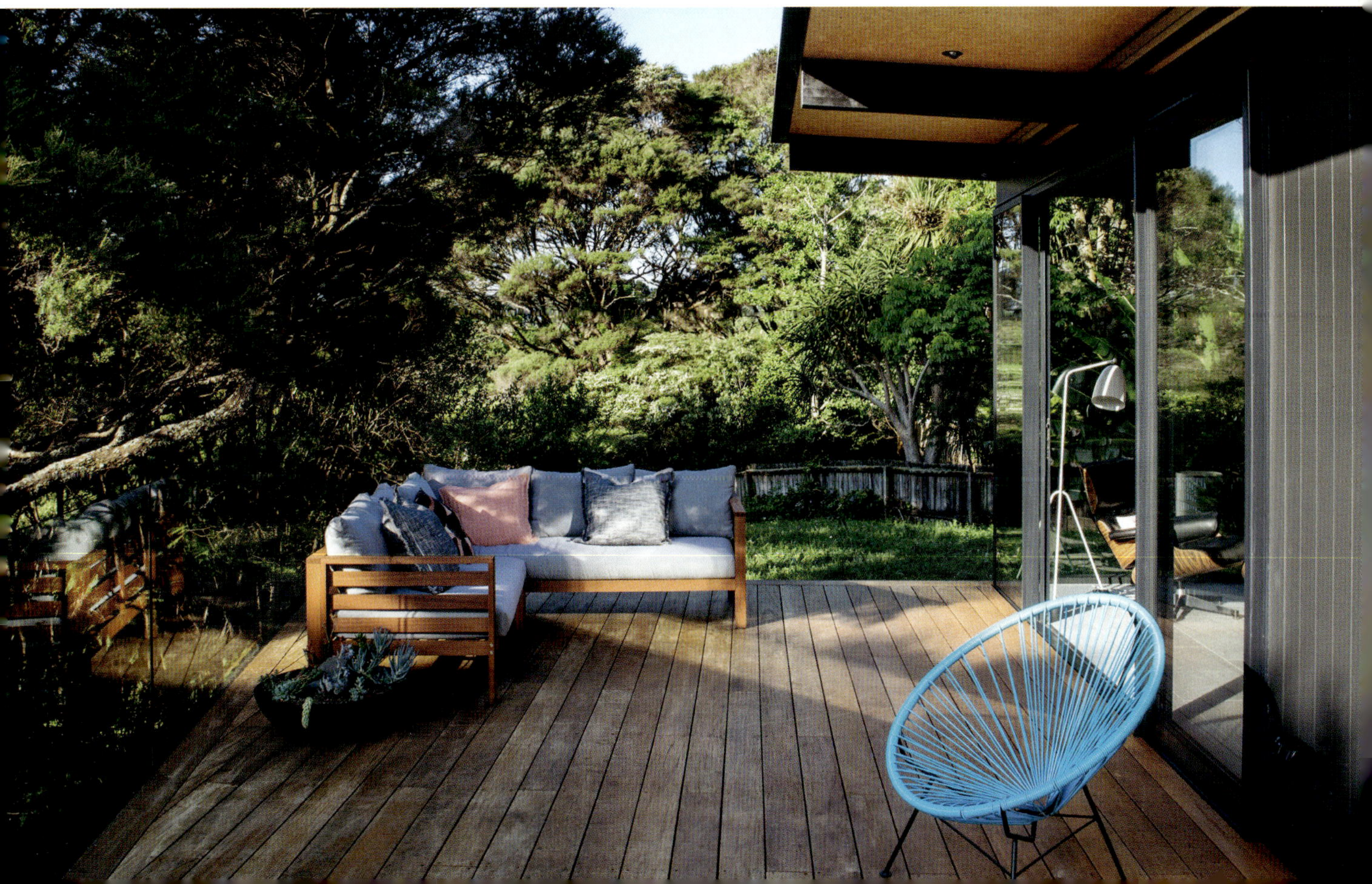

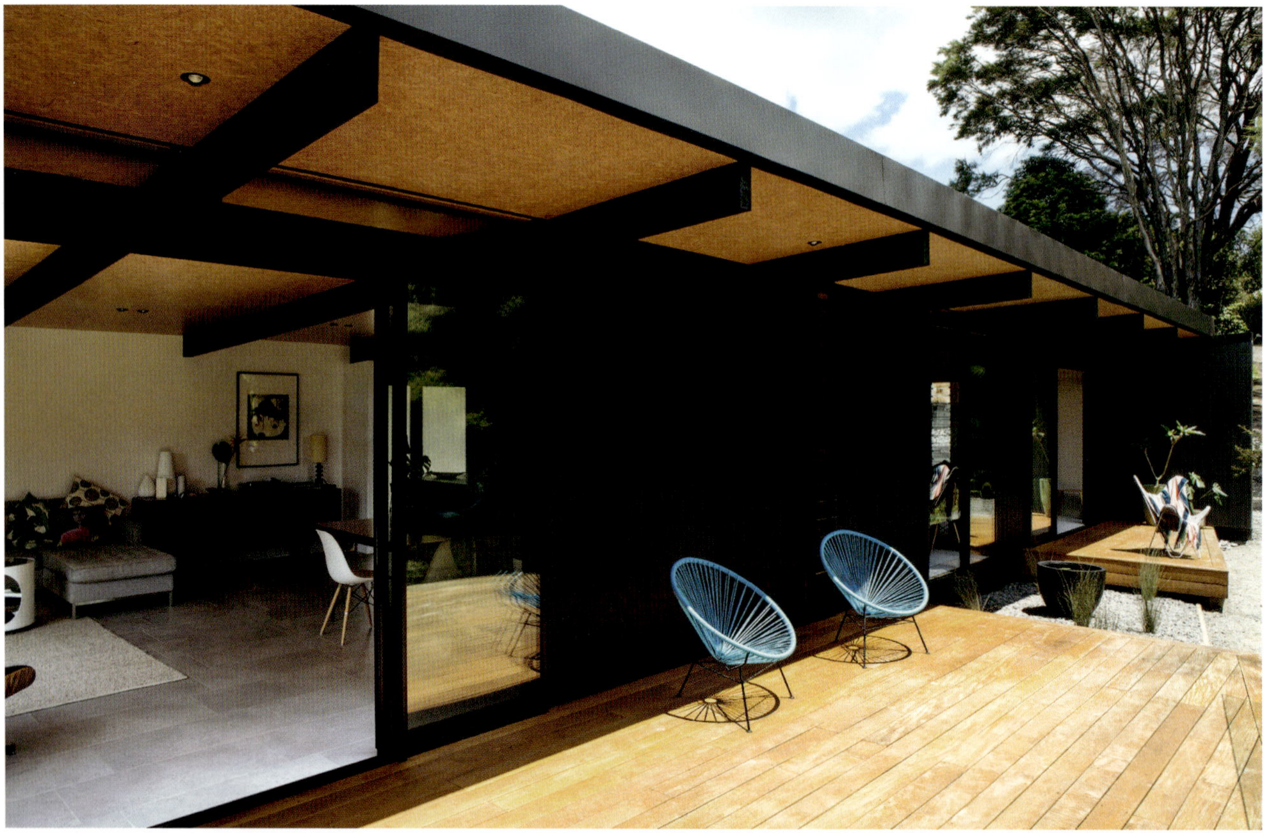

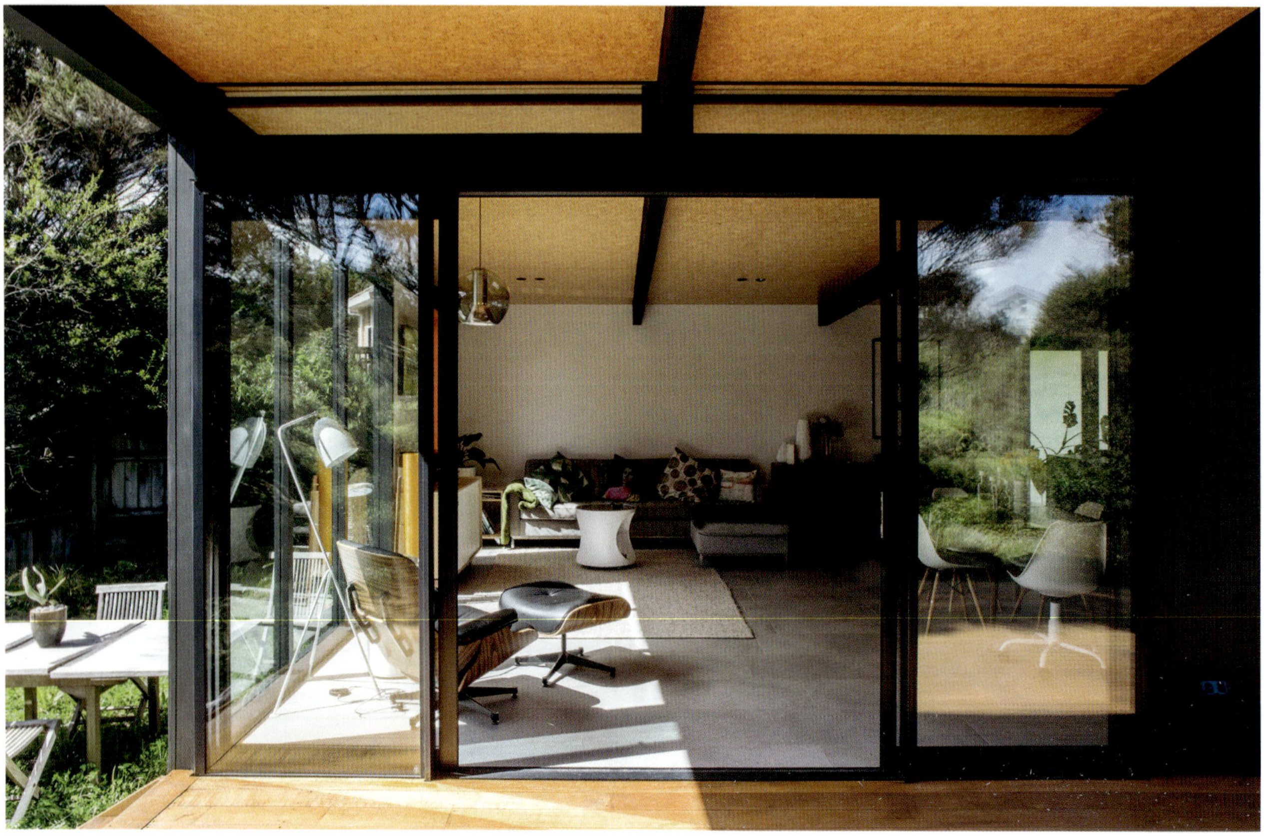

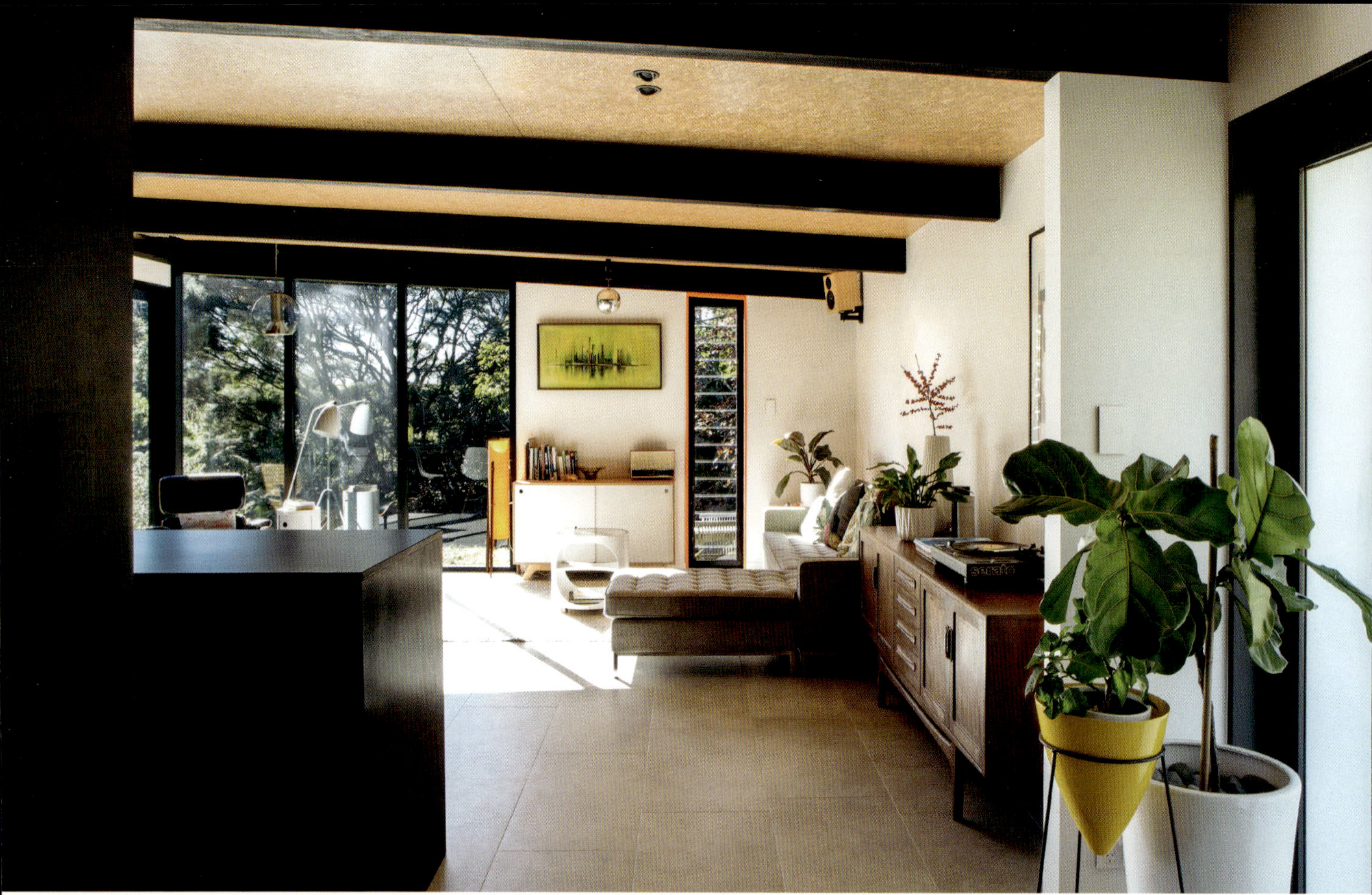

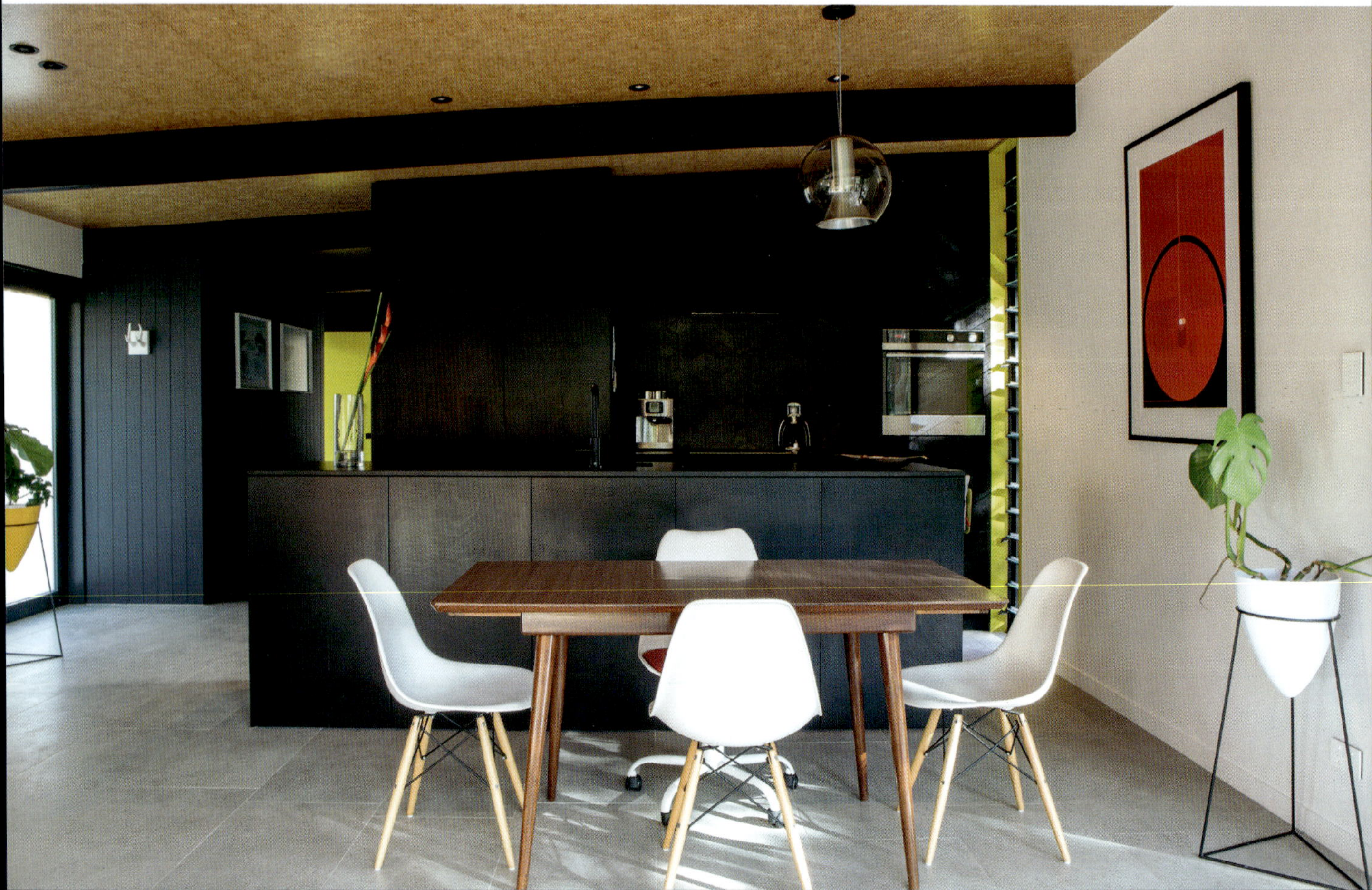

VIKING SEASIDE SUMMER HOUSE

FREAKS ARCHITECTURE
GUILLAUME AUBRY,
CYRIL GAUTHIER & YVES PASQUET

WWW.FREAKSARCHITECTURE.COM

FREAKS is a Paris-France based architecture firm lead by three architects (Guillaume Aubry, Cyril Gauthier & Yves Pasquet) favouring prospection, research and experimentation through projects and building process practices from small scale art installations to large scale architecture competitions. FREAKS has been awarded the AJAP price from the French Ministry of Culture and Communication in 2010 and the 40under40 European price in 2016. Recent projects include the MECA in Bordeaux (in association with BIG) shortlisted for the Mies van der Rohe 2021 Award, the International Glass Blowing Center of Meisenthal (in association with SO-IL), the Fiminco art Foundation in Romainville or the Museum of Natural History of Strasbourg.

FREAKS ist ein in Paris-Frankreich ansässiges Architekturbüro, das von drei Architekten (Guillaume Aubry, Cyril Gauthier & Yves Pasquet) geleitet wird, die Prospektion, Forschung und Experimente durch Projekte und Bauprozesspraktiken von kleinen Kunstinstallationen bis hin zu groß angelegten Architekturwettbewerben favorisieren. FREAKS wurde 2010 mit dem AJAP-Preis des französischen Ministeriums für Kultur und Kommunikation und 2016 mit dem europäischen Preis 40under40 ausgezeichnet. Zu den jüngsten Projekten gehören das MECA in Bordeaux (in Zusammenarbeit mit BIG), das auf der Shortlist für den Mies van der Rohe 2021 Award steht, das Internationale Glasbläserzentrum in Meisenthal (in Zusammenarbeit mit SO-IL), die Fiminco Kunststiftung in Romainville oder das Naturhistorische Museum in Straßburg.

FREAKS ARCHITECTURE

FREAKS est une agence d'architecture basée à Paris et dirigée par trois architectes (Guillaume Aubry, Cyril Gauthier et Yves Pasquet) qui privilégient la prospection, la recherche et l'expérimentation à travers des projets et des processus de construction allant d'installations artistiques à petite échelle à des concours d'architecture à grande échelle. FREAKS a reçu le prix AJAP du ministère français de la Culture et de la Communication en 2010 et le prix européen 40under40 en 2016. Parmi ses projets récents, citons le MECA de Bordeaux (en association avec BIG) sélectionné pour le prix Mies van der Rohe 2021, le Centre international de soufflage de verre de Meisenthal (en association avec SO-IL), la Fondation d'art Fiminco à Romainville ou le Musée d'histoire naturelle de Strasbourg.

FREAKS es un estudio de arquitectura con sede en París, dirigido por tres arquitectos (Guillaume Aubry, Cyril Gauthier e Yves Pasquet) que favorece la prospección, la investigación y la experimentación a través de proyectos y procesos de construcción desde instalaciones artísticas a pequeña escala hasta concursos de arquitectura a gran escala. FREAKS ha recibido el premio AJAP del Ministerio de Cultura y Comunicación francés en 2010 y el premio europeo 40under40 en 2016. Entre sus proyectos más recientes se encuentran el MECA de Burdeos (en asociación con BIG), preseleccionado para el Premio Mies van der Rohe 2021, el Centro Internacional de Soplado de Vidrio de Meisenthal (en asociación con SO-IL), la Fundación de Arte Fiminco de Romainville o el Museo de Historia Natural de Estrasburgo.

VIKING SEASIDE SUMMER HOUSE

12 M² // FERMANVILLE, FRANCE

PHOTOS © JULES COUARTOU

FREAKS was commissioned for the refurbishment of a preexisting concrete fishing shack of ten by fifteen feet, built in the rock during the 1950s. Because of the strict coastal construction regulations, the shack couldn't change in size or shape. The architects realized that the shack's dimensions and ratio were comparable to those of the log cabin on Walden Pond, where philosopher Henry David Thoreau lived alone for two-and-a-half years. During this time, Thoreau focused on nature, his writing, and "to front only the essential facts of life," he wrote. This concept, so profusely revived nowadays through many small house trends, was the starting point for the project, manifesting that downsizing isn't necessarily a sacrifice.

FREAKS wurde für die renovierung einer bereits bestehenden, zehn mal fünfzehn fuß großen fischerhütte aus beton in auftrag gegeben, die in den 1950er jahren in den felsen gebaut wurde. Aufgrund der strengen bauvorschriften an der küste konnte die hütte weder in größe noch form verändert werden. Die architekten erkannten, dass die abmessungen und verhältnisse der hütte mit denen der blockhütte am walden pond vergleichbar waren, wo der philosoph Henry David Thoreau zweieinhalb jahre lang allein lebte. In dieser zeit konzentrierte sich Thoreau auf die natur, seine schriftstellerei und darauf, „nur die wesentlichen tatsachen des lebens vor augen zu haben", wie er schrieb. Dieses konzept, das heutzutage durch viele kleine haustrends wiederbelebt wird, war der ausgangspunkt für das projekt und manifestiert, dass downsizing nicht unbedingt ein verzicht sein muss.

FREAKS a été commandé pour la rénovation d'une cabane de pêche pré-existante en béton de 3 x 4 m construite dans la roche dans les années 1950. En raison des règles strictes de construction sur la côte, la cabane ne pouvait pas changer de taille ou de forme. Les architectes ont réalisé que les dimensions et le rapport de la cabane étaient comparables à ceux de la cabane en rondins de Walden Pond, où le philosophe Henry David Thoreau a vécu seul pendant deux ans et demi. Pendant cette période, Thoreau s'est concentré sur la nature, sur ses écrits et sur le fait de « ne faire face qu'aux faits essentiels de la vie », a-t-il écrit. Ce concept, si abondamment repris de nos jours par de nombreuses tendances de petites maisons, a été le point de départ du projet, manifestant que la réduction de la taille n'est pas nécessairement un sacrifice.

FREAKS recibió el encargo de reformar una cabaña de pesca de hormigón preexistente de 3 x 4 m, construida en la roca en los años cincuenta. Debido a la estricta normativa de construcción costera, la choza no podía cambiar de tamaño ni de forma. Los arquitectos se dieron cuenta de que las dimensiones y la proporción de la choza eran comparables a las de la cabaña de madera de Walden Pond, donde el filósofo Henry David Thoreau vivió solo durante dos años y medio. Durante este tiempo, Thoreau se centró en la naturaleza, en sus escritos y en «afrontar solo los hechos esenciales de la vida», escribió. Este concepto, tan profusamente revivido hoy en día a través de muchas tendencias de casas pequeñas, fue el punto de partida del proyecto, manifestando que la reducción de tamaño no es necesariamente un sacrificio.

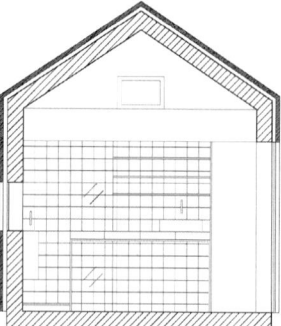

North interior elevation

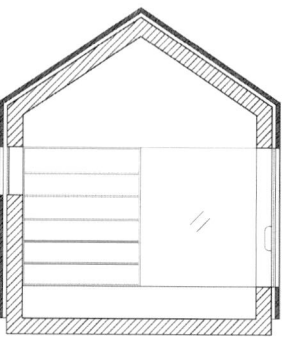

South interior elevation

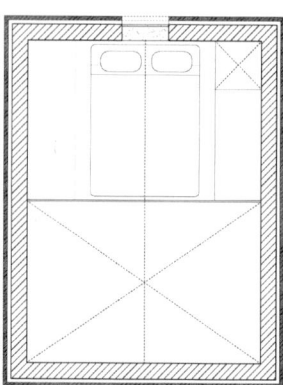

Mezzanine floor plan

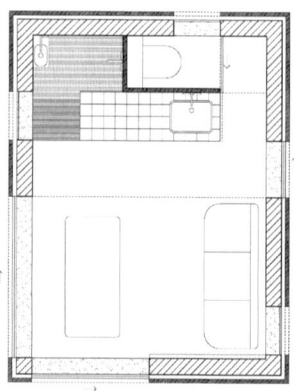

Ground floor plan

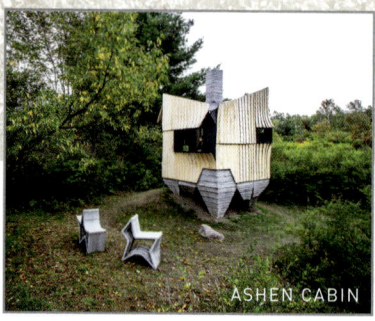

ASHEN CABIN

HANNAH

LESLIE LOK, SASA ZIVKOVIC

WWW.HANNAH-OFFICE.ORG

HANNAH is an experimental design and research studio based in Ithaca, New York, working across scales from furniture to urbanism. From the ground up, digital design and fabrication technologies are intrinsic to the making of our work, facilitating fundamentally new material methods, tectonic articulations, environmental practices, technological affordances, and forms of construction. Led by Leslie Lok & Sasa Zivkovic, HANNAH was named Next Progressives by Architect Magazine in 2018 and won the Architectural League Prize in 2020.

Leslie Lok combines her role as co-principal at HANNAH with a position as an assistant professor at Cornell University College of Architecture, Art, and Planning. Sasa Zivkovic is also an assistant professor at Cornell University AAP where he directs the Robotic Construction Laboratory (RCL).

HANNAH ist ein experimentelles Design- und Forschungs-studio mit Sitz in Ithaca, New York, das von Möbeln bis zum Städtebau arbeitet. Von Anfang an sind digitale Design- und Fertigungstechnologien fester Bestandteil unserer Arbeit und ermöglichen grundlegend neue Materialmethoden, tektonische Artikulationen, Umweltpraktiken, technologische Möglichkeiten und Konstruktionsformen. Unter der Leitung von Leslie Lok & Sasa Zivkovic wurde HANNAH 2018 vom Architect Magazine als Next Progressives ausgezeichnet und gewann 2020 den Architectural League Prize.

Leslie Lok kombiniert ihre Rolle als Co-Direktorin bei HANNAH mit einer Position als Assistenzprofessorin am Cornell University College of Architecture, Art, and Planning. Sasa Zivkovic, Co-Direktor bei HANNAH, ist außerdem Assistenzprofessor an der Cornell University AAP, wo er das Robotic Construction Laboratory (RCL) leitet.

HANNAH

HANNAH est un studio de design et de recherche expérimental basé à Ithaca, New York, travaillant à des échelles allant du mobilier à l'urbanisme. Depuis le début, les technologies de conception et de fabrication numériques sont intrinsèques à la réalisation de notre travail, facilitant des méthodes matérielles, des articulations tectoniques, des pratiques environnementales, des possibilités technologiques et des formes de construction fondamentalement nouvelles.

Dirigé par Leslie Lok & Sasa Zivkovic, HANNAH a été nommé Next Progressives par Architect Magazine en 2018 et a remporté le prix Architectural League en 2020. Leslie Lok combine son rôle de co-principale chez HANNAH avec un poste de professeur adjoint au Collège d'architecture, d'art et de planification de l'Université Cornell. Sasa Zivkovic, co-principal chez HANNAH, est également professeur adjoint à l'Université Cornell AAP, où il dirige le Robotic Construction Laboratory (RCL).

HANNAH es un estudio de diseño e investigación experimental con sede en Ithaca, Nueva York, que trabaja en distintas escalas, desde el mobiliario hasta el urbanismo. Desde su creación, el diseño digital y las tecnologías de fabricación son intrínsecos a la realización de nuestro trabajo, facilitando fundamentalmente nuevos métodos materiales, articulaciones tectónicas, prácticas ambientales, posibilidades tecnológicas y formas de construcción. Dirigido por Leslie Lok y Sasa Zivkovic, HANNAH fue nombrado Next Progressives por Architect Magazine en 2018 y ganó el Architectural League Prize en 2020.

Leslie Lok combina su papel como codirectora de HANNAH con un puesto como profesora adjunta en la Facultad de Arquitectura, Arte y Planificación de la Universidad de Cornell. Sasa Zivkovic, codirector de HANNAH, es también profesor adjunto en la Universidad de Cornell AAP, donde dirige el Laboratorio de Construcción Robótica (RCL).

ASHEN CABIN

10 M² // ITHACA, NEW YORK, UNITED STATES
PHOTOS © HANNAH AND ANDY CHEN

Ashen Cabin is 3D-printed from concrete and clothed in a robotically fabricated envelope made of irregular ash wood logs. The cabin lifts off the ground on 3D printed legs which adjust to the sloped terrain. All concrete components were fabricated on a self-built 3D printer. The cabin utilizes wood infested by the Emerald Ash Borer for its envelope which is widely considered as "waste". By implementing 3D scanning and robotic fabrication technology, HANNAH upcycles infested "waste wood" into an abundantly available and sustainable building material. Architecturally, Ashen Cabin walks the line between familiar and unfamiliar; between technologically advanced and formally elemental. The undulating wooden surfaces are strategically deployed to highlight moments of architectural importance.

Die Ashen-Hütte ist aus Beton 3D-gedruckt und mit einer robotergefertigten Hülle aus unregelmäßigen Eschenstämmen verkleidet. Die Kabine steht auf 3D-gedruckten Beinen, die sich dem schrägen Terrain anpassen. Alle Betonteile wurden auf einem selbst hergestellten 3D-Drucker gefertigt. Die Hütte verwendet für ihre Hülle vom Smaragd-Eschen-Bohrer befallenes Holz, das normalerweise als „Abfall" gilt. Durch die Anwendung von 3D-Scanning und Roboter-Fertigungstechnologie verwandelt HANNAH befallenes „Abfallholz" in einen nachhaltigen und reichlich vorhandenen Baustoff. Architektonisch bewegt sich die Kabine zwischen dem Vertrauten und dem Unvertrauten, zwischen dem technologisch Fortschrittlichen und dem formal Elementaren. Gewellte Holzoberflächen werden strategisch eingesetzt, um architektonisch bedeutsame Momente hervorzuheben.

La cabane des Cendres est imprimée en 3D à partir de béton et habillée d'une enveloppe fabriquée par un robot à partir de bûches de cendres irrégulières. La cabine repose sur des pieds imprimés en 3D qui s'adaptent au terrain en pente. Tous les éléments en béton ont été fabriqués sur une imprimante 3D fabriquée en interne. La cabane utilise pour son enveloppe du bois infesté par l'agrile du frêne, normalement considéré comme un « déchet ». Grâce à l'application de la technologie de numérisation 3D et de fabrication robotisée, HANNAH transforme les « déchets de bois » infestés en un matériau de construction durable et abondamment disponible. Sur le plan architectural, la cabine se déplace entre le familier et l'inconnu, entre le technologiquement avancé et le formellement élémentaire. Les surfaces de bois ondulées sont stratégiquement déployées pour mettre en valeur des moments d'importance architecturale.

La cabaña Ashen está impresa en 3D a partir de hormigón y revestida de una envoltura fabricada robóticamente con troncos de madera de fresno irregulares. La cabaña se levanta sobre unas patas impresas en 3D que se ajustan al terreno inclinado. Todos los componentes de hormigón se fabricaron en una impresora 3D de fabricación propia. La cabaña utiliza para su envoltura madera infestada por el barrenador esmeralda del fresno, que normalmente se considera un «residuo». Mediante la aplicación de la tecnología de escaneado 3D y fabricación robótica, HANNAH convierte la «madera de desecho» infestada en un material de construcción sostenible y abundantemente disponible. Desde el punto de vista arquitectónico, la cabaña se mueve entre lo familiar y lo desconocido, entre lo tecnológicamente avanzado y lo formalmente elemental. Las superficies de madera onduladas se despliegan estratégicamente para resaltar los momentos de importancia arquitectónica.

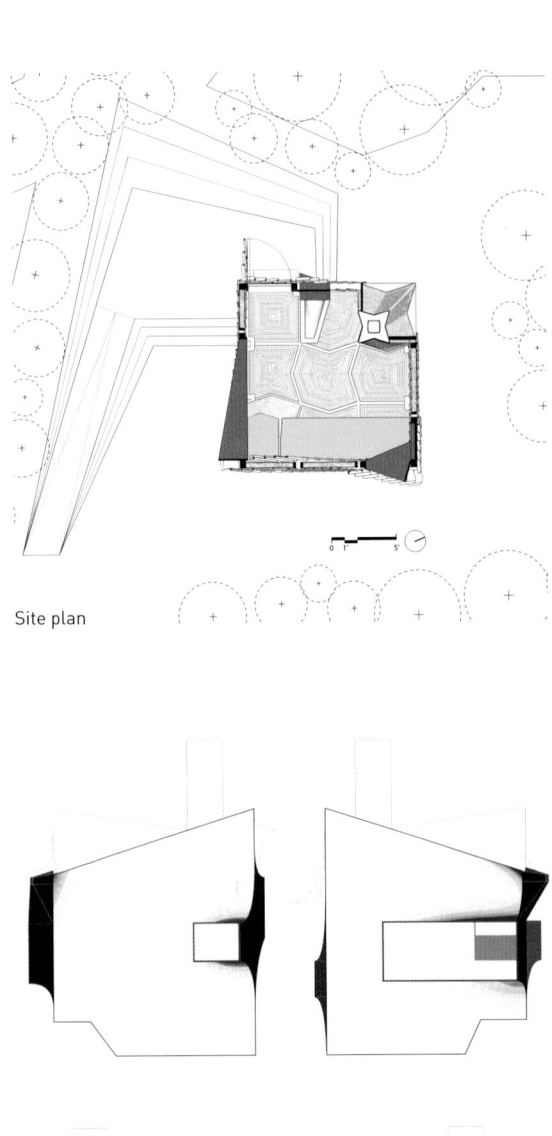

Site plan

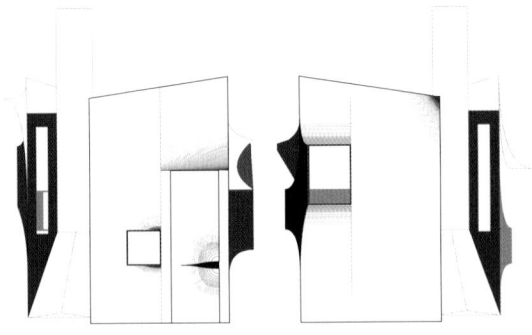

Unrolled elevation diagram

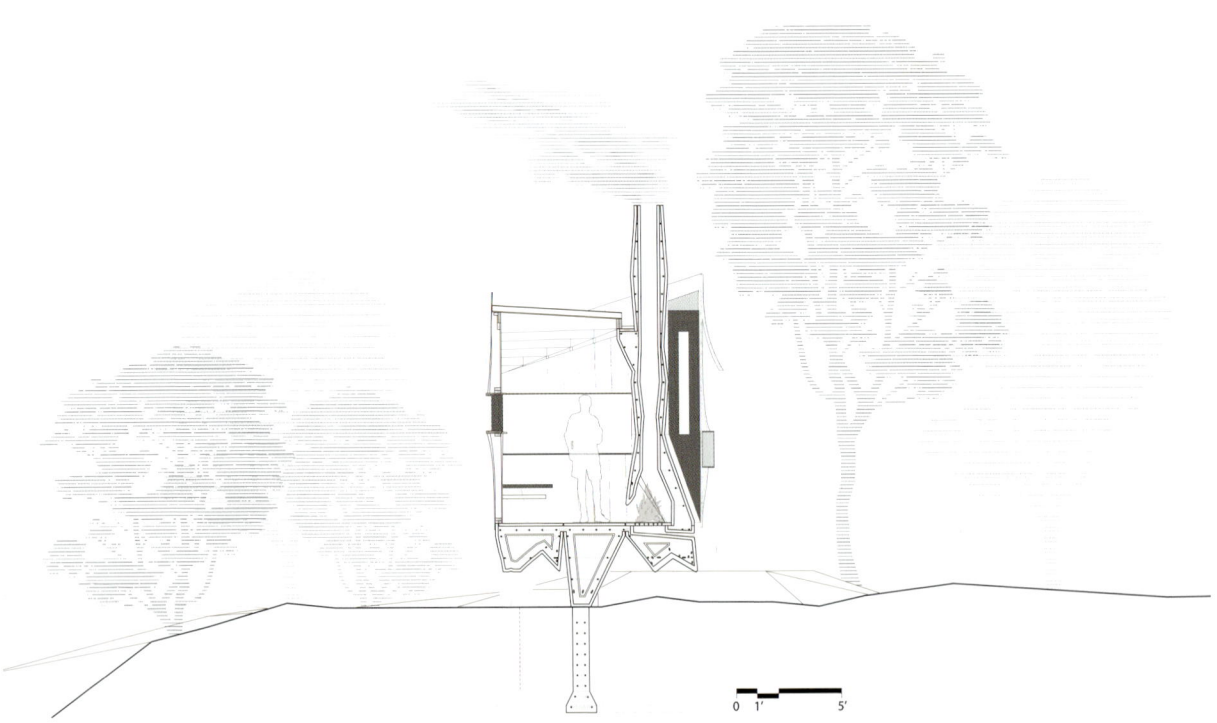

Section through 3D-printed chimney and fireplace

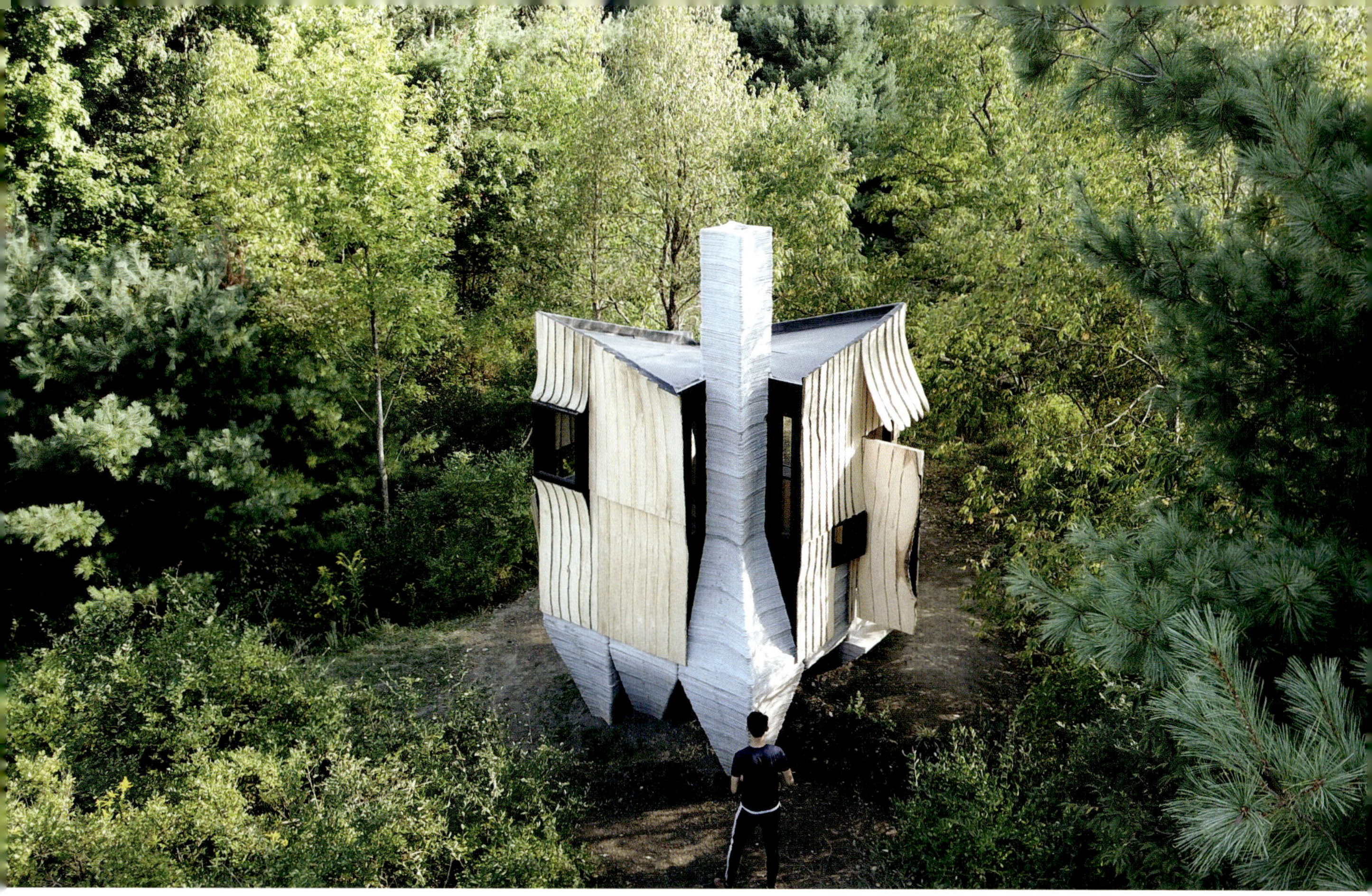

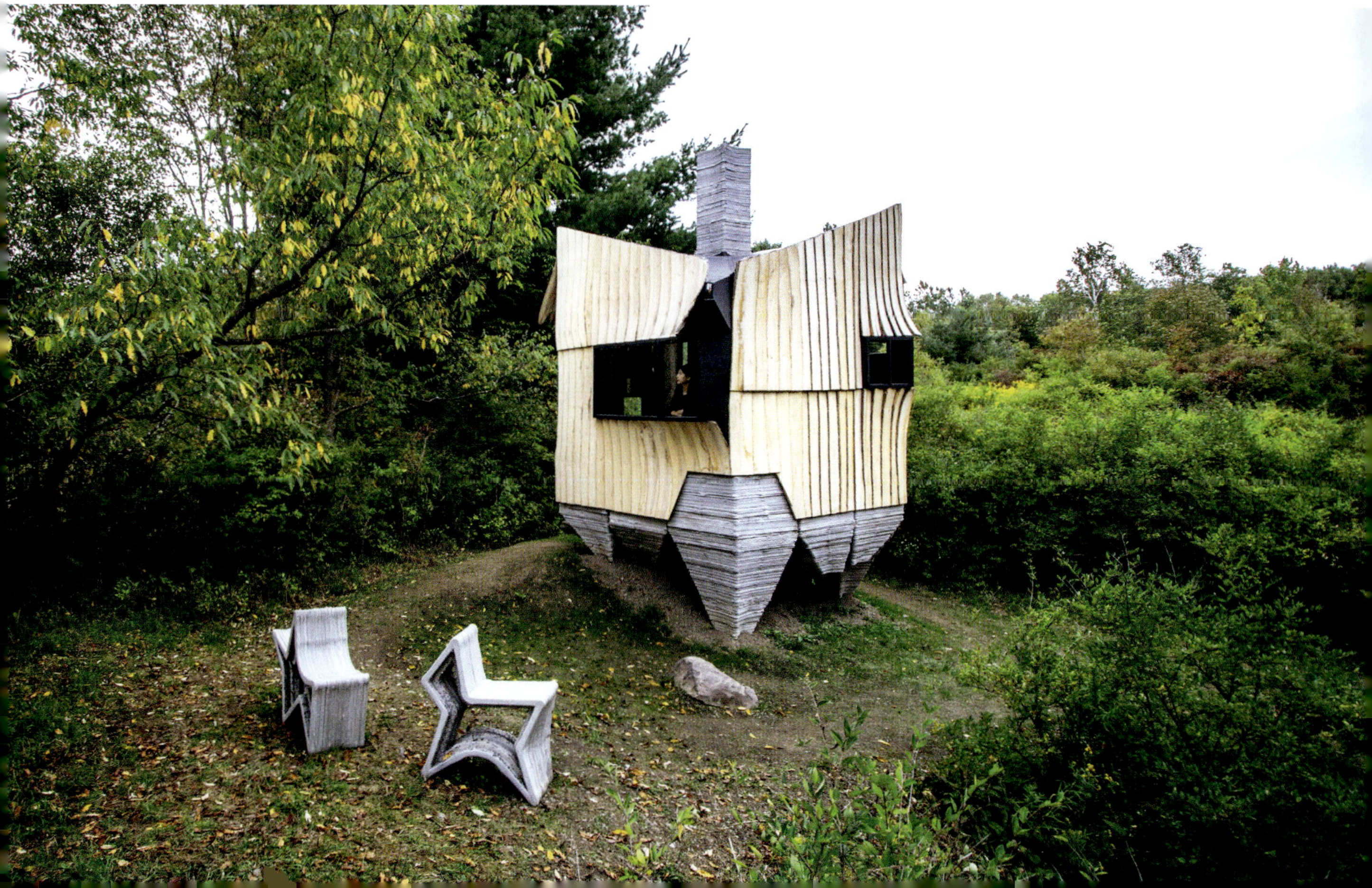

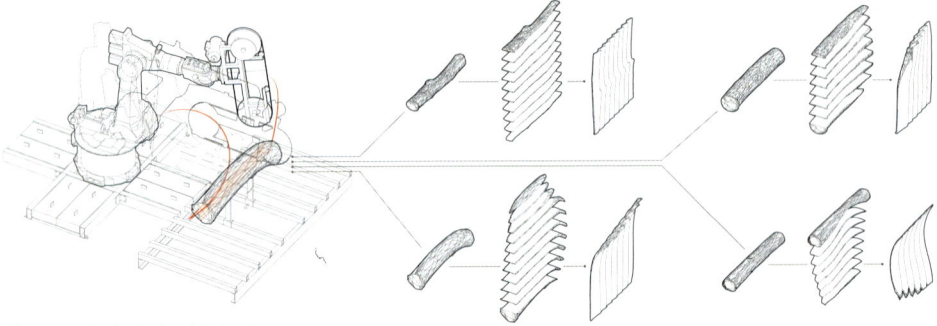

Diagram of robotic log fabrication

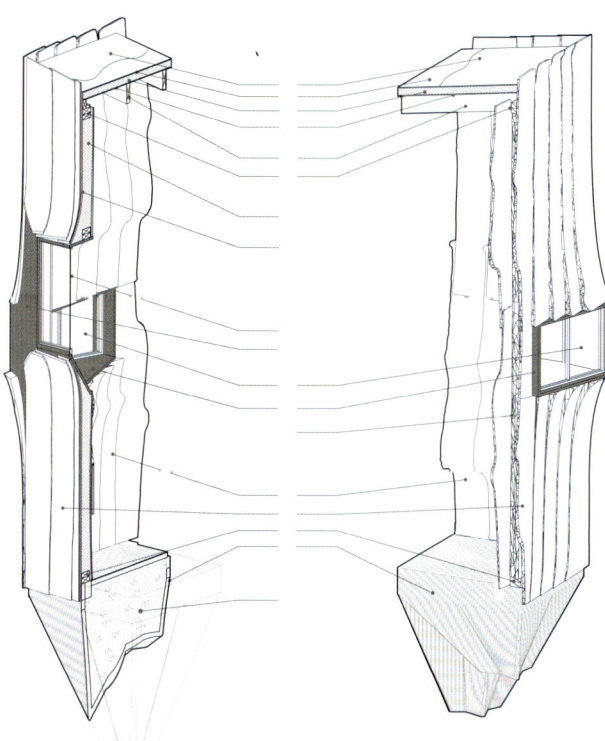

1. Epdm roof membrane
2. Roof coverboard
3. Rigid insulation
4. Plywood sheathing
5. 2 x 6 wood rafter
6. 2 x 4 integral wood top plate
7. Closed cell spray foam insulation
8. Integral corrugated drainage plane
9. Fixed glazing
10. Plywood spandrel
11. Operable glazing
12. Plywood window box
13. Integral log post
14. Interior log sheathing
15. Exterior log sheathing
16. 2 x 4 integral wood bottom plate
17. 3D printed concrete formwork
18. Poured concrete infill

Detail axonometric of corner module

JONATHAN TUCKEY DESIGN
JONATHAN TUCKEY, RYUTA HIRAYAMA

WWW.JONATHANTUCKEY.COM

Jonathan Tuckey Design has garnered an international reputation for working with existing buildings and structures. Our studio has become expert in combining contemporary design with layers of built heritage to explore the ways in which old and new can co-exist and elevate one another. We have worked on a number of commercial, cultural and residential projects within Europe, the United States and South America, developing a clear set of principles and approaches to deal with historic and modern architecture. We embrace an architecture of change and an acute awareness of style and context underpins everything we do. The juxtaposition of contemporary elements with original features creates a dialogue between different eras and allows buildings to establish a new purpose. Re-using existing built stock is the most sustainable approach to the future development of our cities and countryside, retaining a sense of collective heritage.

Jonathan Tuckey Design hat sich einen internationalen Ruf für die Arbeit mit bestehenden Gebäuden und Strukturen erworben. Das Studio versteht es, zeitgenössisches Design mit dem baulichen Erbe zu kombinieren, um die Möglichkeiten zu erforschen, wie Altes und Neues nebeneinander bestehen und sich gegenseitig aufwerten können. Sie haben an einer Reihe von kommerziellen, kulturellen und Wohnprojekten in Europa, den Vereinigten Staaten und Südamerika gearbeitet und dabei klare Prinzipien und Ansätze für den Umgang mit historischer und moderner Architektur entwickelt. Sie setzen sich für eine Architektur des Wandels ein. Die Grundlage für alles, was sie tun, ist ein ausgeprägtes Bewusstsein für Stil und Kontext. Die Gegenüberstellung von zeitgenössischen Elementen mit originalen Merkmalen schafft einen Dialog zwischen verschiedenen Epochen und ermöglicht es den Gebäuden, einen neuen Zweck zu etablieren. Die Wiederverwendung von Gebäuden ist der nachhaltigste Ansatz für die zukünftige Entwicklung von Städten und Landschaften, während gleichzeitig ein Gefühl für das kollektive Erbe erhalten bleibt.

JONATHAN TUCKEY DESIGN

Jonathan Tuckey Design a acquis une réputation internationale en travaillant avec des bâtiments et des structures existants. Le studio est habile à combiner le design contemporain avec le patrimoine bâti pour explorer les façons dont l'ancien et le nouveau peuvent coexister et s'élever l'un l'autre. Ils ont travaillé sur toute une série de projets commerciaux, culturels et résidentiels en Europe, aux États-Unis et en Amérique du Sud, développant un ensemble clair de principes et d'approches pour traiter de l'architecture historique et moderne. Ils prônent une architecture du changement et la base de tout ce qu'ils font est une conscience aiguë du style et du contexte. La juxtaposition d'éléments contemporains et d'éléments originaux crée un dialogue entre différentes époques et permet aux bâtiments d'établir une nouvelle destination. La réutilisation des bâtiments est l'approche la plus durable pour le développement futur des villes et des campagnes, tout en conservant un sens de l'héritage collectif.

Jonathan Tuckey Design se ha ganado una reputación internacional por trabajar con edificios y estructuras ya existentes. El estudio es experto en combinar el diseño contemporáneo con el patrimonio construido para explorar las formas en que lo viejo y lo nuevo pueden coexistir y elevarse mutuamente. Han trabajado en una serie de proyectos comerciales, culturales y residenciales en Europa, Estados Unidos y Sudamérica, desarrollando un conjunto claro de principios y enfoques para tratar la arquitectura histórica y moderna. Abogan por una arquitectura de cambio y la base de todo lo que hacen es una conciencia aguda del estilo y el contexto. La yuxtaposición de elementos contemporáneos con características originales crea un diálogo entre diferentes épocas y permite que los edificios establezcan un nuevo propósito. La reutilización de los edificios es el enfoque más sostenible para el desarrollo futuro de las ciudades y campos, manteniendo un sentido de patrimonio colectivo.

EGG

100 M² // LONDON, UNITED KINGDOM
PHOTOS © JAMES BRITTAIN, DIRK LINDNER

Egg, a London-based fashion boutique, is known for its minimalist design approach to the clothes it stocks and the way they are presented, acting more like a gallery than a traditional shop. This refurbishment created a new pied-à-terre and provided an expansion of the back-of-house for the adjacent shop. Inspired by the minimalism of the boutique and by the informal character of the mews, we have inserted a series of containers within the first floor of the building to accommodate domestic and commercial functions. These boxes sit within the volume of the roof and create the nest-like atmosphere of an attic or store room. A bespoke wooden bath by Studio Anna van der Lei sits within a bathroom that opens to the mews and that doubles as a meeting room.

Egg, eine Modeboutique mit Sitz in London, ist bekannt für ihr minimalistisches Design und die Art und Weise, wie die Kleidungsstücke präsentiert werden. Dabei ähnelt die Boutique eher einer Galerie als einem traditionellen Geschäft. Dieser Umbau führte zu einem neuen Pied-à-Terre und ermöglichte eine Erweiterung der Rückseite des angrenzenden Geschäfts. Inspiriert durch den Minimalismus der Boutique und den informellen Charakter der Farbtöne, fügten wir eine Reihe von Containern im ersten Stock des Gebäudes ein, um häusliche und kommerzielle Funktionen unterzubringen. Diese Kästen werden innerhalb des Dachvolumens platziert und schaffen die Nestatmosphäre eines Penthouses. Eine maßgefertigte Holzbadewanne, hergestellt vom Studio Anna van der Lei, befindet sich in einem Badezimmer, das sich zum Hinterhof hin öffnet.

Egg, une boutique de mode basée à Londres, est connue pour son approche minimaliste des vêtements qu'elle vend et de la façon dont ils sont présentés, se comportant plus comme une galerie que comme un magasin traditionnel. Cette rénovation a donné lieu à un nouveau « pied-à-terre » et a permis d'agrandir l'arrière du magasin adjacent. Inspirés par le minimalisme de la boutique et la nature informelle des teintes, nous avons inséré une série de conteneurs au premier étage du bâtiment pour accueillir des fonctions domestiques et commerciales. Ces boîtes sont placées dans le volume du toit et créent l'atmosphère de nidification du dernier étage. Une baignoire en bois faite sur mesure par le Studio Anna van der Lei se trouve à l'intérieur d'une salle de bain qui s'ouvre sur la cour arrière et sert aussi de salle de réunion.

Egg, una *boutique* de moda con sede en Londres, es conocida por su enfoque de diseño minimalista de las prendas que vende y la forma en que se presentan, actuando más como una galería que como una tienda tradicional. Esta remodelación dio lugar a un nuevo *pied-à-terre* y proporcionó una expansión de la parte trasera de la tienda adyacente. Inspirados por el minimalismo de la boutique y por el carácter informal de los matices, hemos insertado una serie de contenedores en el primer piso del edificio para acomodar las funciones domésticas y comerciales. Estas cajas se sitúan dentro del volumen del tejado y crean la atmósfera de nido propia de un ático. Una bañera de madera, hecha a medida por el Studio Anna van der Lei, se encuentra dentro de un baño que se abre al patio trasero y que sirve también como sala de reuniones.

Site plan

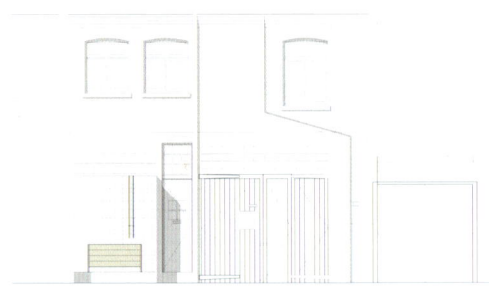

Front elevation

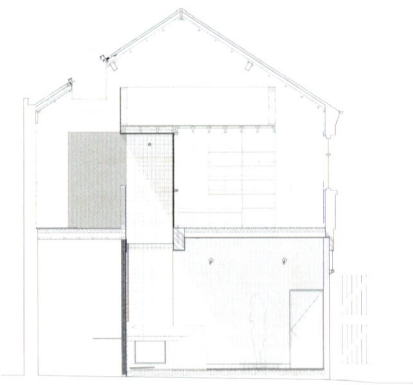

Section

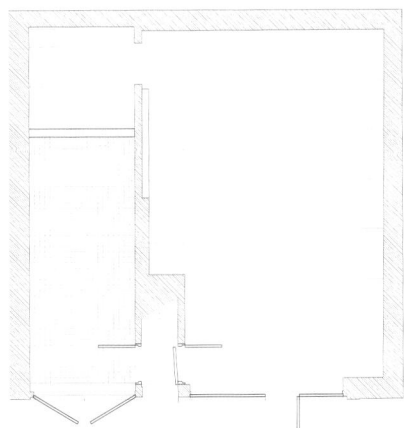

Ground floor plan

Attic plan

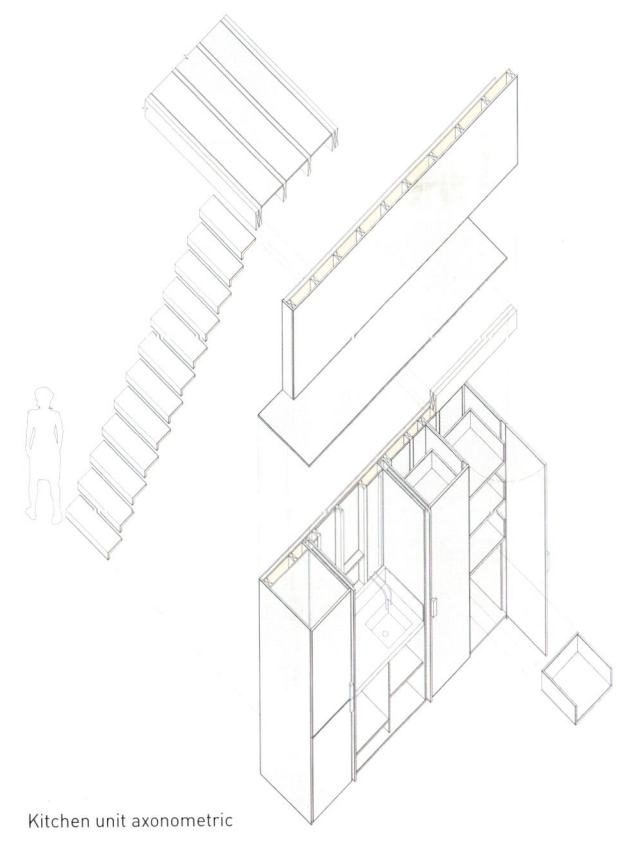

Kitchen unit axonometric

KWK PROMES
ROBERT KONIECZNY

WWW.KWKPROMES.PL

A leader and a founder of KWK Promes Architecture studio in 1999, he is a holder of the award for the House of the Year 2006, (Aatrial House) as the best housing project by World Architecture News. In 2007 the KWK Promes office was listed among 44 best young architects of the world. Year 2008 brought him another prize for The European Center for Architecture Art Design and Urban Studies and The Chicago Athenaeum for Europe's Emerging Young Architects 'Europe 40 under 40'. In 2016 National Museum – Dialogue Centre Przeomy was announced to be The Best Public Space in Europe by Centre de Cultura Contemporània de Barcelona.

Als Leiter und Gründer des KWK Promes Architecture Studios im Jahr 1999 ist Robert Konieczny Träger der Auszeichnung für das Haus des Jahres 2006 (Aatrial House) als bestes Wohnprojekt der World Architecture News. Im Jahr 2007 wurde das Büro KWK Promes unter den 44 besten jungen Architekten der Welt gelistet. Im Jahr 2008 erhielt er einen weiteren Preis für das European Center for Architecture Art Design and Urban Studies und das Chicago Athenaeum for Europe's Emerging Young Architects ‚Europe 40 under 40'. Im Jahr 2016 wurde das Nationalmuseum-Dialogzentrum Przeomy vom Centre de Cultura Contemporània de Barcelona zum besten öffentlichen Raum Europas erklärt.

KWK PROMES

Dirigeant et fondateur du studio KWK Promes Architecture en 1999, il a reçu le prix de la Maison de l'année 2006, (Aatrial House) comme meilleur projet d'habitation par World Architecture News. En 2007, le bureau KWK Promes a été classé parmi les 44 meilleurs jeunes architectes du monde. En 2008, il a reçu un autre prix pour The European Center for Architecture Art Design and Urban Studies et The Chicago Athenaeum for Europe's Emerging Young Architects « Europe 40 under 40 ». En 2016, le Musée National - Centre de Dialogue Przeomy a été proclamé meilleur espace public d'Europe par le Centre de Cultura Contemporània de Barcelona.

Líder y fundador del estudio KWK Promes Architecture en 1999, Robert Konieczny es titular del premio de la Casa del Año 2006 (Aatrial House) como el mejor proyecto de vivienda de World Architecture News. En 2007, la oficina de KWK Promes figuraba entre los 44 mejores jóvenes arquitectos del mundo. El año 2008 le trajo otro premio del Centro Europeo de Arquitectura Diseño de Arte y Estudios Urbanos y El Ateneo de Chicago para los jóvenes arquitectos emergentes de Europa «Europa 40 under 40». En 2016 el Museo Nacional – Centro de Diálogo Przeomy en Szczecin fue anunciado como el Mejor Espacio Público en Europa por el Centro de Cultura Contemporánea de Barcelona.

KONIECZNY'S ARK

138 M² // BRENNA, POLAND

PHOTOS © JAKUB CERTOWICZ, ALEKSANDER RUTKOWSKI (OLO STUDIO)

The argument of this house is the search for the best panoramic views of the impressive surrounding landscape. A one-storey house was developed, the shape of which is reminiscent of old barns, offering the same view from any point inside. Being in the middle of nature posed a security problem. The house was "twisted" in such a way that only one side of the structure touches the ground and the rest is suspended. With this solution, part of the ground floor, where the bedrooms are located, is raised above the level of the first floor. The location of the house on a steep slope could lead to the risk of slippage. To limit the movement of the subsoil, the house was treated as a bridge on which rainwater flows naturally. To stiffen the building the walls were tensioned by the planes of the "inverted" roof slightly raised off the ground, allowing the natural water to flow.

Das Ziel dieses Hauses ist die Suche nach den besten Panoramablicken auf die beeindruckende Landschaft der Umgebung. Es entstand ein eingeschossiges Haus, das in seiner Form an die alten Scheunen erinnert und von jedem Punkt seines Inneren den gleichen Ausblick bietet. Die Lage mitten in der Natur stellt jedoch ein Sicherheitsproblem dar. Das Haus wurde so „verdreht", dass nur eine Seite des Gebäudes den Boden berührt und der Rest aufgehängt ist. Bei dieser Lösung wird ein Teil des Erdgeschosses, in dem sich die Schlafzimmer befinden, über den ersten Stock angehoben. Die Lage des Hauses an einem steilen Hang könnte zu einer Rutschgefahr führen. Um die Bewegung des Untergrunds zu begrenzen, wurde das Haus wie eine Brücke gebaut, über die das Regenwasser auf natürliche Weise fließt. Zur Aussteifung des Gebäudes wurden die Wände durch die leicht vom Boden abgehobenen Ebenen des „umgekehrten" Daches gespannt, wodurch das natürliche Wasser fließen kann.

L'argument de cette maison est la recherche des meilleures vues panoramiques du paysage environnant impressionnant. Une maison de plain-pied a été développée, dont la forme rappelle les anciennes granges, offrant la même vue de n'importe quel point de son intérieur. Étant en pleine nature, un problème de sécurité s'est posé. La maison a été conçue de telle manière qu'un seul côté de la structure touche le sol et que le reste soit suspendu. Avec cette solution, une partie du rez-de-chaussée, où se trouvent les chambres, est surélevée par rapport au niveau du premier étage. L'emplacement de la maison sur une pente raide pourrait entraîner un risque de glissement. Pour limiter le mouvement du sous-sol, la maison a été traitée comme un pont où l'eau de pluie s'écoule naturellement. Pour rigidifier le bâtiment, les murs ont été façonnés par les pans du toit « inversé » légèrement surélevé par rapport au sol, permettant à l'eau naturelle de s'écouler.

El argumento de esta vivienda es la búsqueda delas mejores panorámicas del impresionante paisaje que la rodea. Se desarrolló una casa de una planta, cuya forma recuerda a los antiguos graneros, que ofrece la misma vista desde cualquier punto de su interior. Al estar en medio de la naturaleza se planteó un problema de seguridad. Se «torció» la casa de tal modo que solo un lado de la estructura toca el suelo y el resto queda suspendido. Con esta solución, parte de la planta baja, donde se encuentran los dormitorios, queda como elevada del nivel del primer piso. La ubicación de la casa en una empinada pendiente podría comportar el riesgo de deslizamiento. Para limitar el movimiento del subsuelo se trató la casa como un puente en el cual el agua de lluvia fluye con naturalidad. Para darle rigidez al edificio las paredes fueron tensadas por los planos del tejado «invertido» ligeramente elevado del suelo, permitiendo que el agua natural fluya.

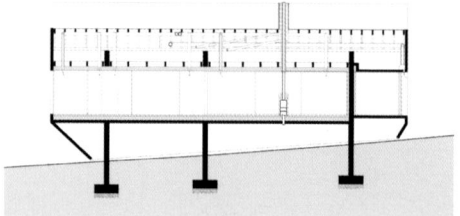

Section A-A

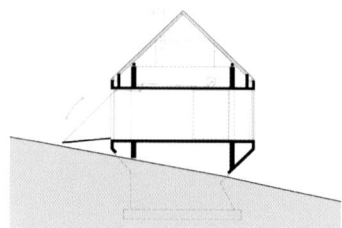

Section 1-1

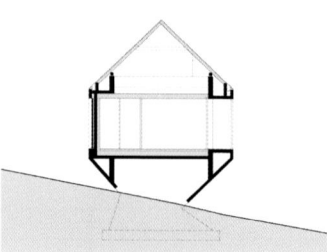

Section 2-2

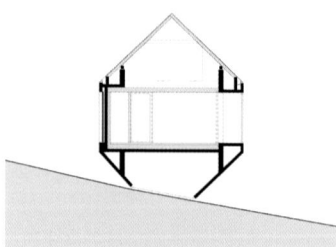

Section 3-3

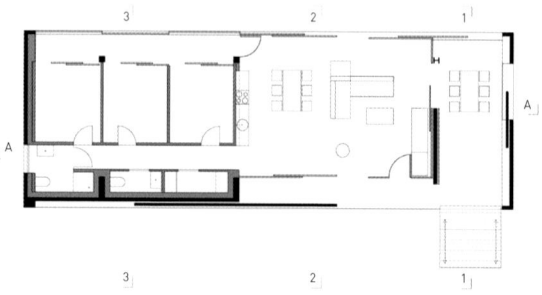

Floor plan

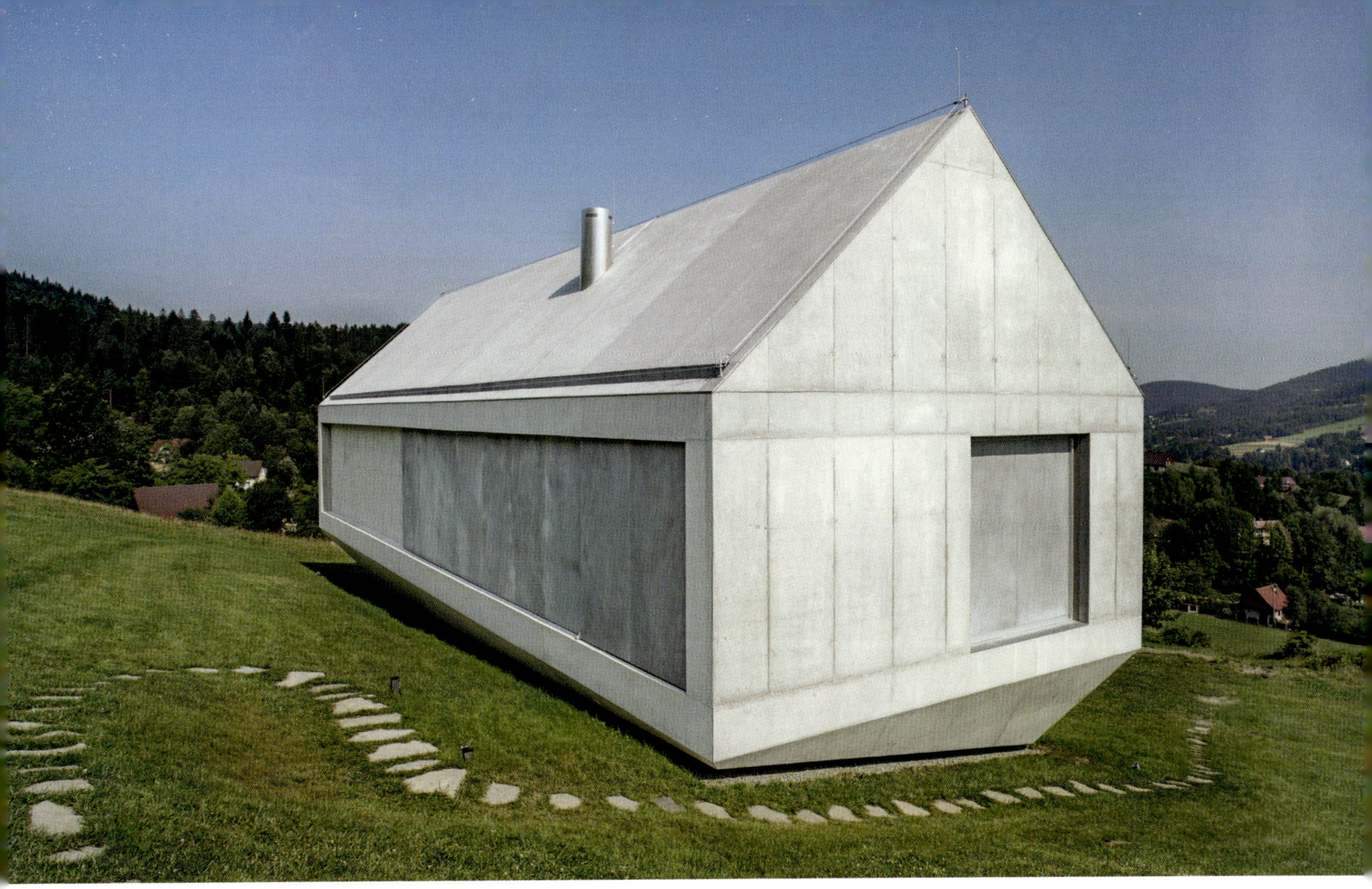
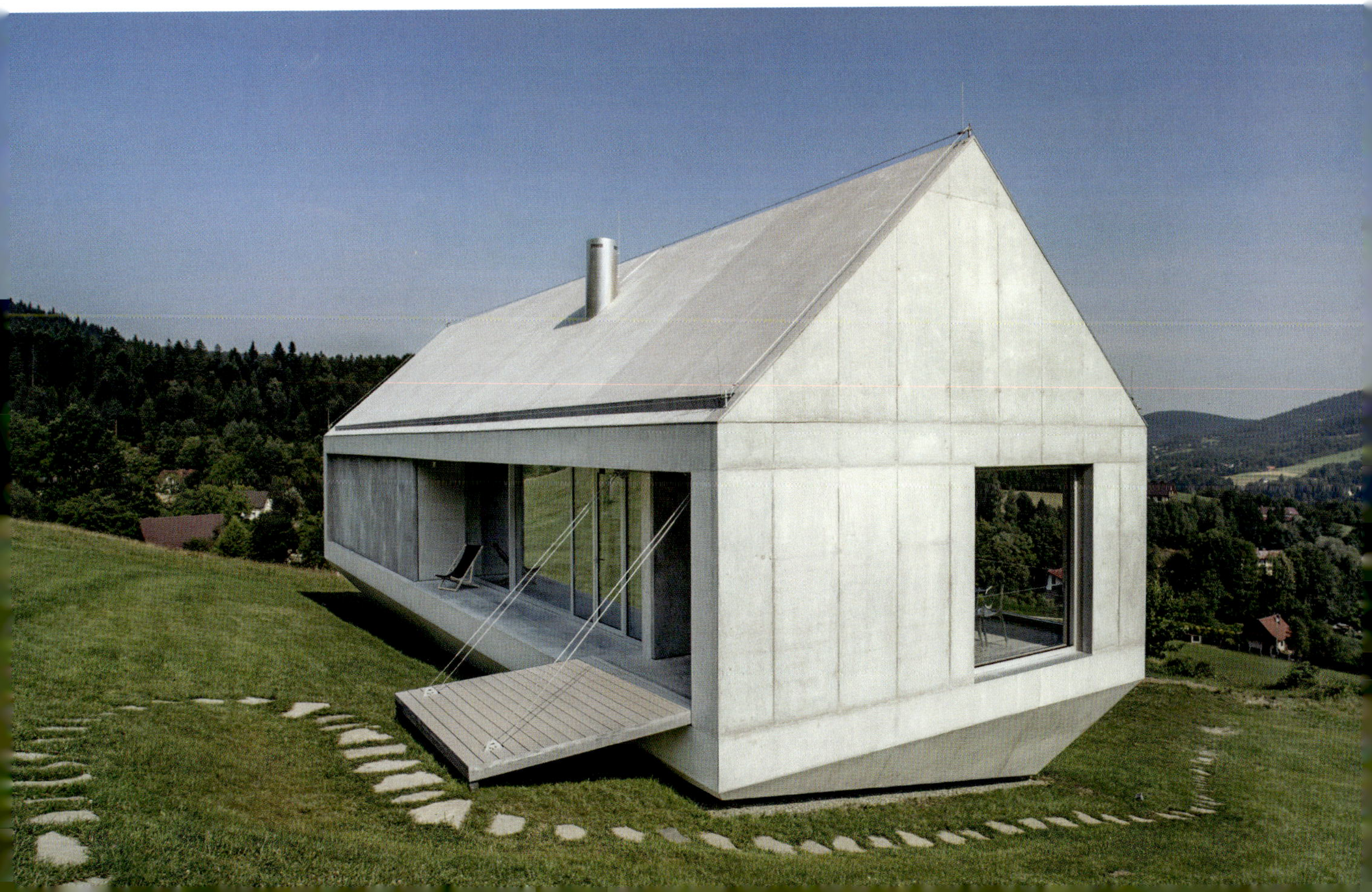

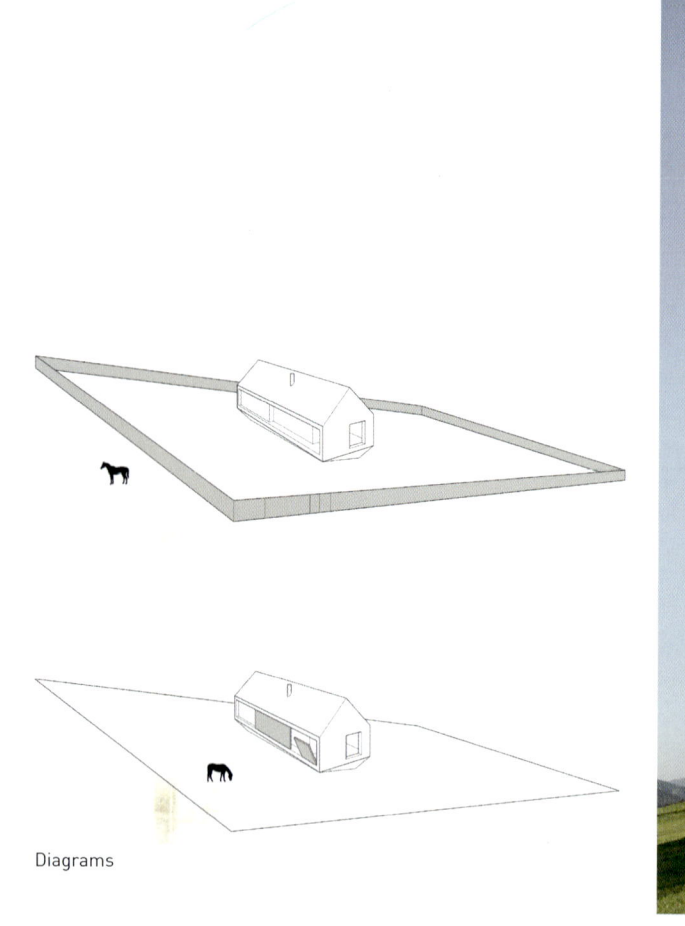

Diagrams

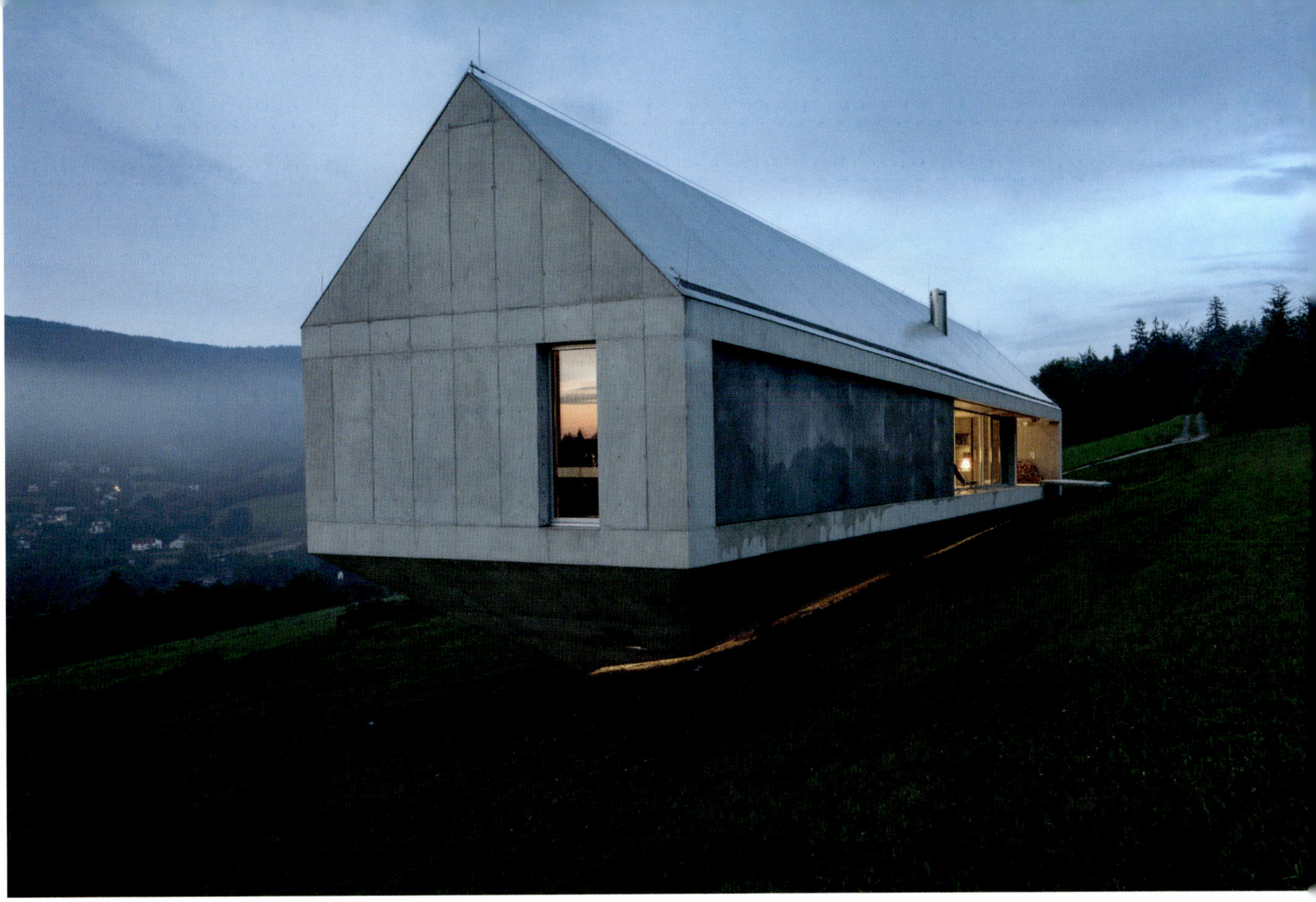

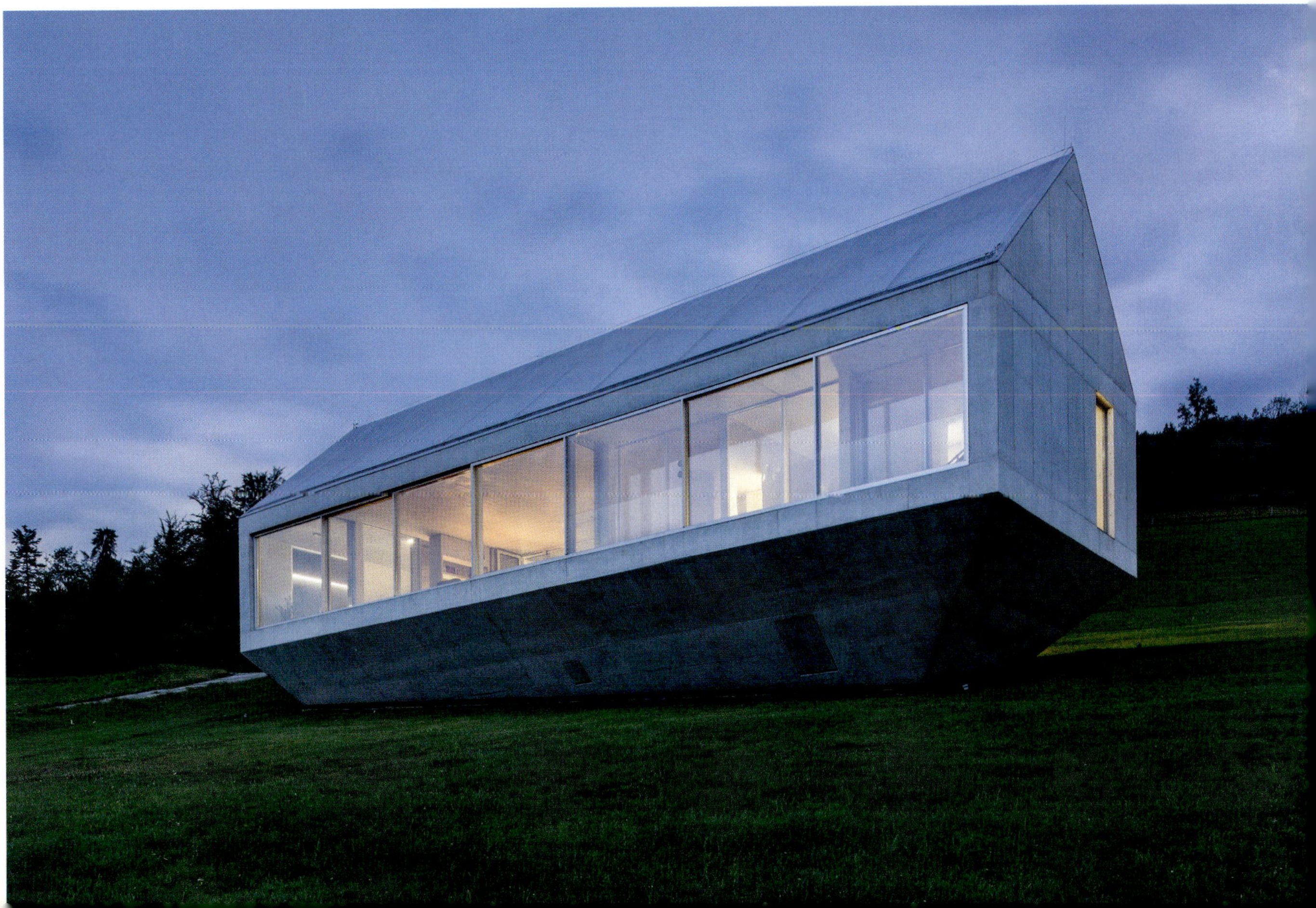

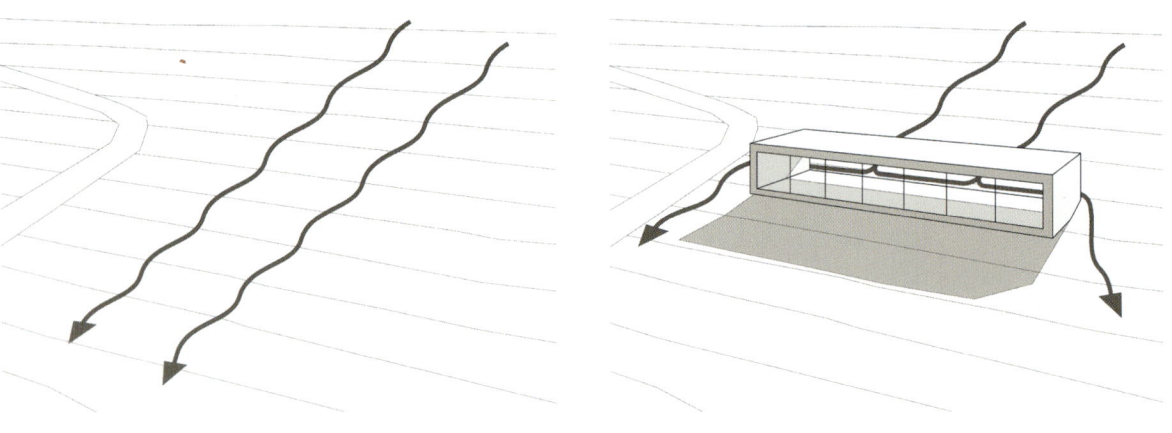

Siting diagrams

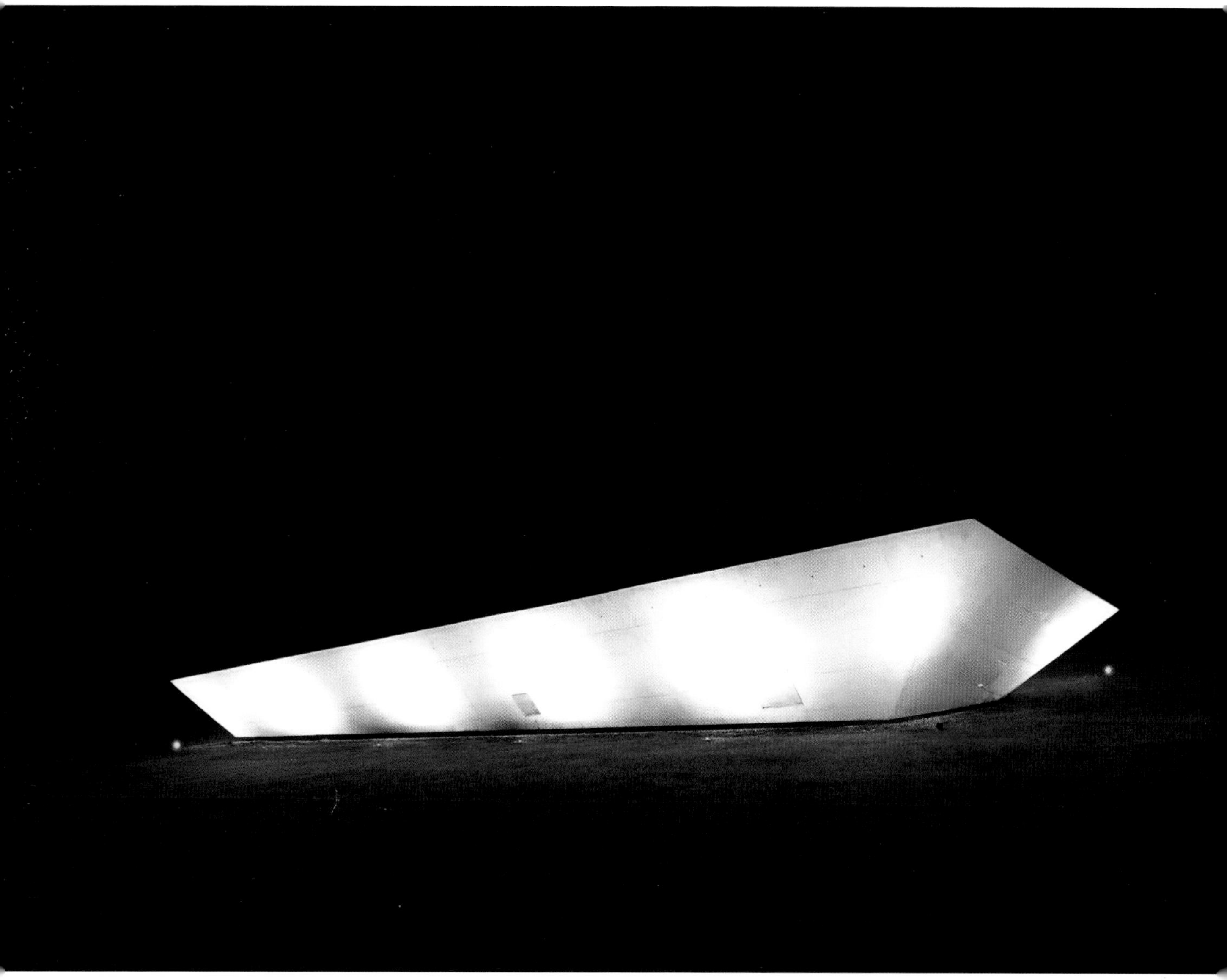

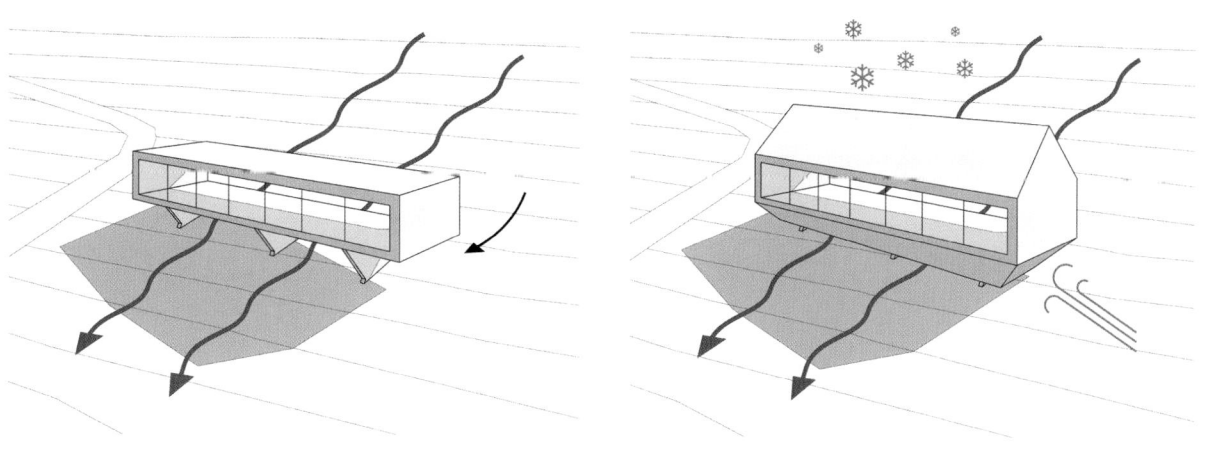

SMALL HOME, SMART HOME

LAAB

OTTO NG, YIP CHUN HANG

WWW.LAAB.PRO

LAAB is a laboratory for Art and Architecture dedicated to spatial innovations, offering forward-thinking design solutions to public space, architecture, interior designs, and digital art experiences. Led by co founders Otto Ng and Yip Chun Hang, the collective of architects, designers, engineers, makers, and sociologists work together with forward-thinking clients and collaborators to bring visionary designs to life.

A precise blend of cutting-edge digital fabrication and traditional craftsmanship drives the team's creative process. Widely recognized projects include "Small Home Smart Home," the "K11 MUSEA and Victoria Dockside," "Leica Flagship Store in Hong Kong and the Asia-Pacific," "f22 foto space," and the "Hong Kong House" in the Japan Echigo Tsumari Art Triennale.

Based in Hong Kong, LAAB has been awarded for design innovation and craftsmanship.

LAAB ist ein Labor für Kunst und Architektur, das sich räumlichen Innovationen widmet und zukunftsweisende Designlösungen für den öffentlichen Raum, Architektur, Innenarchitektur und digitale Kunsterlebnisse anbietet. Unter der Leitung der Mitbegründer Otto Ng und Yip Chun Hang arbeitet das Kollektiv aus Architekten, Designern, Ingenieuren, Machern und Soziologen mit zukunftsorientierten Kunden und Kooperationspartnern zusammen, um visionäre Entwürfe zum Leben zu erwecken.

Eine präzise Mischung aus modernster digitaler Fabrikation und traditioneller Handwerkskunst treibt den kreativen Prozess des Teams an. Zu den weithin anerkannten Projekten gehören „Small Home Smart Home", das „K11 MUSEA und Victoria Dockside", der „Leica Flagship Store in Hongkong und im asiatisch-pazifischen Raum", „f22 foto space" und das „Hong Kong House" in der Japan Echigo Tsumari Art Triennale.

LAAB mit Sitz in Hongkong wurde für Design-Innovation und Handwerkskunst ausgezeichnet.

LAAB

LAAB est un laboratoire d'art et d'architecture dédié aux innovations spatiales, qui propose des solutions de conception avant-gardistes en matière d'espace public, d'architecture, de décoration intérieure et d'expériences artistiques numériques. Dirigé par les cofondateurs Otto Ng et Yip Chun Hang, le collectif d'architectes, de designers, d'ingénieurs, de créateurs et de sociologues travaille avec des clients et des collaborateurs avant-gardistes pour donner vie à des projets visionnaires.

Le processus créatif de l'équipe repose sur un mélange précis de fabrication numérique de pointe et d'artisanat traditionnel. Parmi les projets largement reconnus, citons « Small Home Smart Home », le « K11 MUSEA and Victoria Dockside », le « Leica Flagship Store in Hong Kong and the Asia-pacific », le « f22 foto space » et la « Hong Kong House » de la Japan Echigo Tsumari Art Triennale.

Basé à Hong Kong, LAAB a été récompensé pour son innovation en matière de design et son savoir-faire.

LAAB es un laboratorio de Arte y Arquitectura dedicado a las innovaciones espaciales, que ofrece soluciones de diseño con visión de futuro para el espacio público, la arquitectura, el diseño de interiores y las experiencias de arte digital. Dirigido por los cofundadores Otto Ng y Yip Chun Hang, el colectivo de arquitectos, diseñadores, ingenieros, creadores y sociólogos trabaja junto a clientes y colaboradores con visión de futuro para dar vida a diseños visionarios.

El proceso creativo del equipo se basa en una precisa combinación de fabricación digital de vanguardia y artesanía tradicional. Entre los proyectos más reconocidos se encuentran «Small Home Smart Home», el «K11 MUSEA y Victoria Dockside», «Leica Flagship Store en Hong Kong y Asia-Pacífico», «f22 Foto Space» y la «Hong Kong House» en la Trienal de Arte Echigo Tsumari de Japón.

Con sede en Hong Kong, LAAB ha sido galardonada por la innovación en el diseño y la artesanía.

SMALL HOME, SMART HOME

29 M² // HONG KONG, SAR CHINA

PHOTOS © SOOTAGE VISUAL AND LAAB

This small flat makes the most of limited space without sacrificing comfort. The owners' wish list for the renovation of their flat included a full kitchen, a bathtub, a home cinema, a gym and plenty of storage space. Flexibility and multi-functionality were key to achieving this goal, meaning that the spaces can be transformed depending on their intended use at any given time. The owners also requested that the space be pet-friendly, so materials, details and mechanical systems were strategically designed to keep the spaces dry, clean, cat-friendly and odour-free.

Diese kleine Wohnung macht das Beste aus dem begrenzten Raum, ohne auf Komfort zu verzichten. Auf der Wunschliste der Eigentümer für ihre Wohnungsrenovierung standen eine vollwertige Küche, eine Badewanne, ein Heimkino, ein Fitnessraum und viel Stauraum. Flexibilität und Multifunktionalität waren der Schlüssel zum Erreichen dieses Ziels, d.h. die Räume können je nach Verwendungszweck zu jeder Zeit umgestaltet werden. Die Eigentümer wünschten sich außerdem, dass die Räume haustierfreundlich sind. Daher wurden die Materialien, Details und mechanischen Systeme strategisch so konzipiert, dass die Räume trocken, sauber, katzenfreundlich und geruchsfrei bleiben.

Ce petit appartement permet d'exploiter au mieux l'espace limité sans sacrifier le confort. La liste des souhaits des propriétaires pour la rénovation de leur appartement comprenait une cuisine complète, une baignoire, un home cinéma, une salle de gym et de nombreux espaces de rangement. La flexibilité et la multifonctionnalité étaient essentielles pour atteindre cet objectif, ce qui signifie que les espaces peuvent être transformés en fonction de leur utilisation prévue à un moment donné. Les propriétaires ont également demandé que l'espace soit adapté aux animaux de compagnie. Les matériaux, les détails et les systèmes mécaniques ont donc été stratégiquement conçus pour garder les espaces secs, propres, adaptés aux chats et sans odeurs.

Este pequeño apartamento aprovecha al máximo el espacio limitado sin sacrificar la comodidad. La lista de deseos de los propietarios para la renovación de su apartamento incluía una cocina completa, una bañera, un cine en casa, un gimnasio y mucho espacio de almacenamiento. La flexibilidad y la multifuncionalidad fueron claves para lograr este objetivo, lo cual significa que los espacios se pueden transformar dependiendo del uso que se le quiera dar en cada momento. Los propietarios también pidieron que el espacio fuera apto para mascotas, por eso los materiales, los detalles y los sistemas mecánicos se diseñaron estratégicamente para mantener los espacios secos, limpios, aptos para gatos y libres de malos olores.

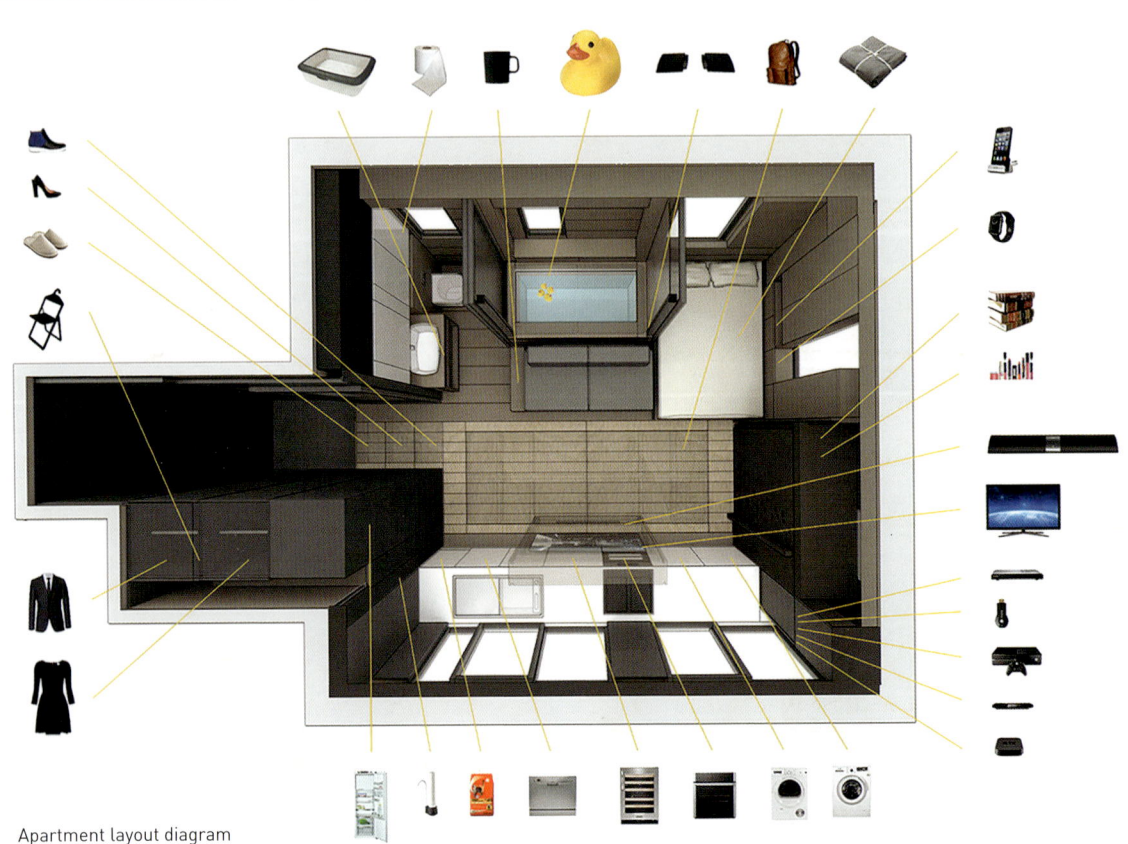

Apartment layout diagram

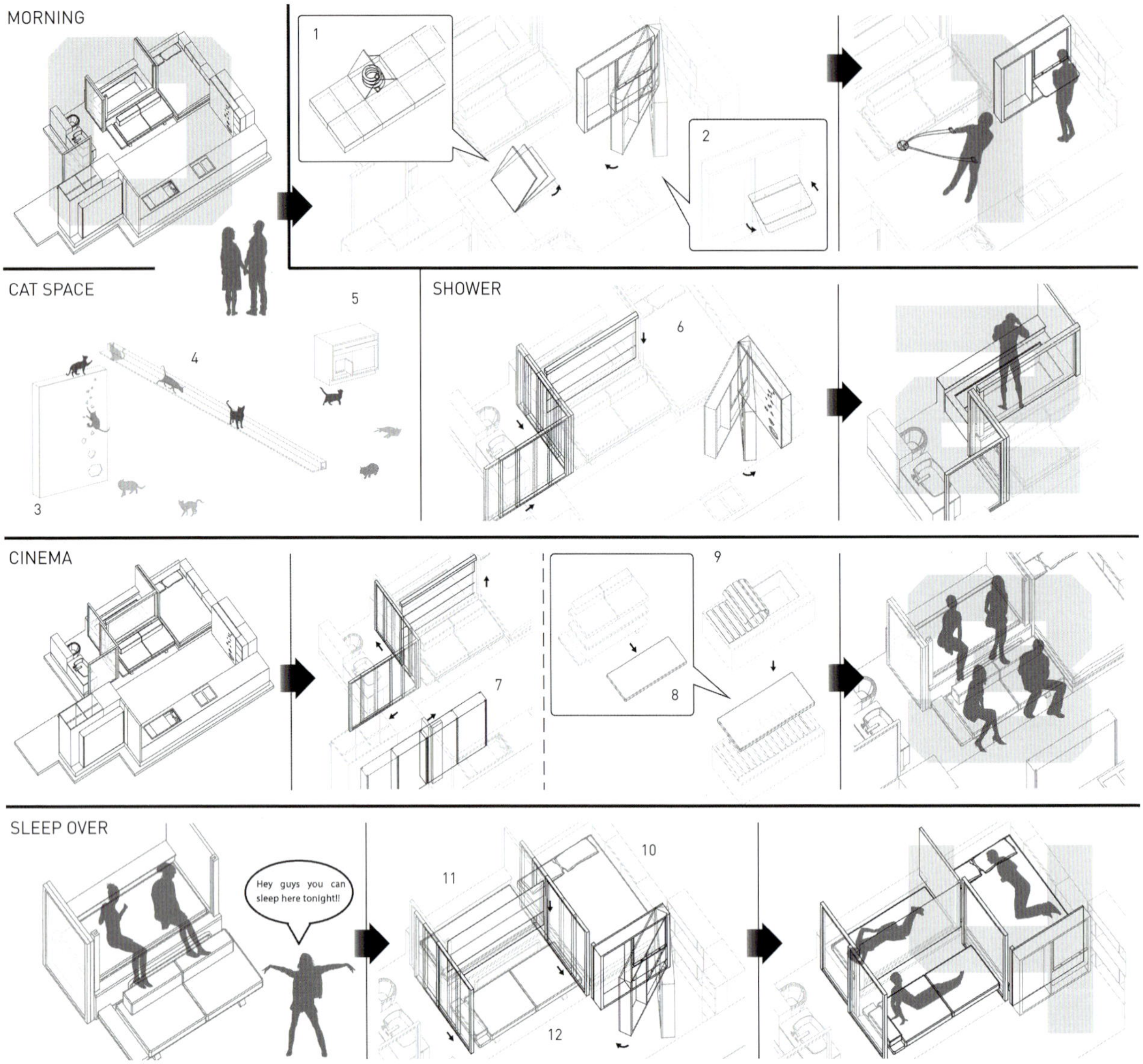

MORNING

1. (inset)
2. (inset)

CAT SPACE

4
5
3

SHOWER

6

CINEMA

9
7
8

SLEEP OVER

Hey guys you can sleep here tonight!!

11
10
12

Functional diagram

1. Gym equipment	5. Litter box	9. Timber deck
2. Make up table	6. Partition screen	10. Bed A
3. Cat ladder	7. Home cinema	11. Bed B
4. Cat walk	8. Cushion	12. Bed C

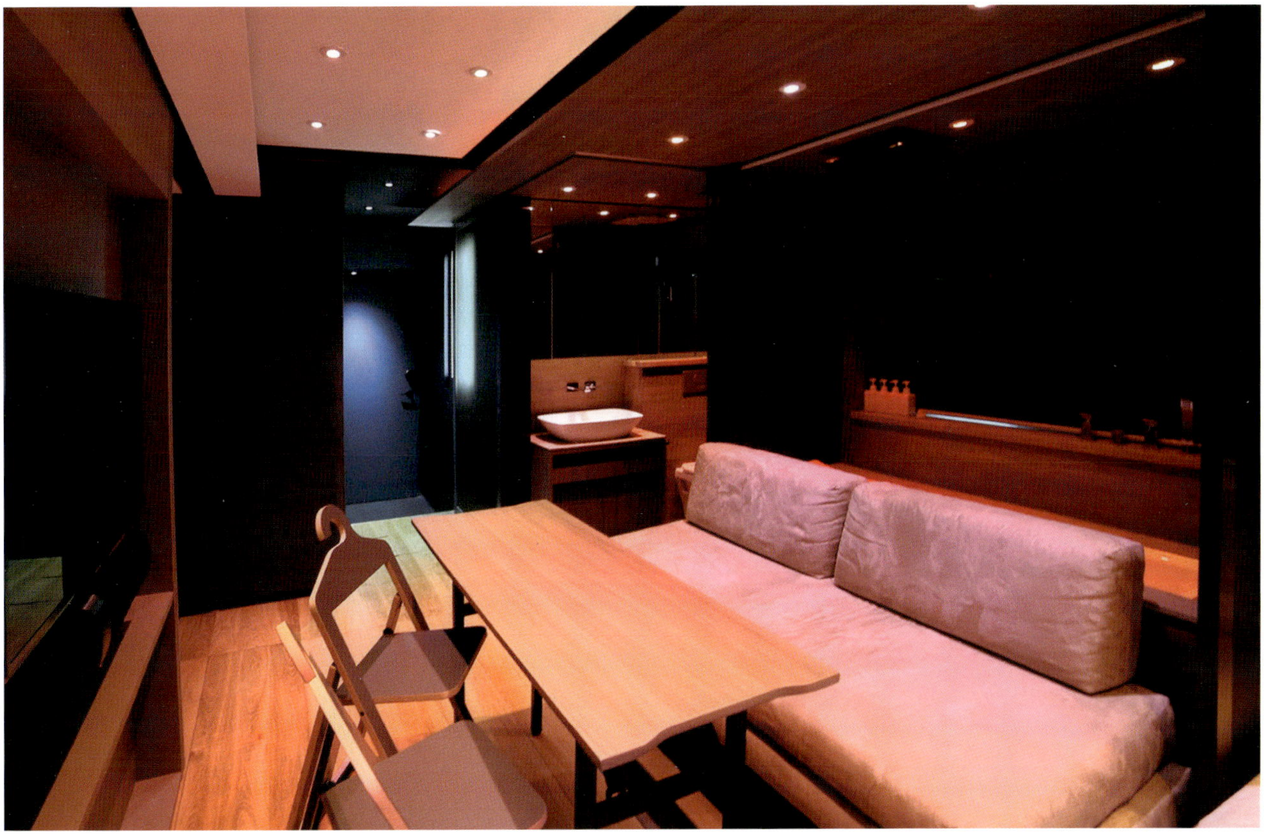

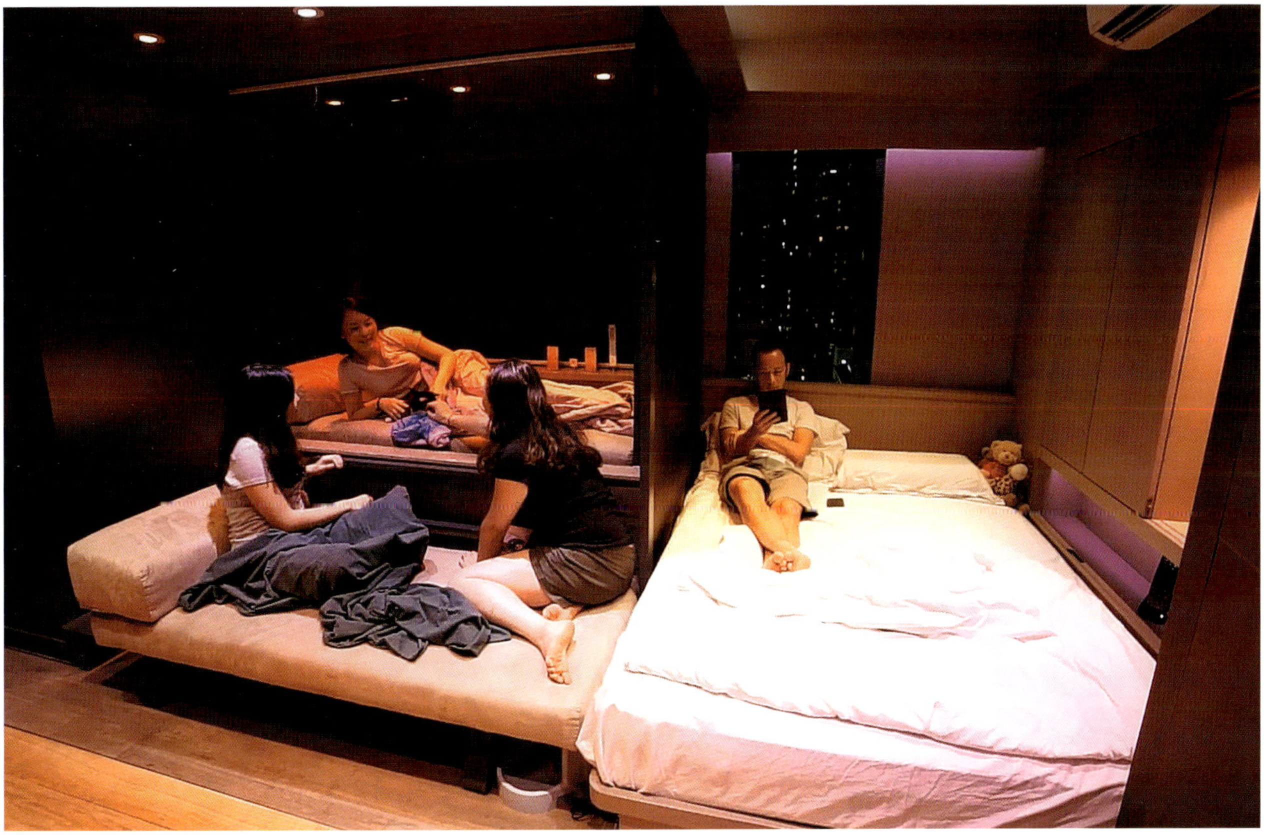

CASETA HOUSE

LICHTSTAD ARCHITECTEN
ROBERT VAN VUGT

LICHTSTADARCHITECTEN.NL

Lichtstad Architecten is a Dutch architecture office founded in 2013 by Robert van Vugt and located in the old Philips Lighting factory in Eindhoven. Lichtstad Architecten regards every building as an experience, sometimes pragmatic and functional, sometimes an eye catcher. Every architectural decision influences this experience, taking into account the location, the user and the materiality. These decisions resonate through time, thus they must be taken prudently for architecture to remain relevant. To achieve this, Lichtstad Architecten advocates for an architecture in which functionality and aesthetics find and strengthen each other. In the design of Caseta House, this approach has resulted in an optimal experience for the users and the sailors passing by.

Lichtstad Architecten ist ein Architekturbüro, das 2013 von Robert van Vugt gegründet wurde und sich in der ehemaligen Lampenfabrik in Eindhoven (Niederlande) befindet. Jedes Gebäude ist ein Erlebnis. Manchmal ist es kommerziell und funktional, manchmal ist es eine Freude für das Auge. Jede Designentscheidung hat einen Einfluss auf dieses Erlebnis. Die Kunst besteht darin, jede Designherausforderung für denjenigen zu realisieren, der sie baut, wo sie gebaut wird und wie sie gebaut wird. Schließlich überdauern die Entscheidungen des Architekten die Zeit. In der Architektur geht es um Form und Inhalt, um Ästhetik und Nutzen, um Kopf und Herz. Lichtstad Architecten steht für Architektur, in der maximale Funktionalität und das richtige Aussehen aufeinander treffen und sich gegenseitig verstärken. Das Ergebnis ist ein optimales Erlebnis für die Bewohner.

LICHTSTAD ARCHITECTEN

Lichtstad Architecten est un cabinet d'architecture fondé en 2013 par Robert van Vugt et situé dans l'ancienne usine de lampes à Eindhoven (Pays-Bas). Chaque bâtiment est une expérience. Parfois, il est commercial et fonctionnel, parfois, il est un plaisir pour les yeux. Chaque choix de design a un effet sur cette création. L'astuce consiste à réaliser chaque défi de conception pour qui le construit, où il est construit et comment il est construit. Après tout, les choix de l'architecte perdurent dans le temps. L'architecture est une question de forme et de contenu, d'esthétique et d'usage, de tête et de cœur. Lichtstad Architecten est l'acronyme de l'architecture dans laquelle la fonctionnalité maximale et l'apparence adéquate se rencontrent et se renforcent mutuellement. Le résultat est une expérience optimale pour l'utilisateur final.

Lichtstad Architecten es un estudio de arquitectura fundado en 2013 por Robert van Vugt y se encuentra en la antigua fábrica de lámparas de Eindhoven (Países Bajos). Cada edificio es una experiencia. A veces es comercial y funcional, a veces es una placer para la vista. Cada elección de diseño tiene un efecto en esa experiencia. El truco es realizar cada desafío de diseño para quien lo construye, donde se construye y cómo se construye. Después de todo, las elecciones del arquitecto perduran a través del tiempo. La arquitectura trata sobre la forma y el contenido, sobre la estética y el uso, sobre la cabeza y el corazón. Lichtstad Architecten representa la arquitectura en la que la máxima funcionalidad y la apariencia correcta se encuentran y se refuerzan mutuamente. El resultado es una experiencia óptima para el usuario final.

CASETA HOUSE

115 M² // GROU, THE NETHERLANDS
PHOTOS © BASEPHOTOGRAPHY

Located on 'De Burd', an island in a protective nature reserve, the brief called for was to design a holiday home that fully engages with the surrounding lake and landscape. The design is inspired by the sails of the "Skûtsjesilen", a traditional Frisian flat-bottom boat. This reference can be found in the edges as well as the subtle curvature of the roof. The mechanism for opening the curtains resembles the mechanism for hoisting the sails. Large windows enhance the experience of the landscape, allowing nature and sunlight to penetrate the space. While a dense facade and the different floor levels provide a sense of privacy. Like the surrounding landscape and the boats passing by, Caseta House changes with the angle of the view. Architecture and nature enter a compositional dialogue.

Auf der Insel De Burd gelegen, bestand die Herausforderung bei diesem Projekt darin, ein Ferienhaus zu entwerfen, das eine maximale Verbindung zur Umgebung - dem Meer und den grünen Wiesen - hat. Das Design ist inspiriert von den Segeln der Skûtsjesilen, die in der Umgebung segeln. Die Linien und Formen der Segel sind subtil in die Kanten des Daches und der Wölbung der Dachfläche eingearbeitet. Der Mechanismus zum Öffnen der Vorhänge ähnelt dem Mechanismus zum Hissen der Segel. Während Sie durch Caseta navigieren, ändert sich das Design mit der Landschaft. In Bezug auf Form und Komposition lässt es sich auf ein Spiel mit den vorbeifahrenden Booten ein. Das Design und die Landschaft werden eins. Große Fenster lassen Sonnenlicht und Natur in den Raum eindringen. Dichte Fassadenabschnitte und die unterschiedliche Höhe der Geschosse sorgen für das Gefühl von Privatsphäre.

Situé sur l'île de De Burd, le défi de ce projet était de concevoir une maison de vacances avec une connexion maximale avec son environnement - la mer et les prairies vertes. Le design est inspiré des voiles des *skûtsjesilen*, qui naviguent dans les environs. Les lignes et les formes des voiles sont subtilement visibles depuis les bords et la courbure de la surface du toit. Le mécanisme d'ouverture des rideaux ressemble au mécanisme de hissage des voiles. Lorsque vous naviguez sur Caseta, le design change en fonction de l'évolution du paysage. En termes de forme et de composition, il s'engage dans un jeu avec les bateaux qui passent. Le dessin et le paysage ne font plus qu'un. De grandes fenêtres permettent de voir la nature ainsi que laisser pénètrer la lumière du soleil. Les façades denses et les différents étages donnent un sentiment d'intimité.

Situada en la isla de De Burd, el desafío de este proyecto era diseñar una casa de vacaciones con una conexión máxima con su entorno –el mar y verdes praderas. El diseño está inspirado en las velas de los *skûtsjesilen*, que navegan por los alrededores. Las líneas y formas de las velas son sutilmente visibles en los bordes del tejado y la curvatura de la superficie del mismo. El mecanismo de apertura de las cortinas se parece al mecanismo de izado de las velas. A medida que se navega por Caseta, el diseño cambia con el cambio del paisaje. En cuanto a la forma y la composición, se involucra en un juego con los barcos que pasan navegando. El diseño y el paisaje se convierten en uno solo. Unos grandes ventanales permiten que la luz del sol y la naturaleza penetren en el espacio. Densas secciones de fachada y diferentes pisos proporcionan la sensación de privacidad.

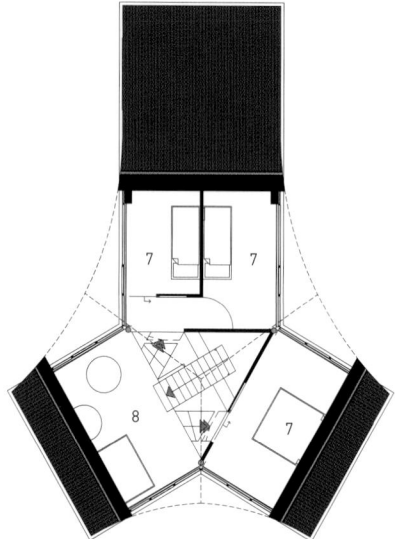

Upper floor plan

Roof plan

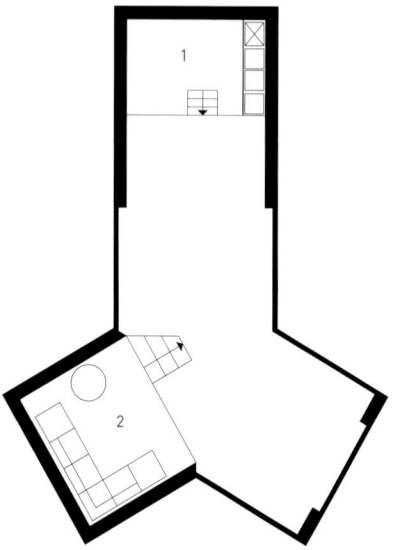

Lower floor plan

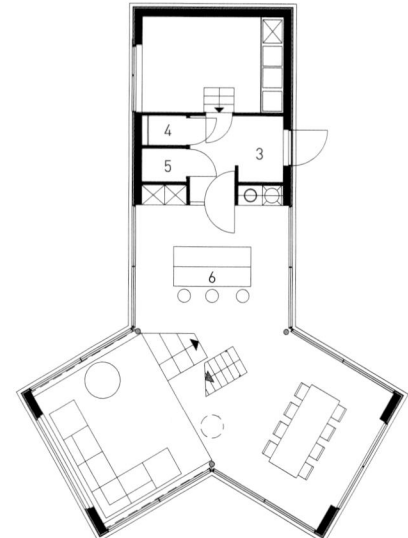

Main floor plan

1. Storage/technical room
2. Sitting area
3. Entry
4. Toilet
5. Shower
6. Kitchen
7. Bedroom
8. Terrace

PIED-À-MER

MICHAEL K CHEN ARCHITECTURE // MKCA

MICHAEL K CHEN

WWW.MKCA.COM

MICHAEL K CHEN ARCHITECTURE // MKCA, established in 2011 in New York City, is an architecture practice dedicated to producing innovative and superbly crafted work integrating architecture, interior design, and product design.

MKCA's approach is deeply informed by curiosity, experimentation, and a love of tinkering, of drawing, of collaboration, and of making. Their methods and capabilities are at the leading edge of research, design, analysis, manufacturing, and construction, and they strive to produce exceptional experiences, intricately choreographed spaces, and works that are unexpected, hyper-useful, intelligent, and full of delight.

MICHAEL K CHEN is founder and principal of MKCA and co-founder of Design Advocates, a network of independent architecture and design firms collaborating on pro-bono projects for small businesses, institutions, and organizations that serve disadvantaged communities to help them adapt their spaces and operations to adapt to COVID-19 and beyond.

MICHAEL K CHEN ARCHITECTURE // MKCA wurde 2011 in New York City gegründet und ist ein Architekturbüro, das sich der Herstellung innovativer und handwerklich hervorragender Arbeiten widmet, die Architektur, Innenarchitektur und Produktdesign integrieren.

Der Ansatz von MKCA ist tief geprägt von Neugier, Experimentieren und der Liebe zum Basteln, Zeichnen, Zusammenarbeiten und Basteln. Ihre Methoden und Fähigkeiten stehen bei Forschung, Design, Analyse, Herstellung und Konstruktion an vorderster Front, um außergewöhnliche Erlebnisse, sorgfältig choreografierte Räume und unerwartete, nützliche, intelligente Arbeiten zu schaffen, die voller Spaß sind.

MICHAEL K CHEN ist Gründer und Direktor von MKCA und Mitbegründer von Design Advocates, einem Netzwerk unabhängiger Architektur- und Designbüros, die an Pro-bono-Projekten für kleine Unternehmen, Institutionen und Organisationen, die benachteiligten Gemeinden dienen, zusammenarbeiten, um sie bei der Anpassung ihrer Räume und Abläufe an COVID-19 und darüber hinaus zu unterstützen.

MICHAEL K CHEN ARCHITECTURE // MKCA

MICHAEL K CHEN ARCHITECTURE // MKCA, créé en 2011 à New York, est un cabinet d'architecture qui se consacre à la production d'un travail innovant et superbement réalisé, intégrant l'architecture, le design d'intérieur et le design de produits.

L'approche de MKCA est profondément informée par la curiosité, l'expérimentation et l'amour du dessin, de la collaboration et de la création. Leurs méthodes et leurs capacités sont à la pointe de la recherche, de la conception, de l'analyse, de la fabrication et de la construction, de façon à produire des expériences exceptionnelles, des espaces minutieusement chorégraphiés et des œuvres inattendues, utiles, intelligentes et pleines de plaisir.

MICHAEL K CHEN est fondateur et directeur de MKCA et co-fondateur de Design Advocates, un réseau de cabinets d'architecture et de design indépendants collaborant sur des projets pro-bono pour les petites entreprises, les institutions et les organisations qui servent les communautés défavorisées, afin de les aider à adapter leurs espaces et leurs opérations pour s'adapter à CO-VID-19 et au-delà.

MICHAEL K CHEN ARCHITECTURE // MKCA, fundado en 2011 en la ciudad de Nueva York, es un estudio de arquitectura dedicado a producir trabajos innovadores y magníficamente elaborados que integran la arquitectura, el diseño de interiores y el diseño industrial.

El enfoque de MKCA está profundamente informado por la curiosidad, la experimentación y el amor por el dibujo, la colaboración y la creación. Sus métodos y capacidades están a la vanguardia de la investigación, el diseño, el análisis, la fabricación y la construcción para producir experiencias excepcionales, espacios intrincadamente coreografiados y obras inesperadas, útiles, inteligentes y llenas de deleite.

MICHAEL K CHEN es fundador y director de MKCA y co-fundador de Design Advocates, una red de empresas independientes de arquitectura y diseño que colaboran en proyectos pro-bono para pequeñas empresas, instituciones y organizaciones que sirven a comunidades desfavorecidas para ayudarles a adaptar sus espacios y operaciones para adaptarse a COVID-19.

PIED-À-MER

55 M² // ABOARD A RESIDENTIAL YACHT

PHOTOS © ALAN TANSY

Playfully dubbed "pied-à-mer," this apartment aboard a residential yacht by Michael K. Chen Architecture (MKCA) is simultaneously adaptable, efficient, and strikingly elegant. The residence serves as a holiday home for a couple and their grown children, transforming seamlessly from a spacious one-bedroom to a two-bedroom apartment through tables and beds that fold away and unfurl as necessary. Drawing from Le Corbusier's interest in streamlined, mid-twentieth-century steamship design, the space is also reflective of MKCA's own expertise in creating compact, multifunctional spaces in contemporary urban environments.

Diese spielerisch als „pied-à-mer" bezeichnete Wohnung an Bord einer Wohnyacht von Michael K. Chen Architecture (MKCA) ist gleichzeitig anpassungsfähig, effizient und auffallend elegant. Die Residenz dient als Ferienhaus für ein Paar und ihre erwachsenen Kinder und verwandelt sich nahtlos von einem geräumigen Apartment mit einem Schlafzimmer in ein Apartment mit zwei Schlafzimmern durch Tische und Betten, die sich nach Bedarf zusammenklappen und entfalten lassen. Aufgrund des Interesses von Le Corbusier an einem optimierten Dampfschiffdesign aus der Mitte des 20. Jahrhunderts spiegelt der Raum auch das Know-how von MKCA bei der Schaffung kompakter, multifunktionaler Räume in modernen städtischen Umgebungen wider.

Surnommé de manière ludique « pied-à-mer », cet appartement à bord d'un yacht résidentiel de Michael K. Chen Architecture (MKCA) est à la fois adaptable, efficace et d'une élégance saisissante. La résidence, qui sert de maison de vacances pour un couple et leurs enfants adultes, peut se transformer facilement d'un spacieux appartement d'une chambre à un appartement de deux chambres grâce à des tables et des lits qui se replient et se déplient si nécessaire. Puisant dans l'intérêt de Le Corbusier pour la conception épurée des navires à vapeur du milieu du XXe siècle, l'espace reflète également la propre expertise de MKCA dans la création d'espaces compacts et multifonctionnels dans les environnements urbains contemporains.

Apodado «pied-à-mer», este.apartamento a bordo de un yate residencial de Michael K. Chen Architecture (MKCA) es a la vez adaptable, eficiente y sorprendentemente elegante. La residencia sirve como casa de vacaciones para una pareja y sus hijos adultos, transformándose fácilmente en un espacioso apartamento de un dormitorio a uno de dos mediante mesas y camas que se pliegan y despliegan según sea necesario. Partiendo del interés de Le Corbusier en el diseño aerodinámico de los barcos de vapor de mediados del siglo XX, el espacio también refleja la propia experiencia de MKCA en la creación de espacios compactos y multifuncionales en entornos urbanos contemporáneos.

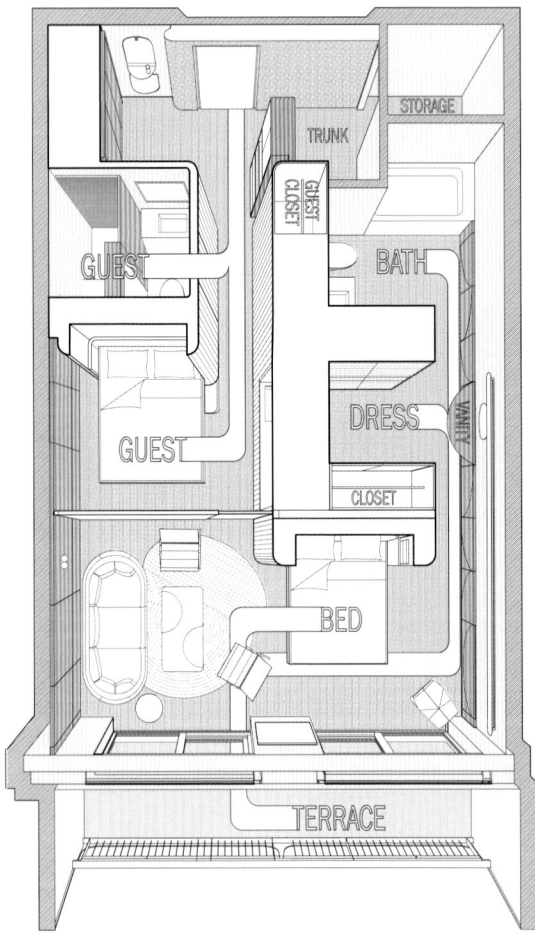

Perspective floor plan

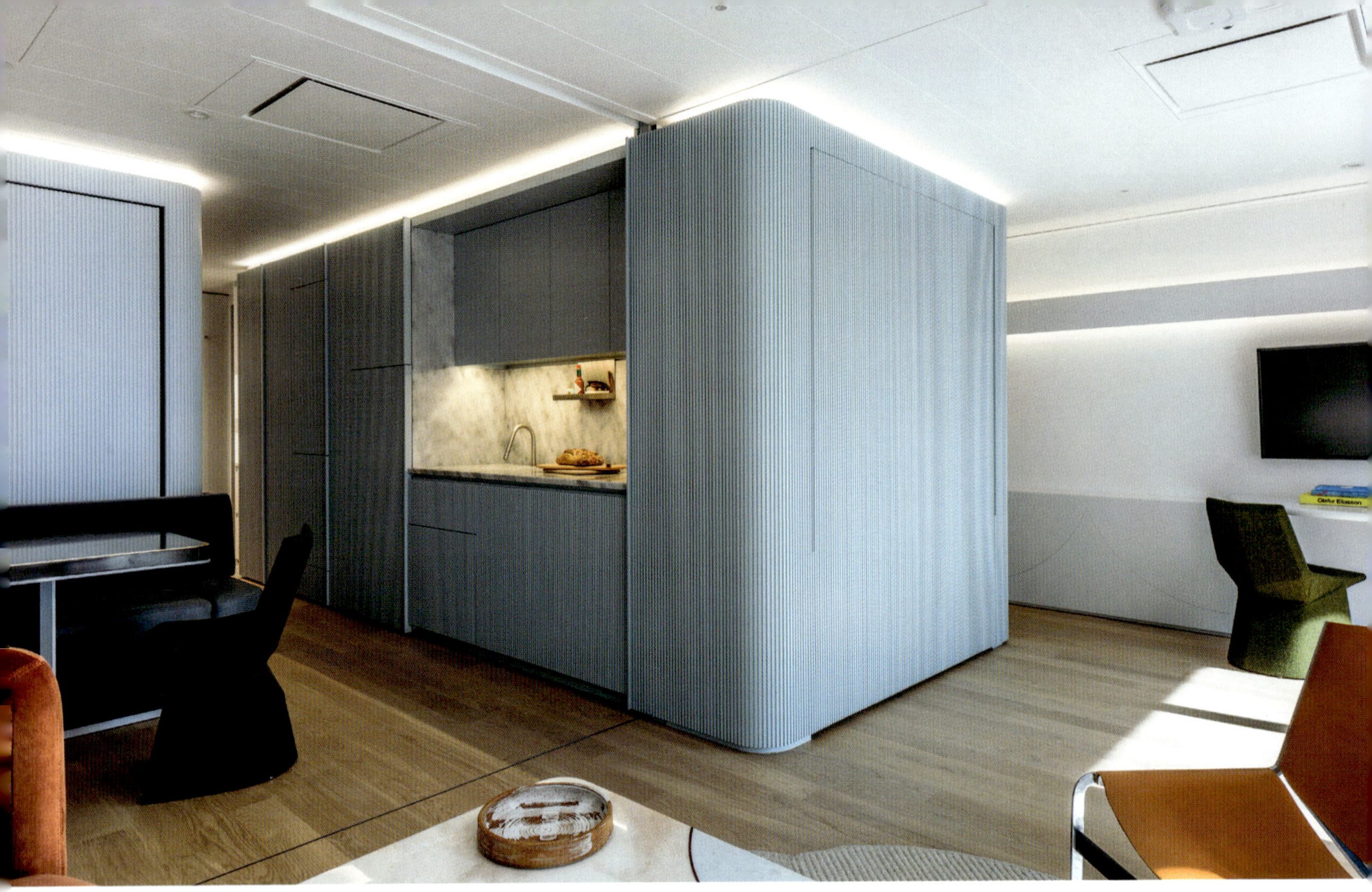

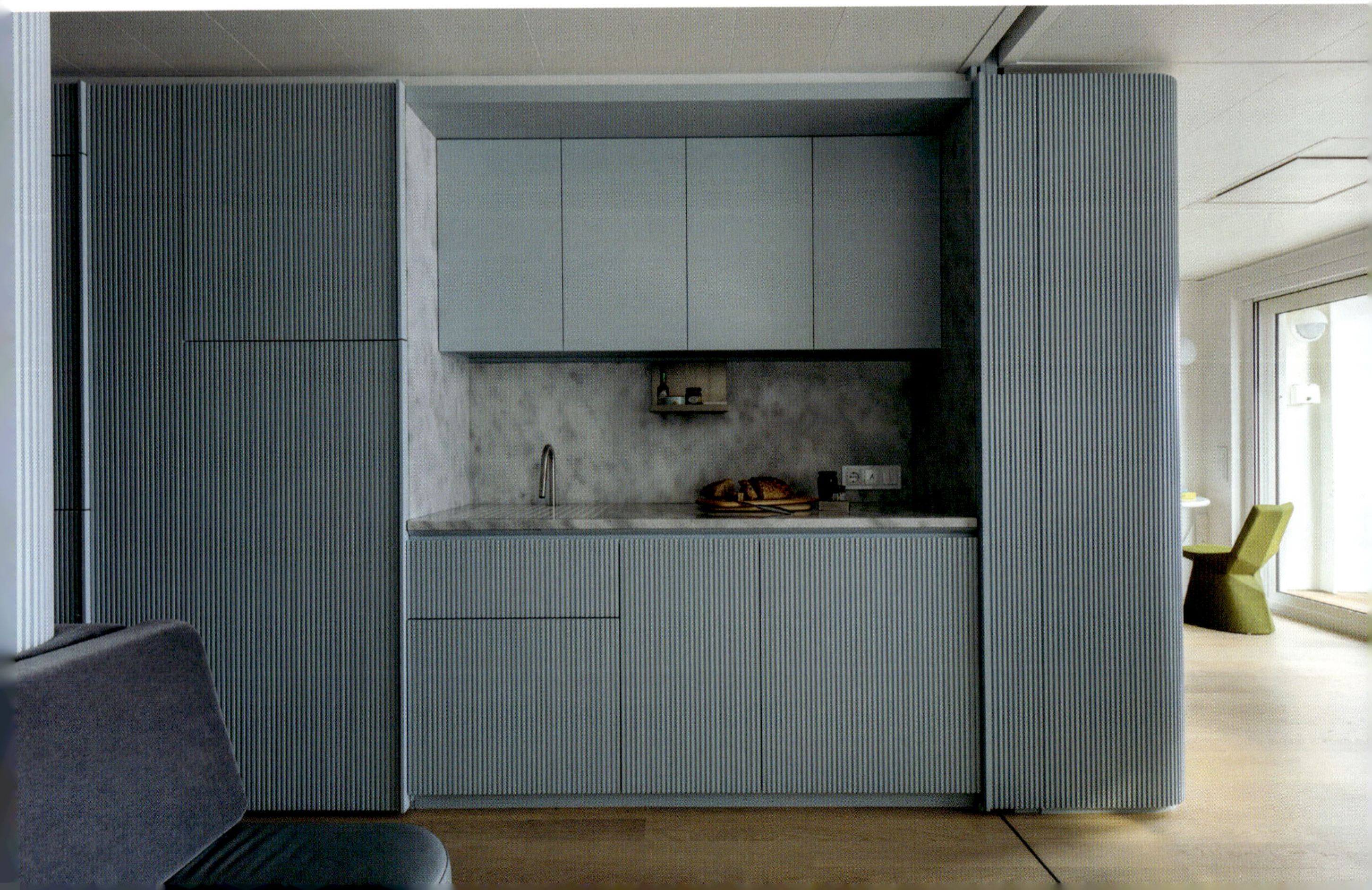

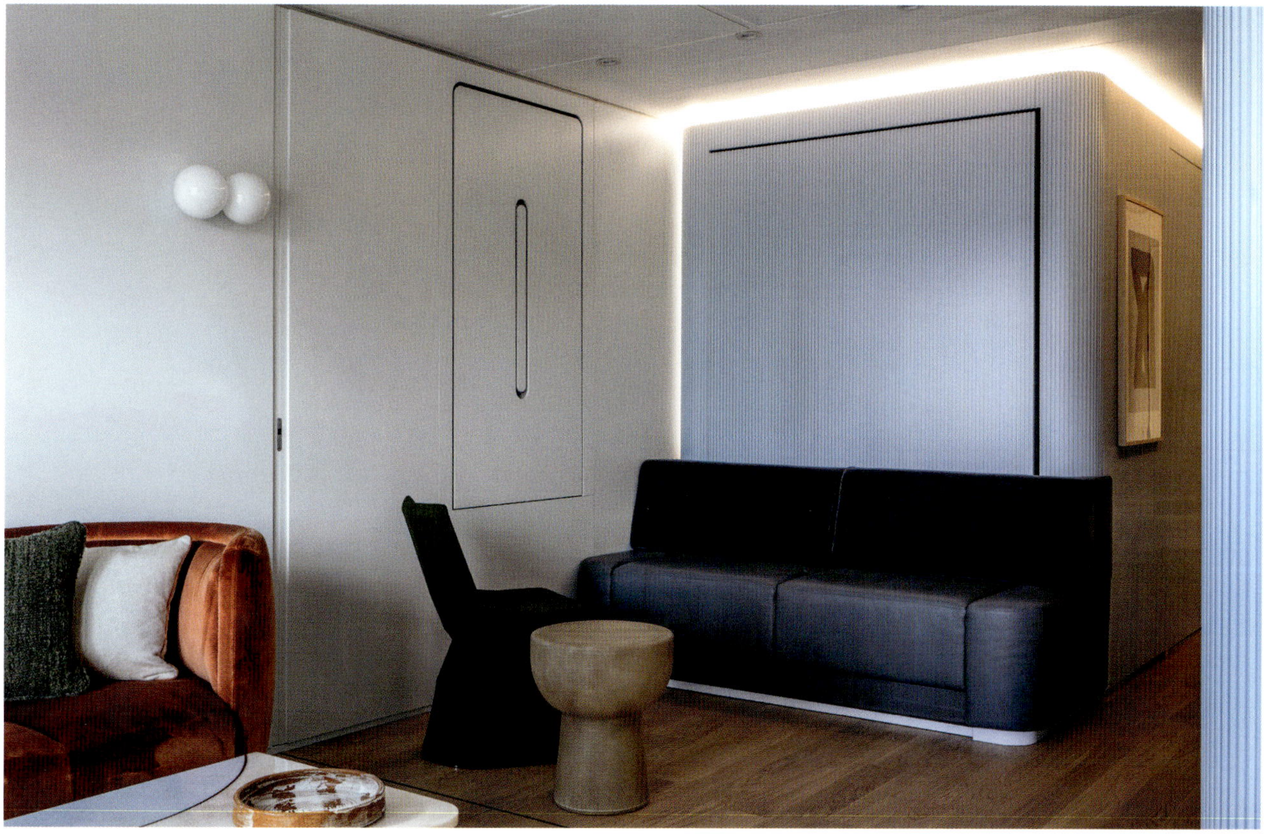

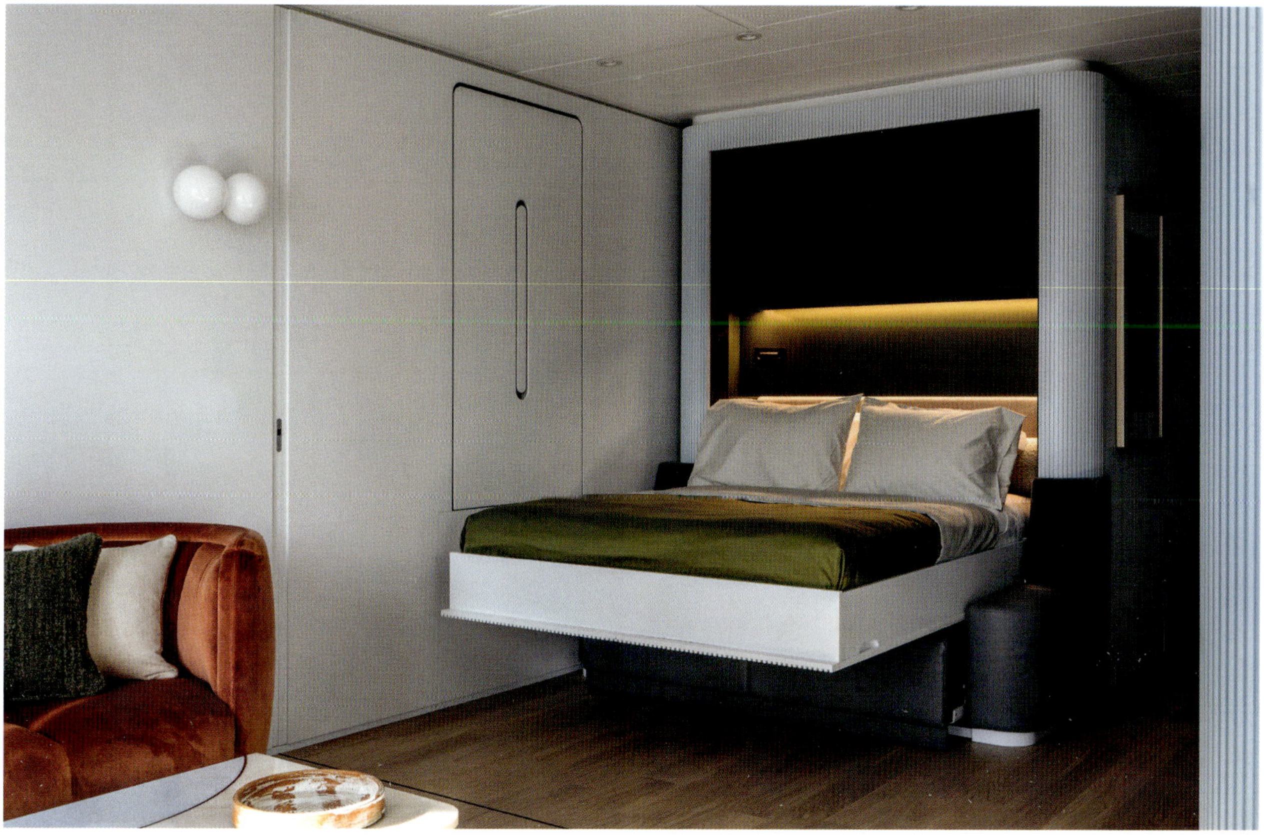

MYLLA CABIN

SKIGARD HYTTE

MORK-ULNES ARCHITECTS
CASPER MORK-ULNES

WWW.MORKULNES.COM

Mork-Ulnes Architects, is an international firm with offices in California and Norway. We approach projects with both Scandinavian practicality and a Californian spirit of innovation. Our work is characterised by playfulness and restraint, the result of a rigorous, concept-driven process that thrives on an economy of means and materials. Since it was founded by Casper Mork-Ulnes in 2005, MUA has built on three continents and worked on projects on a variety of scales. It has also received numerous accolades, including the 2020 Emerging Voices Award from the Architectural League of New York, nominated twice for the EU Prize for Contemporary Architecture, and the 2015 Design Vanguard Award from Architectural Record. The studio has also been featured in international publications such as Detail, The New York Times, Wallpaper*, Architectural Record, Domus, Architizer, Dezeen, Abitare and Dwell Magazine.

Mork-Ulnes Architects ist ein internationales Büro mit Niederlassungen in Kalifornien und Norwegen. Wir gehen Projekte sowohl mit skandinavischer Sachlichkeit als auch mit kalifornischem Innovationsgeist an. Unsere Arbeit zeichnet sich durch Verspieltheit und Zurückhaltung aus. Sie ist das Ergebnis eines rigorosen, konzeptgesteuerten Prozesses, der von einer Ökonomie der Mittel und Materialien lebt. Seit der Gründung durch Casper Mork-Ulnes im Jahr 2005 hat MUA auf drei Kontinenten gebaut und an Projekten in unterschiedlichen Größenordnungen gearbeitet. Es hat auch zahlreiche Auszeichnungen erhalten, darunter den 2020 Emerging Voices Award der Architectural League of New York, zwei Nominierungen für den EU Contemporary Architecture Award und den 2015 Design Vanguard Award von Architectural Record. Das Studio wurde auch in internationalen Publikationen wie Detail, The New York Times, Wallpaper*, Architectural Record, Domus, Architizer, Dezeen, Abitare und Dwell Magazine vorgestellt.

MORK-ULNES ARCHITECTS

Mork-Ulnes Architects, est un cabinet international qui possède des bureaux en Californie et en Norvège. Nous abordons les projets à la fois avec un sens pratique scandinave et un esprit d'innovation californien. Notre travail se caractérise par le jeu et la retenue, résultat d'un processus rigoureux, axé sur le concept, qui se nourrit d'une économie de moyens et de matériaux. Depuis sa création par Casper Mork-Ulnes en 2005, MUA s'est développé sur trois continents et a travaillé sur des projets à différentes échelles. Il a également reçu de nombreuses récompenses, notamment le prix 2020 Emerging Voices de l'Architectural League of New York, nominé à deux reprises pour le prix d'architecture contemporaine de l'UE, et le prix 2015 Design Vanguard de l'Architectural Record. Le studio a également été présenté dans des publications internationales telles que Detail, The New York Times, Wallpaper*, Architectural Record, Domus, Architizer, Dezeen, Abitare et Dwell Magazine.

Mork-Ulnes Architects, es una firma internacional con oficinas en California y Noruega. Abordamos los proyectos tanto con la practicidad escandinava como con el espíritu californiano de innovación. Nuestro trabajo se caracteriza por el juego y la moderación, resultado de un proceso riguroso y basado en conceptos, que se nutre de una economía de medios y materiales. Desde que fue fundada por Casper Mork-Ulnes en 2005, MUA ha construido en tres continentes y ha trabajado en proyectos a diversas escalas. Además ha recibido numerosos reconocimientos, entre ellos el premio 2020 Emerging Voices de la Architectural League of New York, nominado dos veces para el Premio de Arquitectura Contemporánea de la UE, y el premio Design Vanguard 2015 de Architectural Record. El estudio también ha aparecido en publicaciones internacionales como Detail, The New York Times, Wallpaper*, Architectural Record, Domus, Architizer, Dezeen, Abitare y Dwell Magazine.

MYLLA CABIN

84 M² // JEVNAKER COUNTY, NORWAY
PHOTOS © BRUCE DAMONTE

Designed as a retreat for a geologist and his family, this cottage sits on a hilltop surrounded by an imposing forest. Although planning regulations called for a gable roof, this house has four shed roofs arranged in a pinwheel configuration, creating two outdoor spaces sheltered from wind and snow. The exterior is clad in untreated pine planks. The compact interior, finished in plywood and unified with a continuous roof, can accommodate up to ten people in three bedrooms and two bathrooms. The furnishings, also of plywood, are custom-made. Each of the house's wings faces a different aspect of the landscape: the master bedroom overlooks the neighboring forest, the guest bedroom faces the hillside, the children's bedroom looks up to the sky, and the living room has a view of Lake Mylla.

Als rückzugsort für einen geologen und seine familie entworfen, liegt dieses haus auf einer hügelkuppe, umgeben von einem imposanten wald. Obwohl die planungsvorschriften ein satteldach vorsahen, hat dieses haus vier pultdächer, die in einer pinwheel-konfiguration angeordnet sind und zwei vor wind und schnee geschützte außenbereiche schaffen. Das äußere ist mit unbehandelten kiefernbrettern verkleidet. Der kompakte innenraum, der mit sperrholz verkleidet und mit einem durchgehenden dach verbunden ist, bietet platz für bis zu zehn personen in drei schlafzimmern und zwei bädern. Die möblierung, ebenfalls aus sperrholz, ist eine sonderanfertigung. Jeder flügel des hauses ist einem anderen aspekt der landschaft zugewandt: das hauptschlafzimmer blickt auf den angrenzenden wald, das gästezimmer auf den hang, das kinderzimmer in den himmel und das wohnzimmer auf den Mylla-see.

Conçu comme une retraite pour un géologue et sa famille, ce chalet se trouve au sommet d'une colline entourée d'une imposante forêt. Bien que la réglementation en matière de planification prévoyait un toit à deux versants, cette maison est dotée de quatre toits en appentis disposés en étoile, créant ainsi deux espaces extérieurs à l'abri du vent et de la neige. L'extérieur est revêtu de planches de pin non traitées. L'intérieur compact, fini en contreplaqué et unifié par un toit continu, peut accueillir jusqu'à dix personnes dans trois chambres et deux salles de bain. L'ameublement, également en contreplaqué, est fait sur mesure. Chacune des ailes de la maison fait face à un aspect différent du paysage : la chambre principale donne sur la forêt voisine, la chambre d'amis fait face à la colline, la chambre des enfants regarde vers le ciel et le salon a une vue sur le lac Mylla.

Diseñada como refugio para un geólogo y su familia, esta casa de campo se encuentra en la cima de una colina rodeada de un imponente bosque. Aunque los reglamentos de planificación exigían un tejado a dos aguas, esta casa tiene cuatro tejados en forma de molinete que crean dos espacios exteriores protegidos del viento y la nieve. El exterior está revestido de tablas de pino sin tratar. El interior compacto, acabado en madera contrachapada y unificado con un techo continuo, puede albergar hasta diez personas en tres dormitorios y dos baños. El mobiliario, también de madera contrachapada, está hecho a medida. Cada una de las alas de la casa está orientada a un aspecto diferente del paisaje: el dormitorio principal tiene vistas al bosque vecino, el dormitorio de invitados está orientado a la ladera, el dormitorio de los niños se abre al cielo y el salón tiene vistas al lago Mylla.

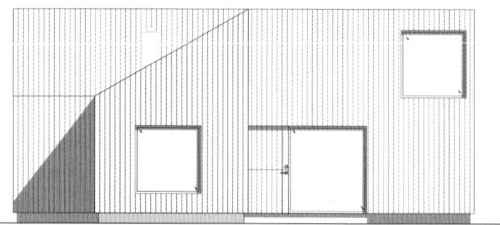

North elevation

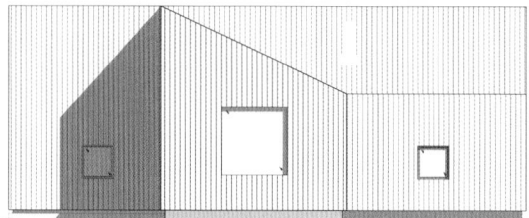

East elevation

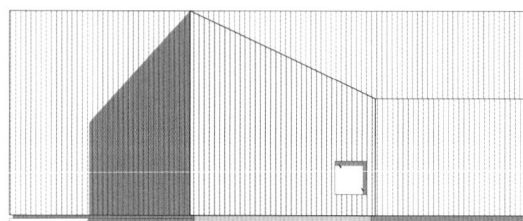

West elevation

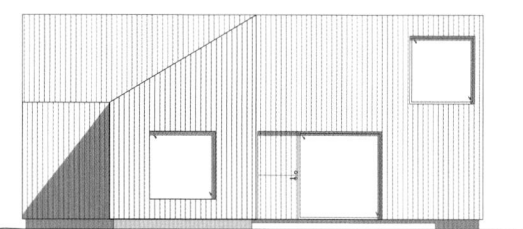

South elevation

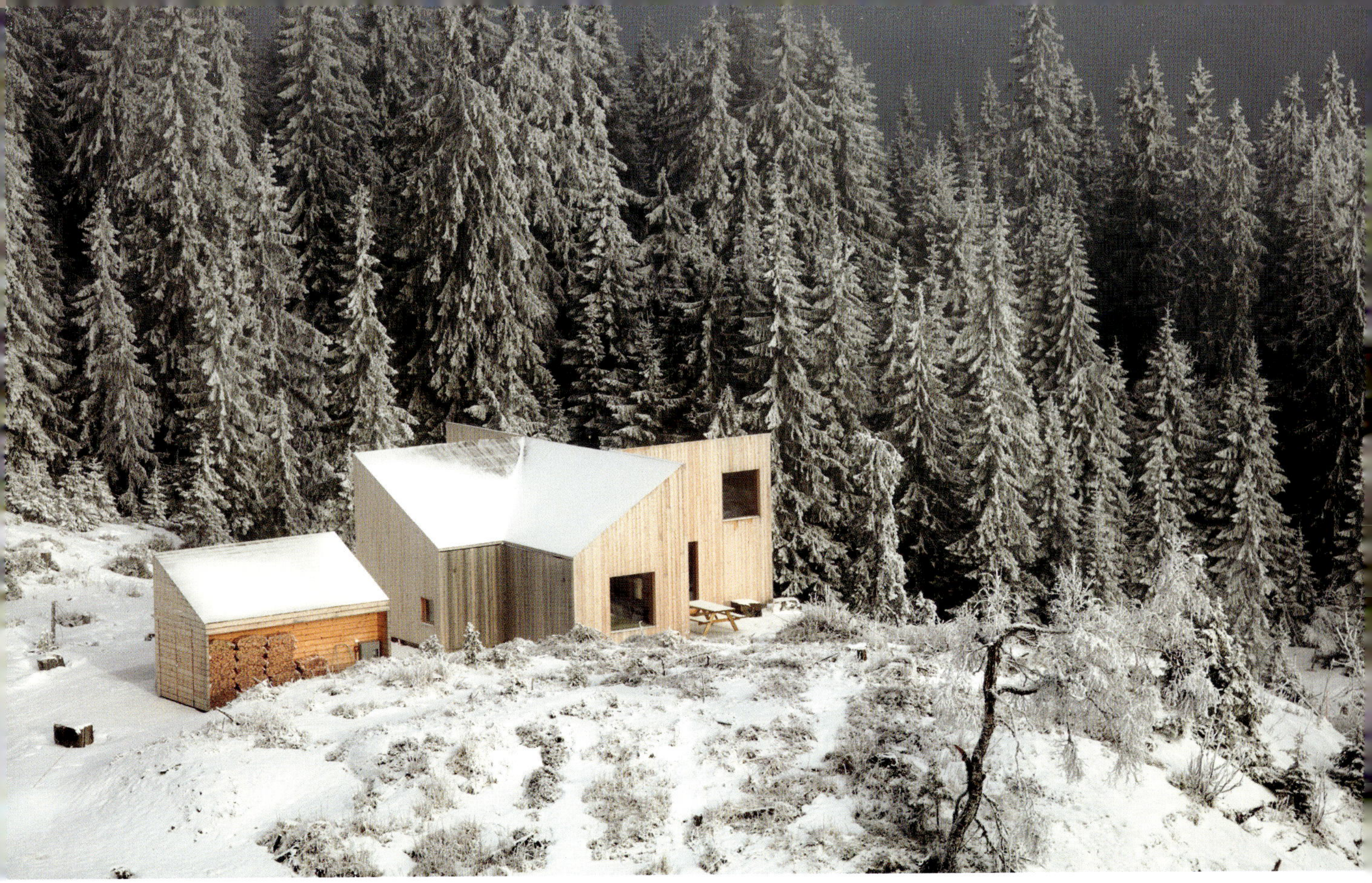

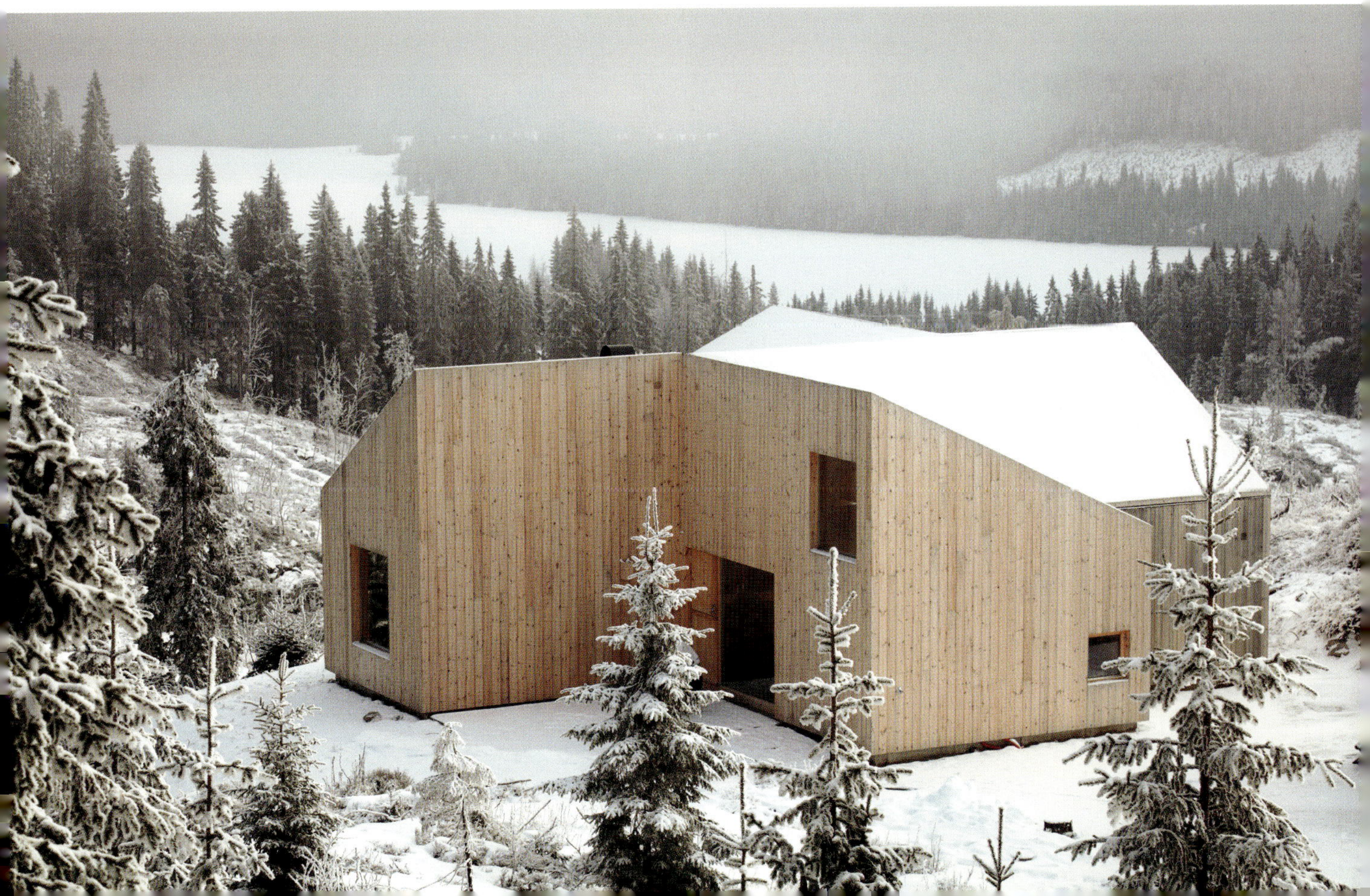

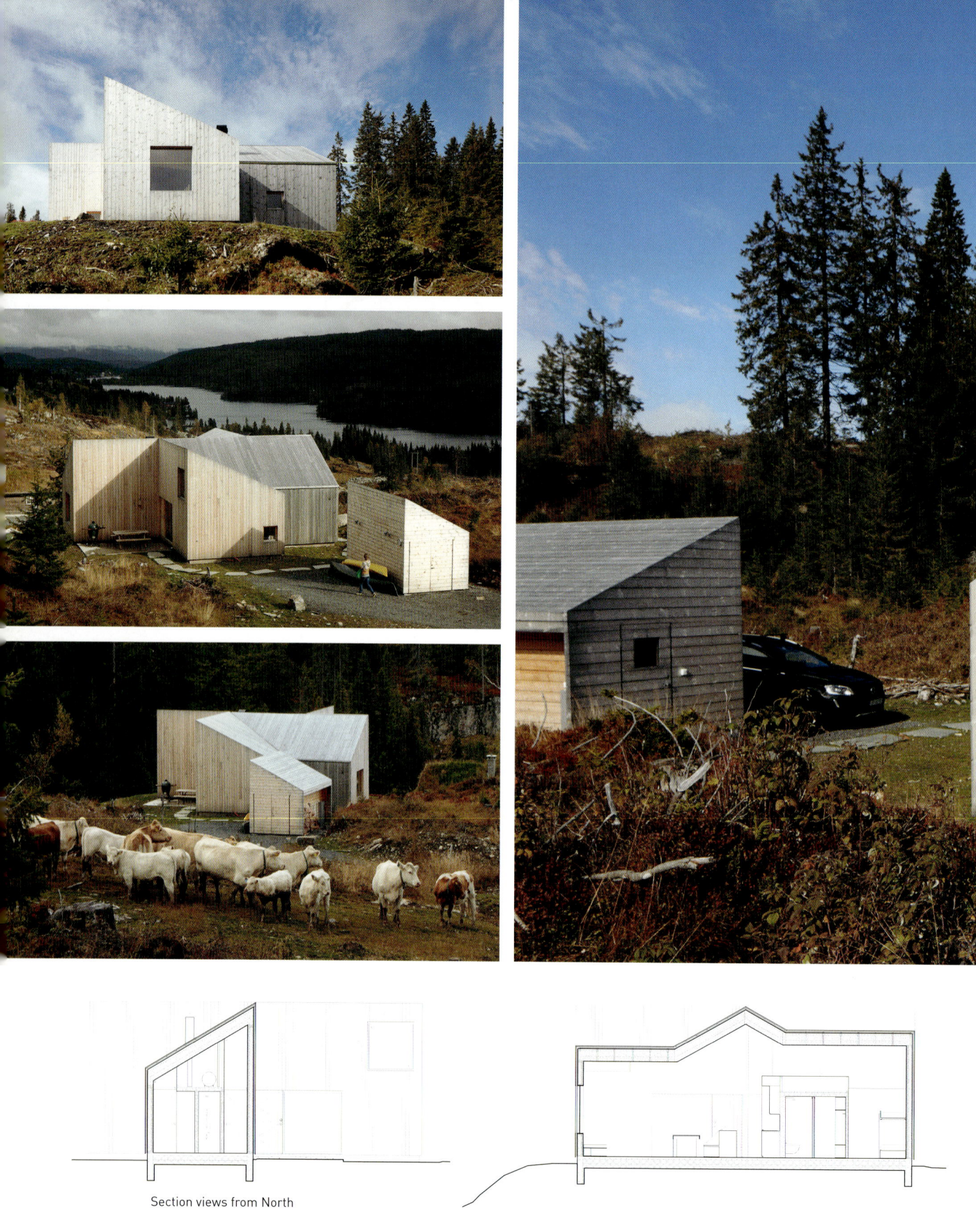

Section views from North

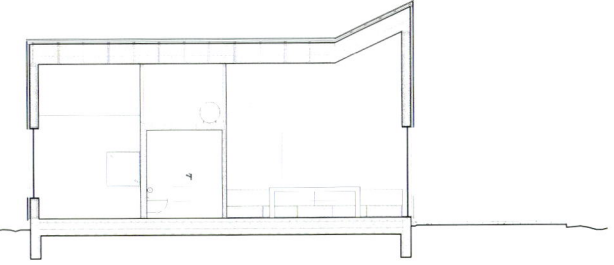

Section view from West

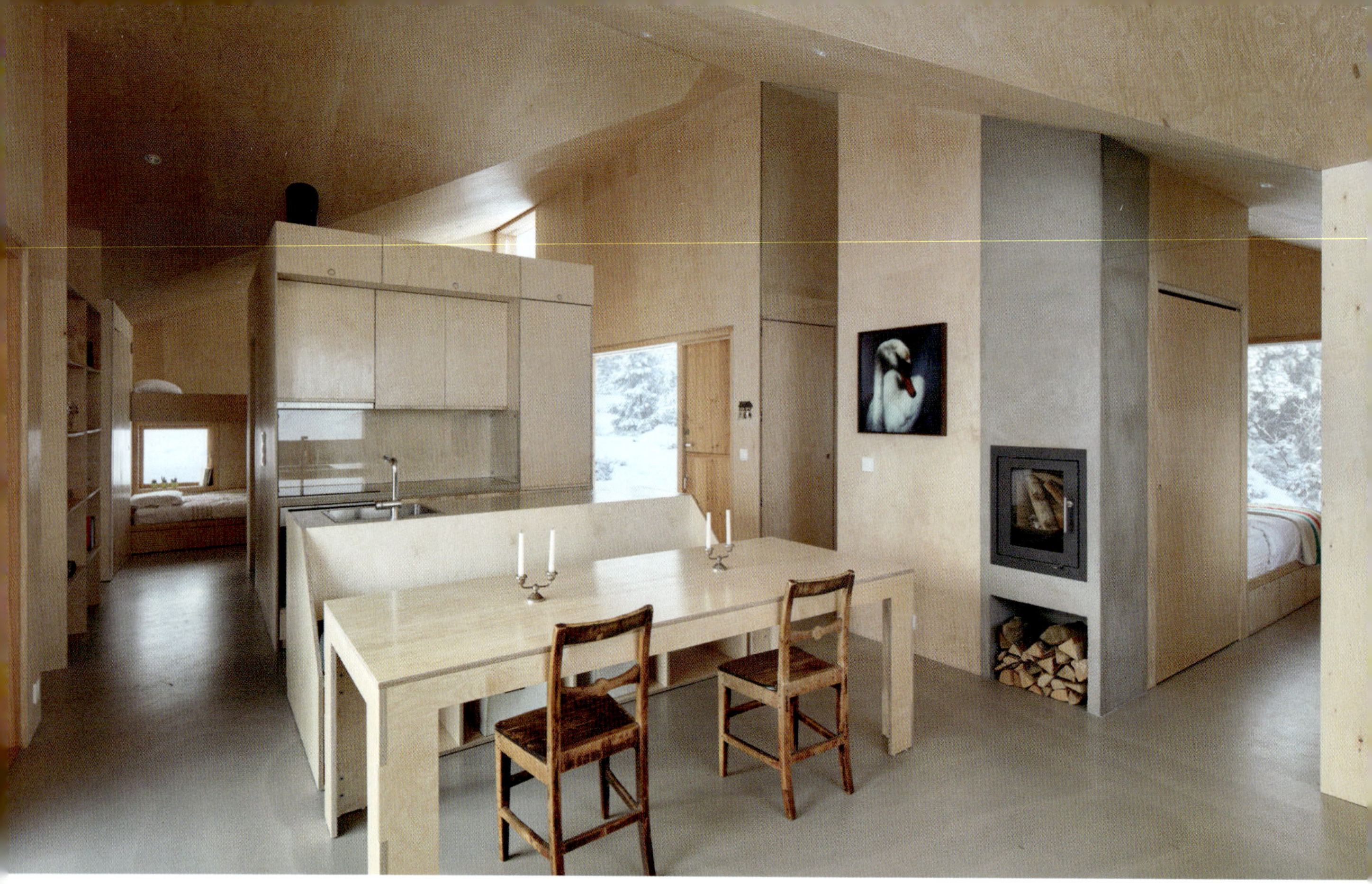

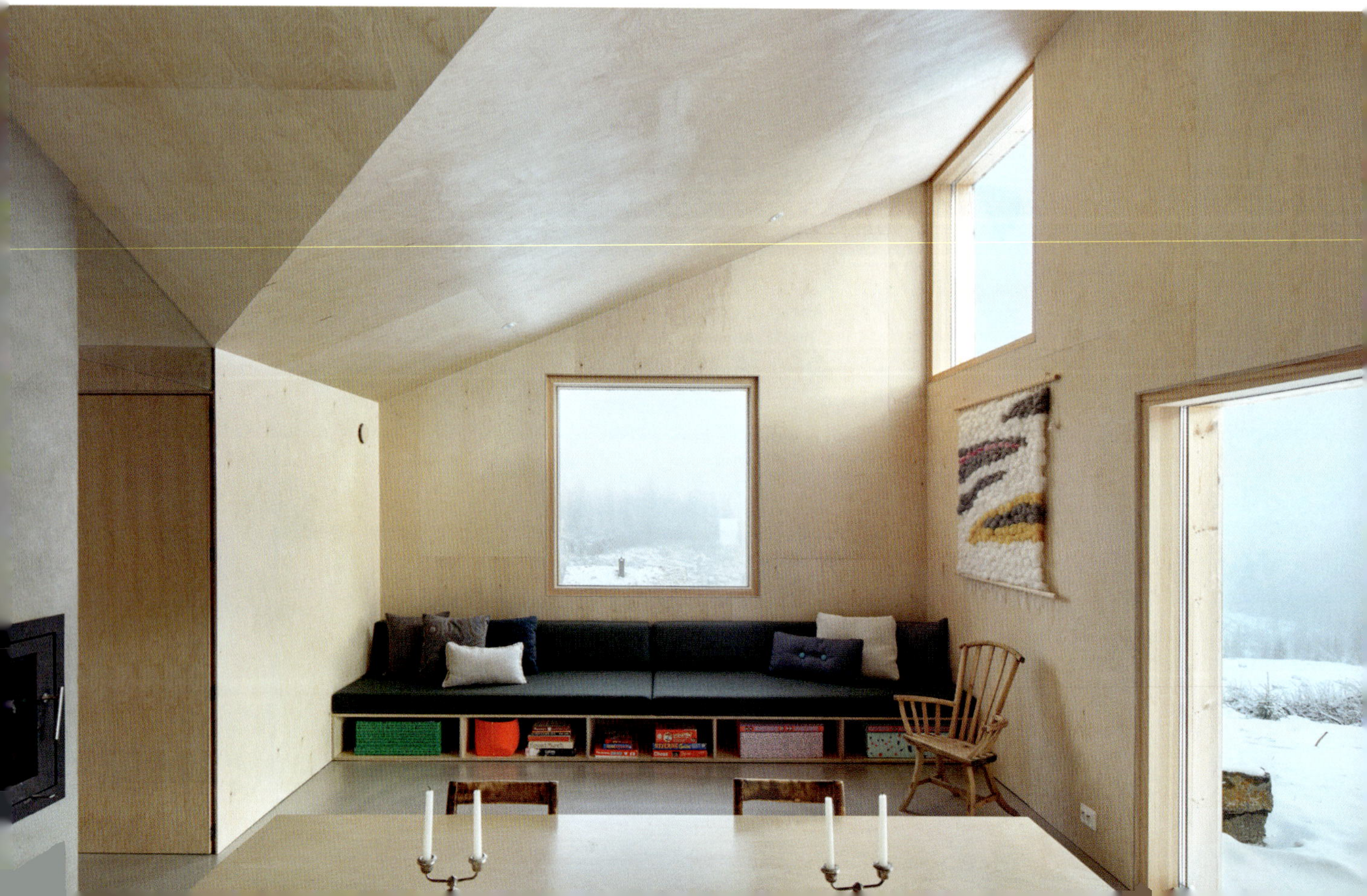

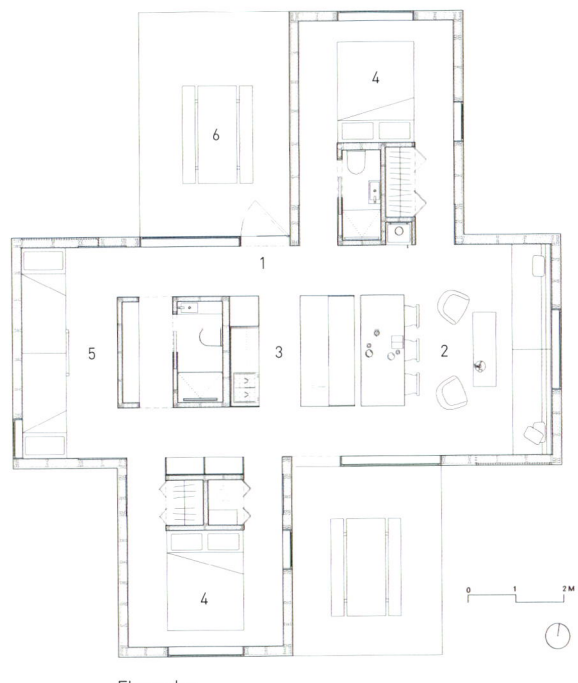

Floor plan

1. Entrance
2. Living/dining room
3. Kitchen
4. Bedroom
5. Bunk room
6. Patio

SKIGARD HYTTE

144 M² // KVITFJELL, NORWAY
PHOTOS © BRUCE DAMONTE

On top of a mountain in Kvitfjell, Norway is a regular grid of 45 wooden columns. The columns lift a 144 square meter cabin 1.5 meters above the ground, allowing native grasses that sheep and cows graze on to grow below. The columns are clad with skigard, a long and narrow, quarter cut tree log that is traditionally laid out diagonally by Norwegian farmers as fencing.The roof is overgrown with the same native grasses found on the ground below and on century's old Norwegian buildings. The cabin is accessed through a series of wide wooden steps that lead to a veranda, which frames the view of a valley and river below. Internally, the wood cabin is divided along its length into four smaller spaces, each housed under a frustum ceiling capped with a skylight. The spaces are scaled intimately but open visually and physically to the landscape below and a small grove of trees the cabin is nestled in.

Auf einem Berggipfel in Kvitfjell, Norwegen, befindet sich ein regelmäßiges Gitter aus 45 Säulen, die mit Skigard verkleidet sind, einem langen, schmalen, in Viertel geschnittenen Baumstamm, den norwegische Bauern traditionell diagonal als Zaun aufstellen. Die Säulen heben eine 144 Quadratmeter große Hütte 1,5 Meter über den Boden, so dass darunter einheimisches Gras wachsen kann, auf dem Schafe und Kühe grasen. Das Dach ist mit dem gleichen Gras gedeckt, das auch bei den norwegischen Gebäuden des letzten Jahrhunderts zu finden war. Der Zugang zur Hütte erfolgt über eine Reihe von breiten Holzstufen, die zu einer Veranda führen, die den Blick auf ein Tal und den darunter liegenden Fluss einrahmt. Im Inneren ist die Kabine der Länge nach in vier kleinere Räume unterteilt, die jeweils von einem Holzdach mit Oberlicht überdacht sind. Die Räume sind intim, aber gleichzeitig visuell und physisch offen zur darunterliegenden Landschaft und dem kleinen Baumhain, in dem die Hütte liegt.

Au sommet d'une montagne à Kvitfjell, en Norvège, on trouve une grille régulière de 45 colonnes recouvertes de *skigard*, un long tronc d'arbre étroit coupé en quartiers que les agriculteurs norvégiens placent traditionnellement en diagonale comme une clôture. Sur les colonnes s'élève un chalet de 144 mètres carrés à 1,5 mètre du sol, permettant à l'herbe indigène de pousser en dessous, sur laquelle paissent les moutons et les vaches. Le toit est recouvert de la même herbe que celle que l'on trouve dans les bâtiments norvégiens du siècle dernier. On accède au chalet par une série de larges marches en bois menant à un porche qui encadre la vue sur une vallée et une rivière en contrebas. À l'intérieur, l'édifice est divisée sur sa longueur en quatre espaces plus petits, chacun couvert par un toit en bois surmonté d'une lucarne. Les espaces sont intimes mais en même temps ouverts visuellement et physiquement au paysage.

En la cima de una montaña en Kvitfjell, Noruega, hay una cuadrícula regular de 45 columnas revestidas con *skigard*, un tronco de árbol largo y estrecho cortado en cuartos que los granjeros noruegos colocan tradicionalmente en diagonal como valla. Las columnas levantan una cabaña de 144 metros cuadrados a 1,5 metros del suelo, permitiendo que crezca debajo la hierba autóctona en la que pastan ovejas y vacas. El tejado está cubierto con la misma hierba que también se encontraba en los edificios noruegos del siglo pasado. Se accede a la cabaña a través de una serie de amplios escalones de madera que conducen a un porche que enmarca la vista de un valle y un río más abajo. Internamente, la cabaña se divide a lo largo de su longitud en cuatro espacios más pequeños, cada uno ellos cubierto por un techo de madera cubierto con un tragaluz. Los espacios son íntimos pero a la vez están abiertos visual y físicamente al paisaje.

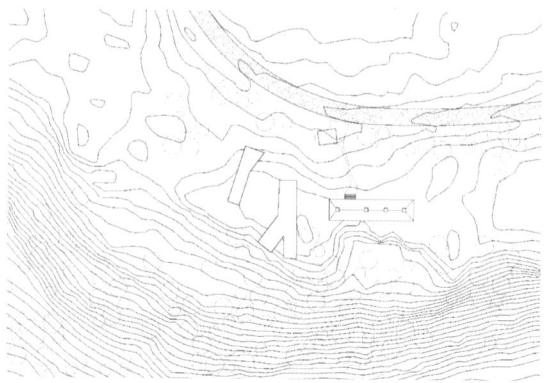
Site plan

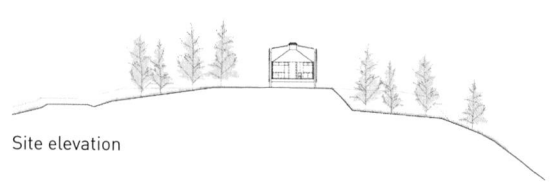
Site elevation

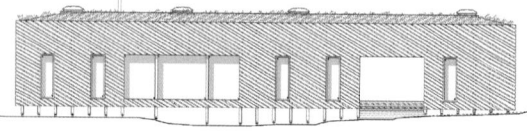
North elevation

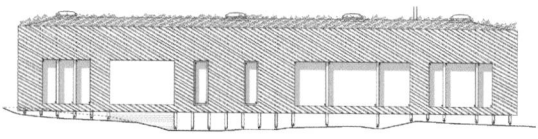
South elevation

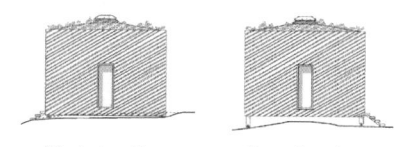
West elevation   East elevation

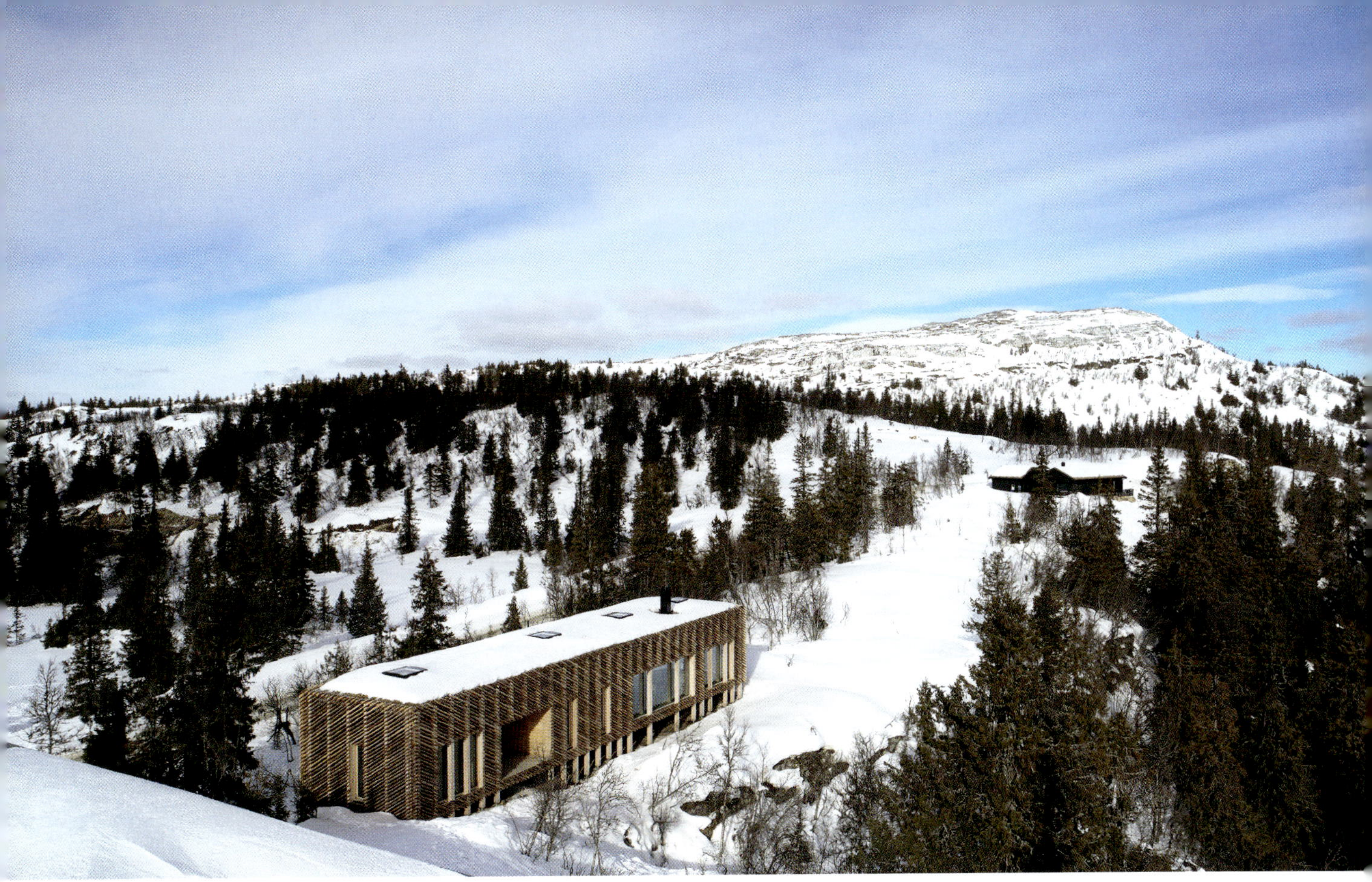

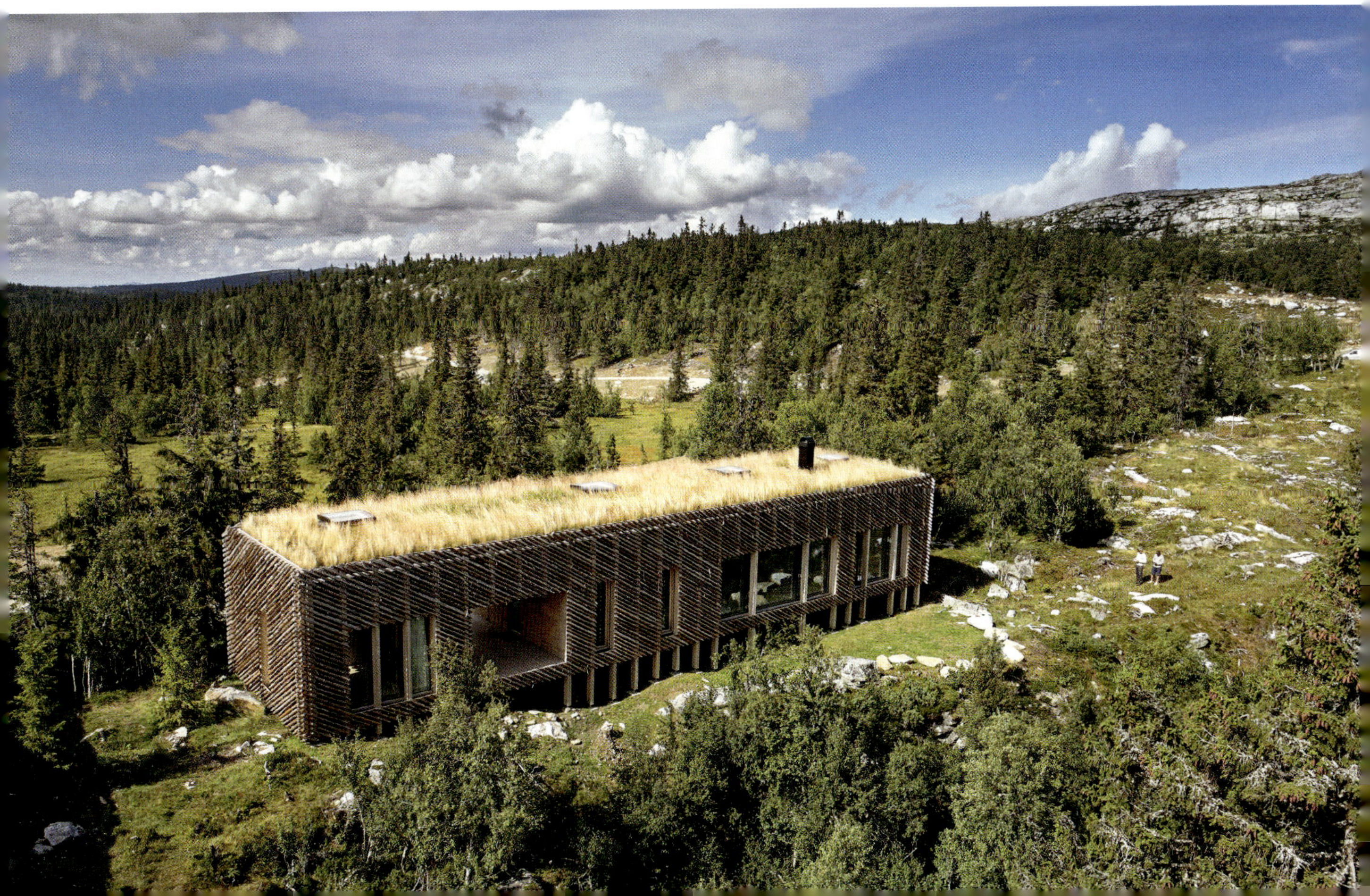

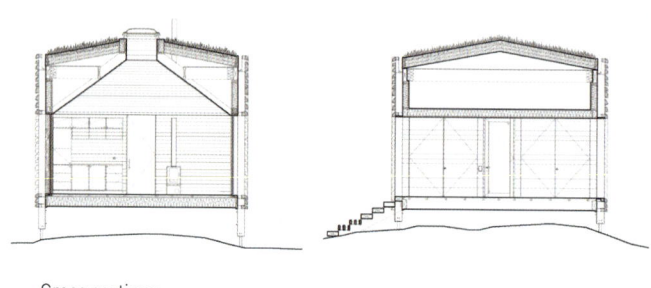

Cross sections

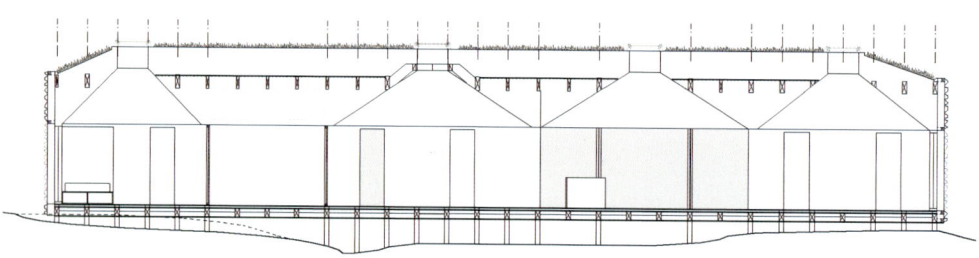

Transversal sections

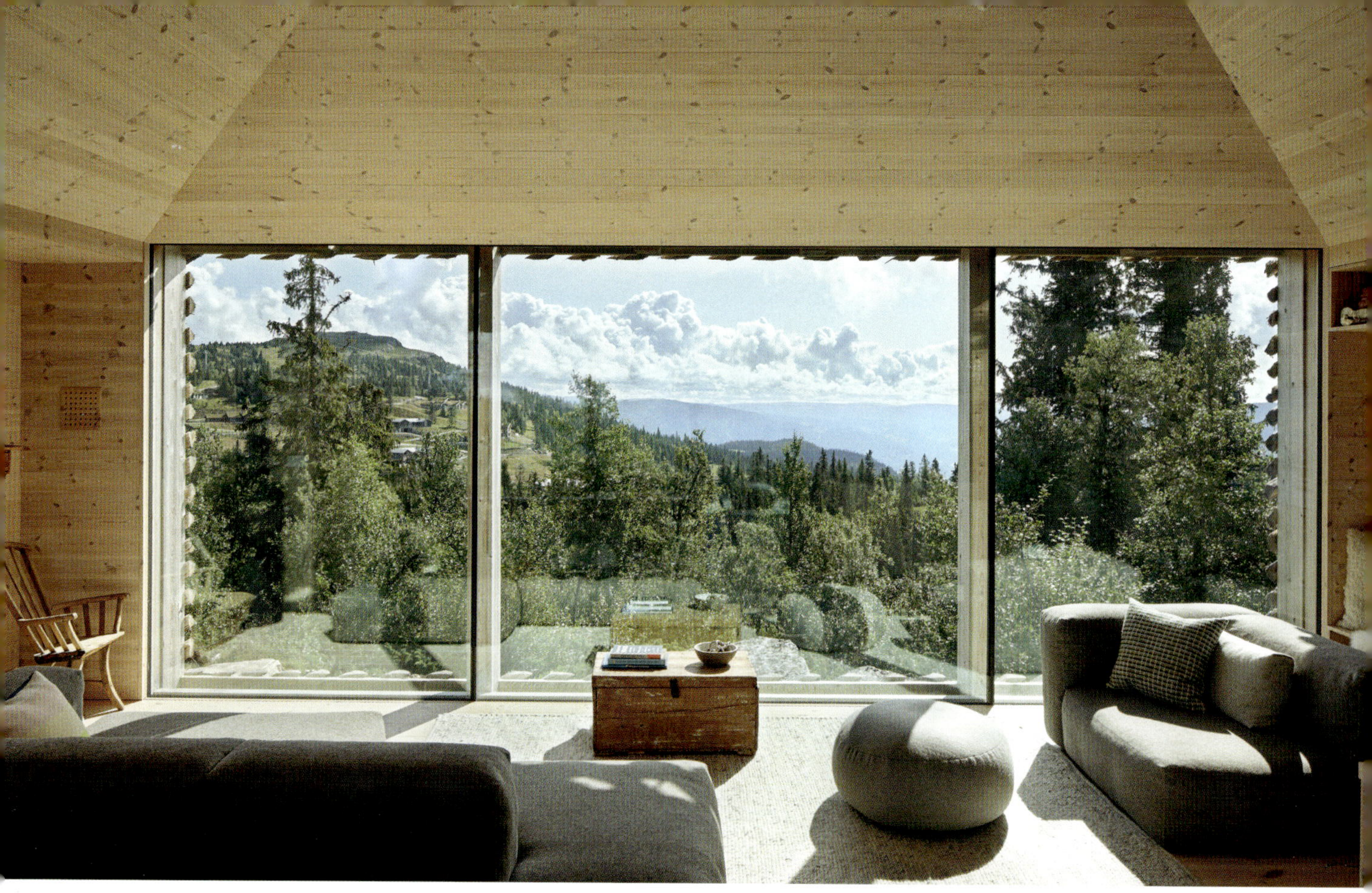

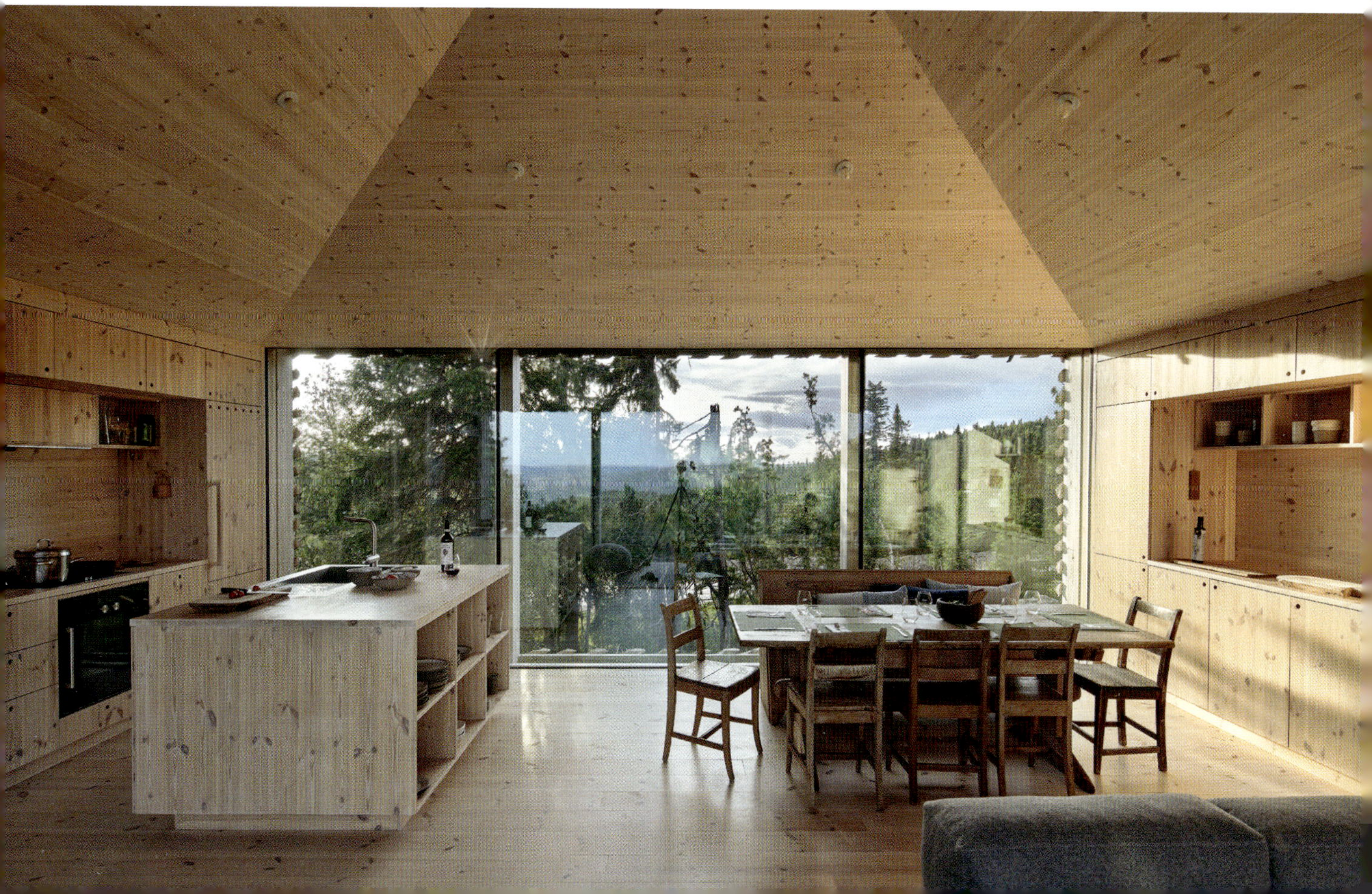

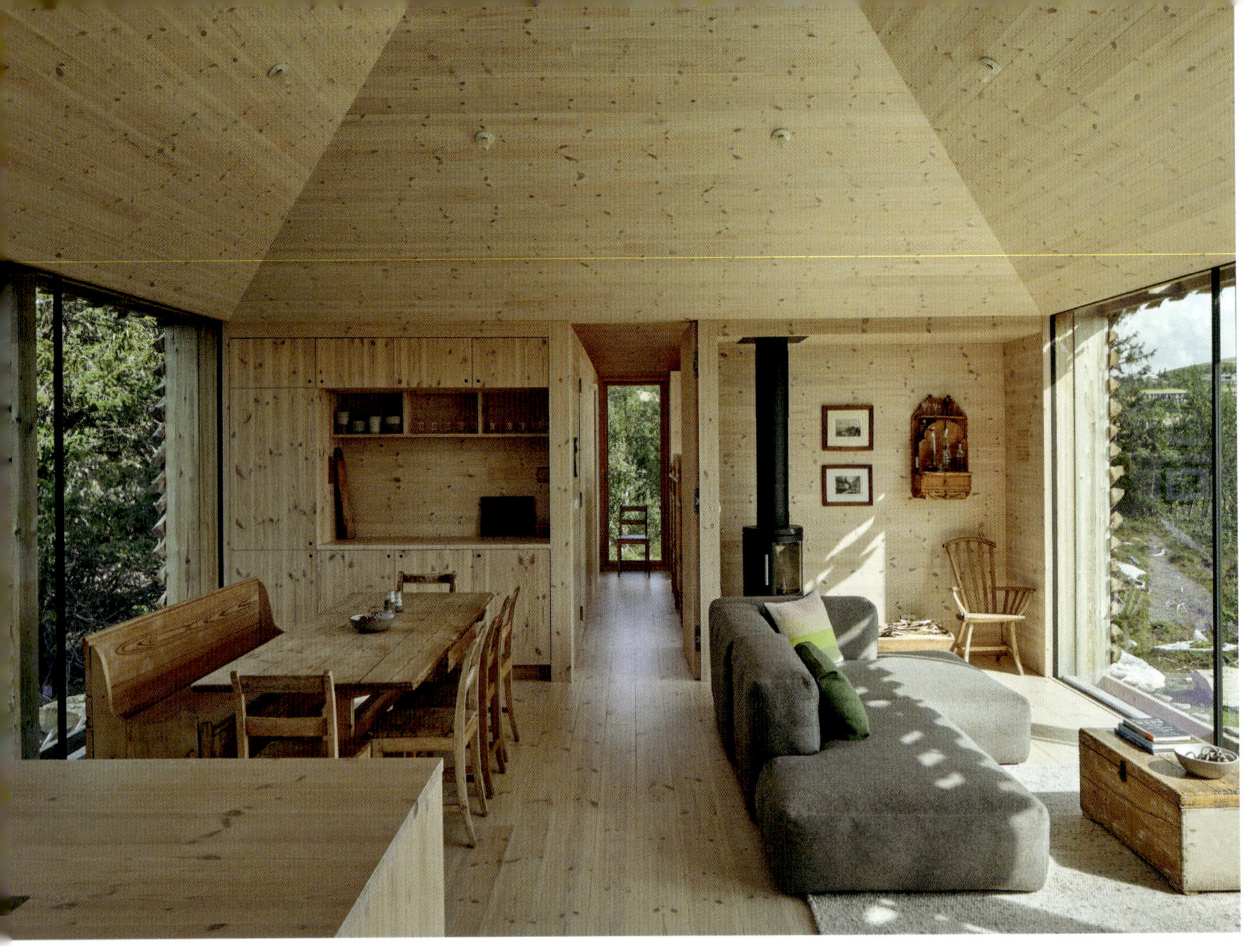

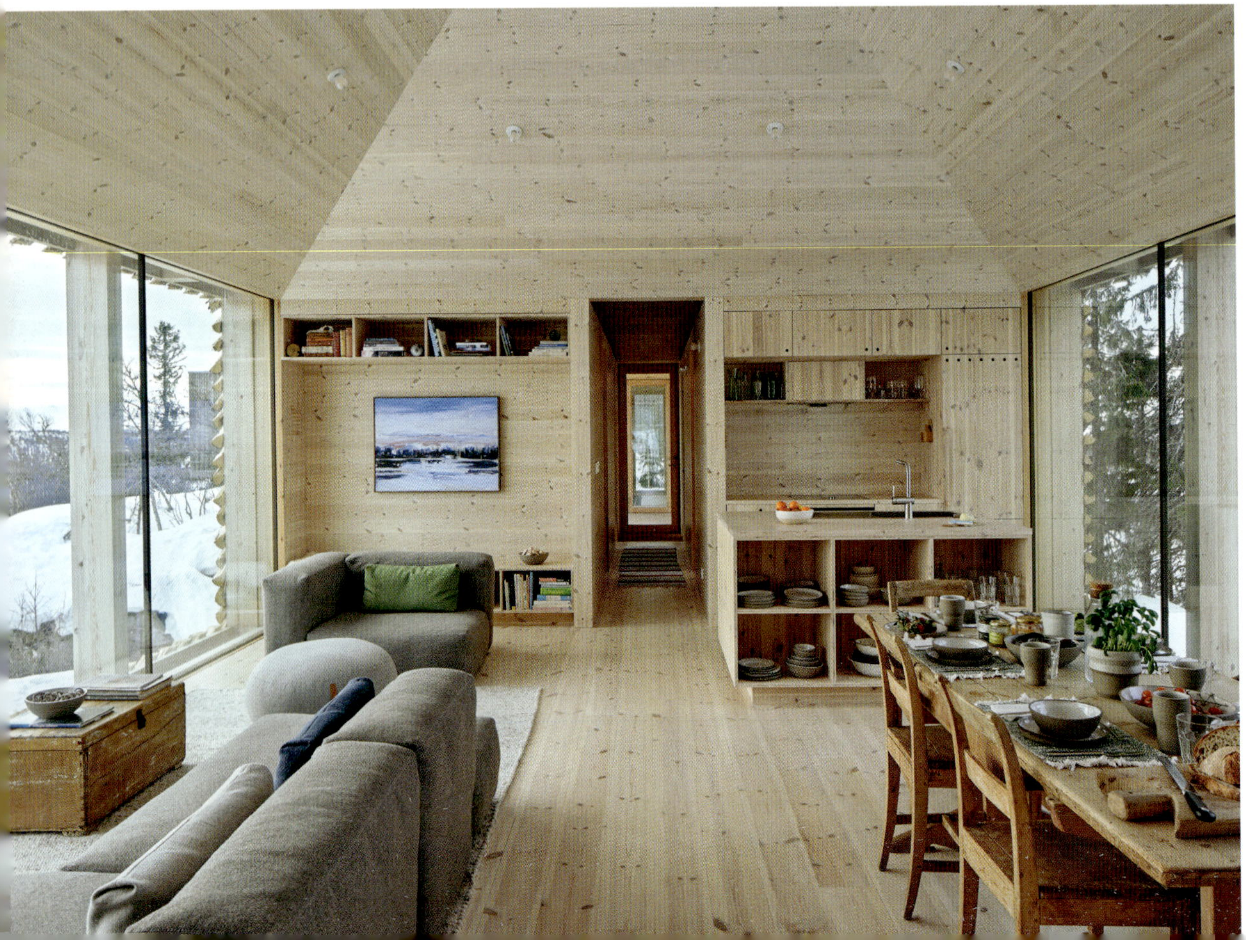

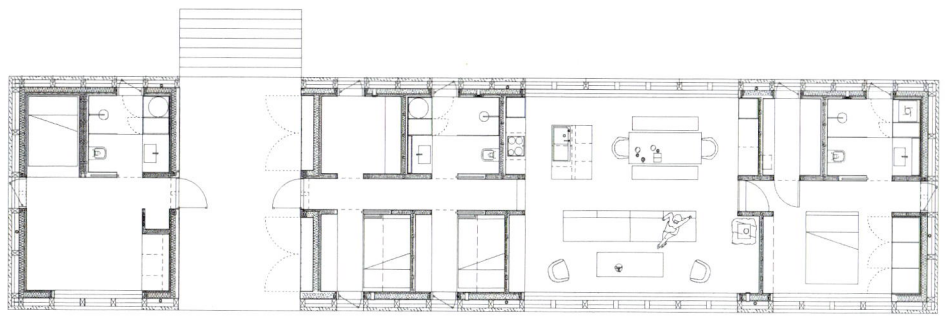

Floor plan

THE STUDIO

NICHOLAS GURNEY

WWW.NICHOLASGURNEY.COM.AU

Nicholas Gurney established his eponymous design studio in 2010 after completing a Bachelor of Industrial Design. The works of his practice are allied with the concepts of reductivism and beautility. Projects are highly functional and considered, delivering dynamic and clever solutions with a focus on the organisation of space. Through design and innovation, Nicholas aims to dispel conventional notions surrounding compact design and small space living. Gurney employs a strong conceptual focus and the needs of his clients are heavily embedded in the outcomes.

Nicholas Gurney gründete sein gleichnamiges Designstudio im Jahr 2010, nachdem er einen Bachelor in Industriedesign abgeschlossen hatte. Die Arbeiten seines Büros sind mit den Konzepten des Reduktionismus und der Schönheit verbunden. Die Projekte sind hochgradig funktional und durchdacht und liefern dynamische und clevere Lösungen mit einem Fokus auf die Organisation von Raum. Durch Design und Innovation zielt Nicholas darauf ab, konventionelle Vorstellungen von kompaktem Design und Wohnen auf kleinem Raum zu zerstreuen. Gurney hat einen starken konzeptionellen Fokus und die Bedürfnisse seiner Kunden sind stark in die Ergebnisse eingebettet.

NICHOLAS GURNEY

Nicholas Gurney a créé son studio de design éponyme en 2010 après avoir obtenu une licence en design industriel. Les œuvres de son cabinet sont alliées aux concepts de réductivité et de beauté. Les projets sont hautement fonctionnels et réfléchis, offrant des solutions dynamiques et astucieuses qui mettent l'accent sur l'organisation de l'espace. Par le biais du design et de l'innovation, Nicholas vise à dissiper les notions conventionnelles entourant le design compact et la vie dans les petits espaces. Gurney a recours à une approche conceptuelle forte et les besoins de ses clients sont fortement pris en compte dans les résultats.

Nicholas Gurney fundó su estudio de diseño homónimo en 2010, tras finalizar su licenciatura en diseño industrial. Las obras de su estudio se alían con los conceptos de reductivismo y belleza. Los proyectos son altamente funcionales y considerados, ofreciendo soluciones dinámicas e inteligentes con un enfoque en la organización del espacio. A través del diseño y la innovación, Nicholas pretende disipar las nociones convencionales que rodean el diseño compacto y la vida en espacios reducidos. Gurney emplea un fuerte enfoque conceptual y las necesidades de sus clientes están fuertemente integradas en los resultados.

THE STUDIO

27 M² // SYDNEY, NEW SOUTH WALES, AUSTRALIA
PHOTOS © KATHERINE LU

This project offers a proposal for future high-density urban living for single families; the fastest growing demographic group.

With a tight budget and a four-week construction deadline, the client simply asked for a flexible space for everyday living. To conserve space, light and views of the city skyline, a timber "container" was inserted into an open space to solve the problems of privacy, storage and lack of living space inherent in small flats. The sturdy structure features wall-to-wall sliding doors and houses an entrance hall, storage, laundry and sleeping areas. The open-plan quality of the studio provides a configuration that is fit for purpose, while clever storage solutions keep the home tidy and organised.

Dieses Projekt bietet einen Vorschlag für zukünftiges städtisches Wohnen mit hoher Dichte für Einfamilienhäuser; die am schnellsten wachsende Bevölkerungsgruppe.

Mit einem knappen Budget und einem vierwöchigen Bautermin wünschte sich der Bauherr einfach einen flexiblen Raum für das tägliche Leben. Um Platz, Licht und Ausblicke auf die Skyline der Stadt zu erhalten, wurde ein Holz-"Container" in einen offenen Raum eingefügt, um die Probleme der Privatsphäre, des Stauraums und des Mangels an Wohnraum zu lösen, die in kleinen Wohnungen auftreten. Die robuste Struktur verfügt über Wand-zu-Wand-Schiebetüren und beherbergt einen Eingangsbereich, Stauraum, Waschküche und Schlafbereiche. Der offene Grundriss des Studios bietet eine zweckmäßige Konfiguration, während clevere Stauraumlösungen für Ordnung sorgen.

Ce projet propose une proposition pour la future vie urbaine à haute densité pour les familles monoparentales, la population qui connaît la croissance la plus rapide.

Avec un budget serré et un délai de construction de quatre semaines, le client a simplement demandé un espace flexible pour la vie quotidienne. Afin de préserver l'espace, la lumière et la vue sur la ville, un « conteneur » en bois a été inséré dans un espace ouvert pour résoudre les problèmes d'intimité, de stockage et de manque d'espace de vie inhérents aux petits appartements. La structure robuste est dotée de portes coulissantes mur à mur et abrite un hall d'entrée, des espaces de rangement, de lavage et de couchage. La qualité de l'espace ouvert du studio permet une configuration adaptée à l'objectif, tandis que des solutions de rangement intelligentes permettent de garder la maison bien rangée.

Este proyecto ofrece una propuesta para la futura vida urbana de alta densidad para las familias unipersonales; el grupo demográfico de más rápido crecimiento.

Con un presupuesto ajustado y un plazo de cuatro semanas para la construcción, el cliente simplemente pidió un espacio flexible para la vida diaria. Para conservar el espacio, la luz y las vistas del horizonte de la ciudad, en un espacio abierto se insertó un «contenedor» de madera para resolver los problemas de privacidad, almacenamiento y falta de espacio vital inherentes a los apartamentos pequeños. La robusta estructura cuenta con puertas correderas de pared a pared y alberga un vestíbulo de entrada, un almacén, una zona de lavado y otra de descanso. La calidad abierta del estudio proporciona una configuración adecuada para su uso, mientras que las ingeniosas soluciones de almacenamiento mantienen el hogar ordenado.

Floor plan

0   1   2   3

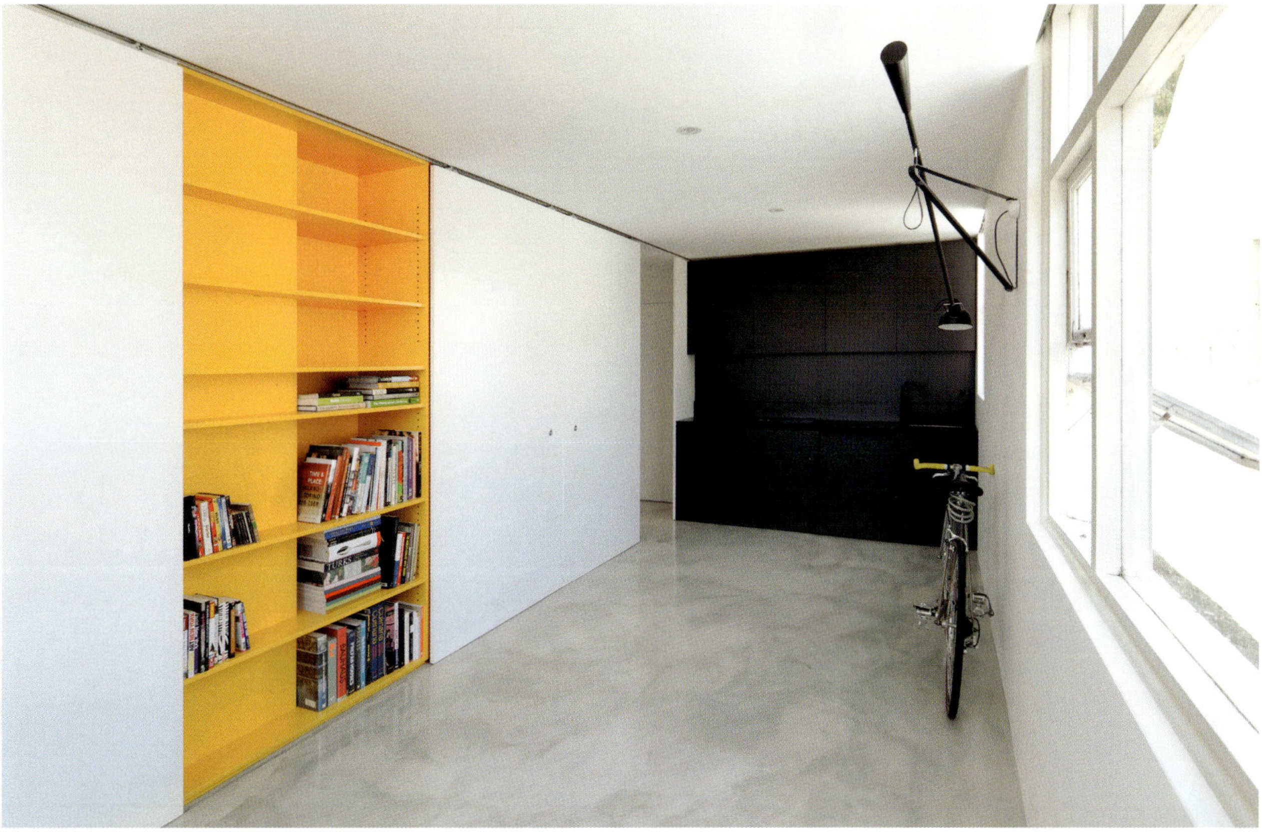

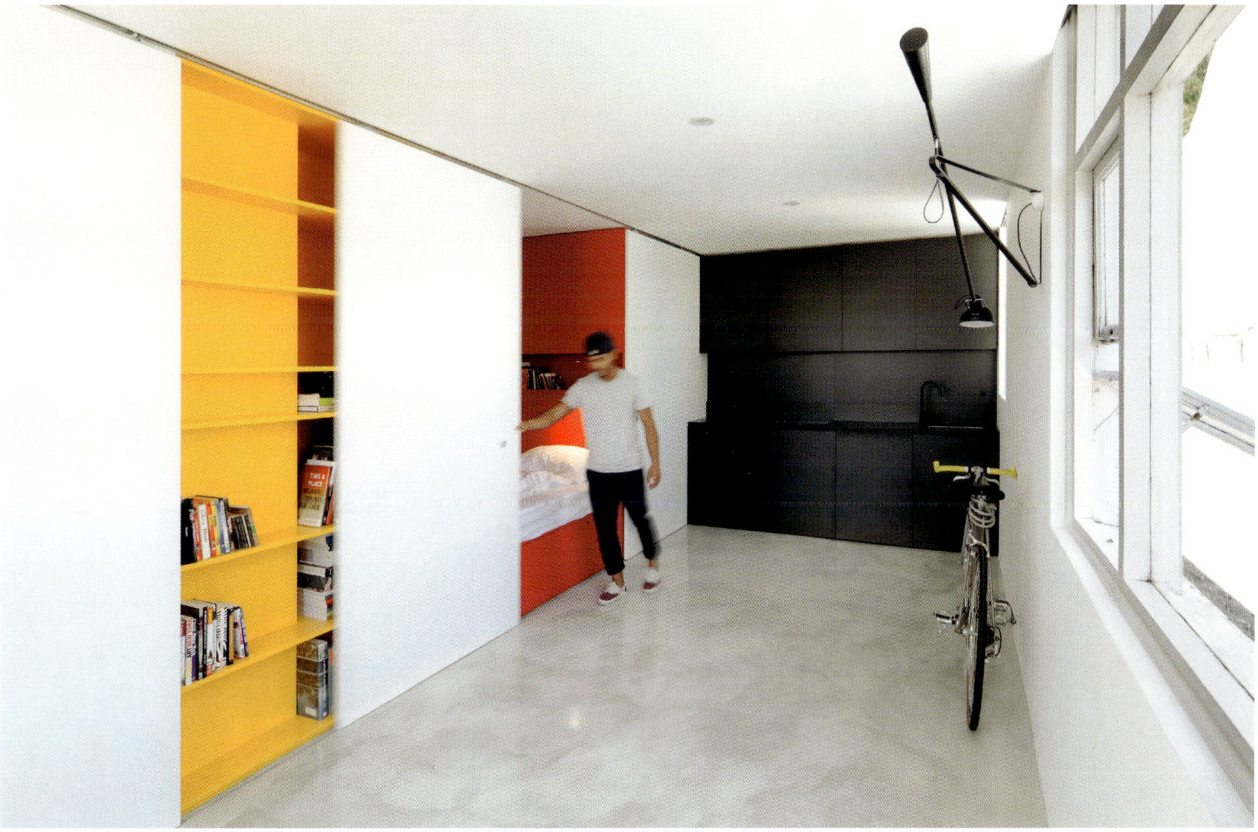

MOORMANN'S KAMMERSPIEL

NILS HOLGER MOORMANN AND B&O GROUP
NILS HOLGER MOORMANN

WWW.MOORMANN.DE

The Nils Holger Moorman Möbel GmbH positions itself somewhere between conventions. The company has, from 1982 onwards, developed with a number of mostly young, unknown designers furniture which exhibits a reduced formal language and precise solutions to detail. The key thoughts are simplicity, intelligence and innovation. From the company headquarters in Aschau to the purist design of FNP, a classic in its own right, and the unusual guesthouse "berge", any new ideas and deliberations will certainly not be put off until tomorrow.

Die Nils Holger Moormann Möbel GmbH positioniert sich gerne zwischen den Konventionen. Seit 1982 entwickelt die Firma mit einer Reihe von meist jungen, unbekannten Designern Möbel, die eine reduzierte Formensprache und präzise Detaillösungen aufweisen. Die Leitgedanken sind Einfachheit, Intelligenz und Innovation. Vom Firmensitz in Aschau über das puristische Design der FNP, einem Klassiker für sich, bis hin zum ungewöhnlichen Gästehaus „berge" werden neue Ideen und Überlegungen sicher nicht auf morgen verschoben.

NILS HOLGER MOORMANN AND B&O GROUP

Le Nils Holger Moormann Möbel GmbH se positionne quelque part entre les conventions. Depuis 1982, la société développe des meubles avec un certain nombre de jeunes pour la plupart, des designers inconnus qui ont un langage de conception réduite et des solutions de détail précises. Les pensées clés sont la simplicité, l'intelligence et l'innovation. Du siège de l'entreprise à Aschau au design puriste de FNP, un classique en soi, en passant par la maison d'hôtes inhabituelle « Berge », les nouvelles idées et réflexions ne seront certainement pas remises à demain.

Nils Holger Moormann se sitúa en algún lugar entre las convenciones. Desde 1982, la compañía ha estado desarrollando muebles con una serie de diseñadores, en su mayoría jóvenes y desconocidos, que tienen un lenguaje de diseño reducido y soluciones de detalle precisas. Las ideas clave son la sencillez, la inteligencia y la innovación. Desde la sede de la empresa en Aschau hasta el diseño purista de la FNP, un clásico por derecho propio, pasando por la insólita casa de huéspedes «berge», las nuevas ideas y deliberaciones no se dejarán para mañana.

MOORMANN'S KAMMERSPIEL

41 M² // PROTOTYPE
PHOTOS © JULIA ROTTER

In his Kammerspiel—intimate theater—, the designer Nils Holger Moormann has playfully addressed the subject of "living in a small space" with one single large piece of furniture as a centerpiece. This piece of furniture, shaped like a cube, concentrates various household functions to maximize the openness of the space around it. Most domestic functions find their own specific place in the cube. Sleeping, eating, working, and reading are organized on the exterior sides, while everyday essentials, as well as a walk-in wardrobe, have their place in the interior. The composition of the cube can, however, be customized adapting to the lifestyle and habits of the user.

In seinem Kammerspiel hat der Designer Nils Holger Moormann das Thema „Wohnen auf kleinem Raum" auf spielerische und raffinierte Weise mit einem einzigen großen Möbelstück als Herzstück aufgegriffen. Dieses würfelförmige Möbelstück konzentriert verschiedene Funktionen des Hauses, um die Offenheit des umgebenden Raumes zu maximieren. Die meisten Haushaltsfunktionen finden ihren spezifischen Platz im Würfel. An den Außenseiten sind Schlafen, Essen, Arbeiten und Lesen organisiert, während im Inneren Alltagsgegenstände (Staubsauger, Putzmittel, Getränke...) sowie eine Kommode ihren Platz haben. Die Zusammensetzung des Würfels kann jedoch individuell an den Lebensstil und die Gewohnheiten des Anwenders angepasst werden.

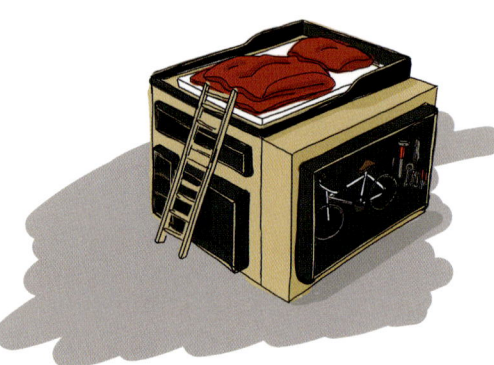

Dans son Kammerspiel - théâtre intime -, le designer Nils Holger Moormann a abordé le thème de la «vie dans un petit espace» de manière amusante et ingénieuse, avec un seul grand meuble comme pièce maîtresse. Ce meuble en forme de cube concentre diverses fonctions de la maison pour maximiser l'ouverture de l'espace environnant. La plupart des fonctions ménagères trouvent leur place spécifique dans le cube. Dormir, manger, travailler et lire sont organisés sur les côtés extérieurs, tandis que les objets de la vie quotidienne (aspirateur, produits de nettoyage, boissons...), ainsi qu'une commode, ont leur place à l'intérieur. Toutefois, la composition du cube peut être personnalisée pour s'adapter au style de vie et aux habitudes de l'utilisateur.

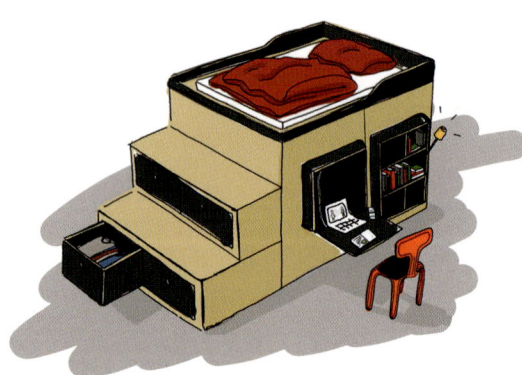

En su Kammerspiel –teatro íntimo–, el diseñador Nils Holger Moormann ha abordado de forma divertida e ingeniosa el tema de «vivir en un espacio pequeño» con un único mueble de gran tamaño como pieza central. Este mueble, con forma de cubo, concentra varias funciones del hogar para maximizar la apertura del espacio que lo rodea. La mayoría de las funciones domésticas encuentran su lugar específico en el cubo. Dormir, comer, trabajar y leer se organizan en los lados exteriores, mientras que los objetos de uso cotidiano (aspiradora, productos de limpieza, bebidas...), así como un vestidor, tienen su lugar en el interior. No obstante, la composición del cubo puede personalizarse adaptándose al estilo de vida y los hábitos del usuario.

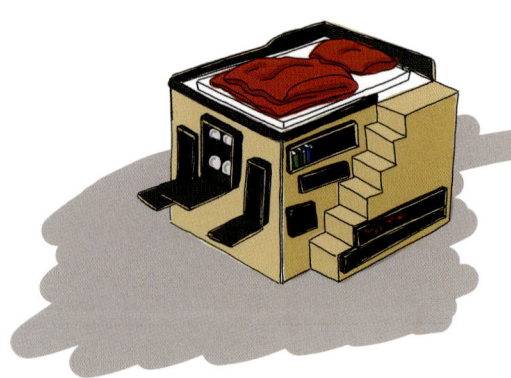

Design development sketches

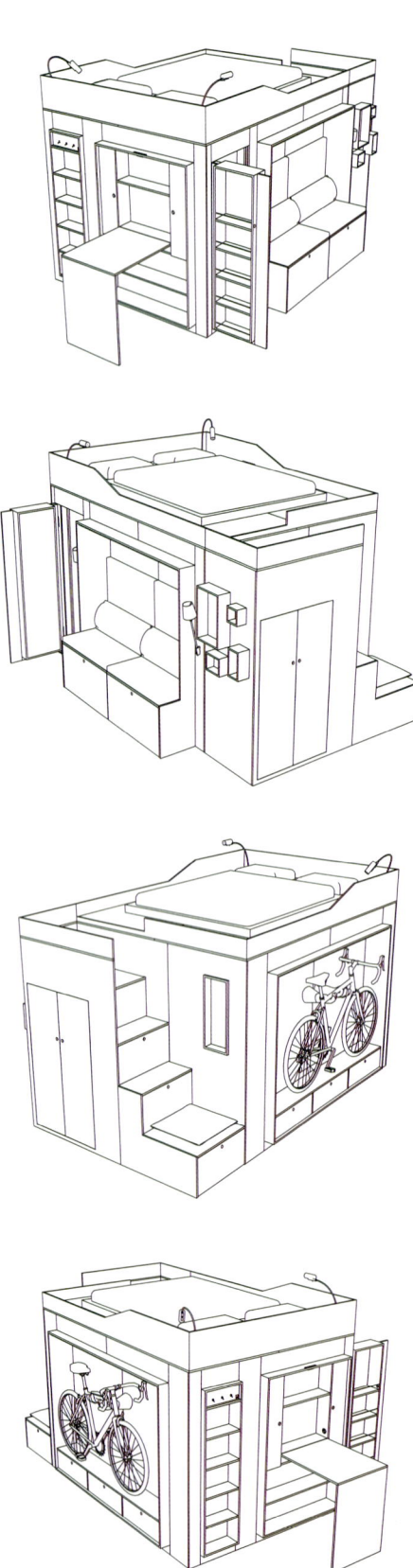

Axonometric views

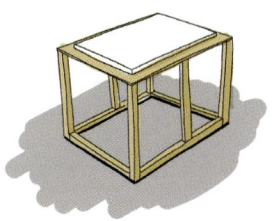

Design development sketches

Floor plan

THE HUG

REACT ARCHITECTS

NATASHA DELIYIANNI, YIORGOS SPIRIDONOS

WWW.RE-ACT.GR

REACT ARCHITECTS is a studio that aims at a theoretical approach to architecture through a research-oriented procedure. Architecture is confronted in its entirety in collaboration with all the specialities that complement the constructive and artistic creation. The office studies small and large scale projects, both public and private. Their experience in a broad spectrum of projects allows them to propose design applications with originality and uniqueness. They strive to combine the archetypes found in Greek architecture with design ideas that meet the demands of 21st century needs. Thus, by experimenting with an aesthetic vocabulary they create the link between ideas and construction. The studio's projects have been published in Greek and European magazines. Its founding members have participated in Greek and international competitions winning prizes and distinctions.

REACT ARCHITECTS ist ein Studio, das durch eine forschungsorientierte Vorgehensweise einen theoretischen Zugang zur Architektur anstrebt. Die Architektur wird in ihrer Gesamtheit in Zusammenarbeit mit allen Fachgebieten betrachtet, die das konstruktive und künstlerische Schaffen ergänzen. Das Büro unternimmt kleine und große Projekte, sowohl im öffentlichen als auch im privaten Bereich. Ihre Erfahrung in einem breiten Spektrum von Projekten ermöglicht es ihnen, Designs mit Originalität und Einzigartigkeit zu schaffen. Sie streben danach, die Archetypen der griechischen Architektur mit Designideen zu kombinieren, die den Anforderungen des 21. Jahrhunderts entsprechen. Indem sie mit einem ästhetischen Vokabular experimentieren, schaffen React die Verbindung zwischen Idee und Konstruktion. Die Projekte des Studios wurden in griechischen und europäischen Zeitschriften veröffentlicht. Seine Gründungsmitglieder haben an griechischen und internationalen Wettbewerben teilgenommen und Preise und Auszeichnungen gewonnen.

REACT ARCHITECTS

REACT ARCHITECTS est un studio qui vise à une approche théorique de l'architecture, par une procédure orientée vers la recherche. L'architecture est abordée dans sa globalité en collaboration avec toutes les spécialités qui complètent la création constructive et artistique. Le bureau étudie des projets de petite et de grande envergure, tant publics que privés. Leur expérience dans un large éventail de projets leur permet de proposer des applications de conception avec originalité et unicité. Ils s'efforcent de combiner les archétypes de l'architecture grecque avec des idées de design qui répondent aux besoins du XXIᵉ siècle. Ainsi, en expérimentant un vocabulaire esthétique, ils créent l'union entre les idées et la construction. Les projets du studio ont été publiés dans des magazines grecs et européens. Ses membres fondateurs ont participé à des concours grecs et internationaux et ont remporté des prix et des distinctions.

REACT ARCHITECTS es un estudio que tiene como objetivo un enfoque teórico de la arquitectura, a través de un procedimiento orientado a la investigación. La arquitectura se enfrenta en su totalidad en colaboración con todas las especialidades que complementan la creación constructiva y artística. La oficina estudia proyectos de pequeña y gran escala, tanto públicos como privados. Su experiencia en un amplio espectro de proyectos les permite proponer aplicaciones de diseño con originalidad y singularidad. Se esfuerzan por combinar los arquetipos que se encuentran en la arquitectura griega con ideas de diseño que satisfagan las exigencias de las necesidades del siglo XXI. Así, experimentando con un vocabulario estético crean la unión entre las ideas y la construcción. Los proyectos del estudio han sido publicados en revistas griegas y europeas. Sus miembros fundadores han participado en competiciones griegas e internacionales donde han ganado premios y distinciones.

THE HUG

150 M² // PAROS, CYCLADES, GREECE
PHOTOS © GEORGE MESSARITAKIS

Located on the island of Paros, the site has an east facing orientation, overlooking the sea and the bay of Naoussa. The complex consists of two buildings with a shared open space and a swimming pool. The large volume of a single building is divided into two and fits harmoniously into the terrain. The volumes are arranged facing each other, and between them the central courtyard has been created, adapted to the slope of the terrain and protected from the north winds, which organises the functions by creating a core with direct reference to the masses of buildings. The stone walls surround and "embrace" the building, protecting it from prying eyes. The transformation of the morphological features of Cycladic architecture with a view to creating a contemporary architectural language is, together with its integration into the natural landscape, the guiding principle of the design.

Die Anlage befindet sich auf der Insel Paros und ist nach Osten ausgerichtet, mit Blick auf das Meer und die Bucht von Naoussa. Der Komplex besteht aus zwei Gebäuden mit einer gemeinsamen Freifläche und einem Schwimmbad. Das große Volumen eines einzelnen Gebäudes wird in zwei Teile geteilt und passt sich harmonisch dem Gelände an. Die Gebäudeteile sind einander zugewandt angeordnet, und zwischen ihnen wurde der zentrale Hof geschaffen, der an die Neigung des Geländes angepasst und vor den Nordwinden geschützt ist. Dies ermöglicht eine Trennung der Funktionen und schafft einen Kern mit direktem Bezug zu den Gebäudemassen schafft. Die Steinmauern umgeben und „umarmen" das Gebäude und schützen es vor neugierigen Blicken. Die Transformation der morphologischen Merkmale der kykladischen Architektur mit dem Ziel, eine zeitgemäße Architektursprache zu schaffen, ist zusammen mit der Einbindung in die natürliche Landschaft das Leitprinzip des Entwurfs.

Situé sur l'île de Paros, le site est orienté à l'est et donne sur la mer et la baie de Naoussa. Le complexe se compose de deux bâtiments avec un espace ouvert commun et une piscine. Le grand volume d'un seul bâtiment est divisé en deux et s'adapte harmonieusement au terrain. Les volumes sont disposés face à face, et entre eux a été créée la cour centrale, adaptée à la pente du terrain et protégée des vents du nord, qui organise les fonctions en créant un noyau en référence directe aux masses des bâtiments. Les murs de pierre entourent et « embrassent » le bâtiment, le protégeant ainsi des regards indiscrets. La transformation des caractéristiques morphologiques de l'architecture cycladique en vue de créer un langage architectural contemporain est, avec son intégration dans le paysage naturel, le principe directeur de la conception.

Situada en la isla de Paros, la obra tiene una orientación hacia el este, con vistas al mar y la bahía de Naoussa. El complejo consta de dos edificios con un espacio abierto compartido y una piscina. El gran volumen de un solo edificio se divide en dos y se adapta armoniosamente al terreno. Los volúmenes están dispuestos de cara a la vista, y entre ellas se ha creado el patio central, adaptado a la pendiente del terreno y protegido de los vientos del norte, que organiza las funciones creando un núcleo con referencia directa a las masas de edificios. Los muros de piedra rodean y «abrazan» el edificio, protegiéndolo de las miradas indiscretas. La transformación de los rasgos morfológicos de la arquitectura cicládica con vistas a crear un lenguaje arquitectónico contemporáneo es, junto con su integración en el paisaje natural, el principio rector del diseño.

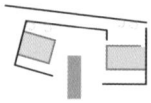

Site plan

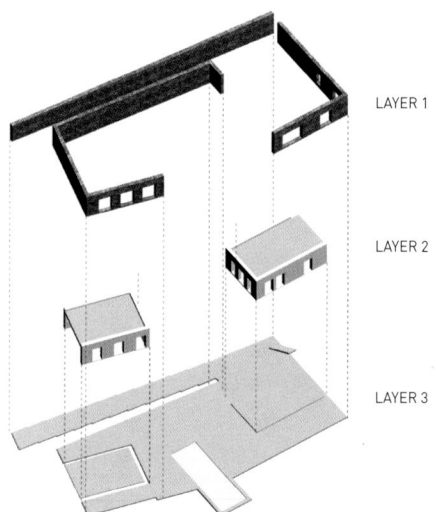

LAYER 1

LAYER 2

LAYER 3

Exploded axonometric

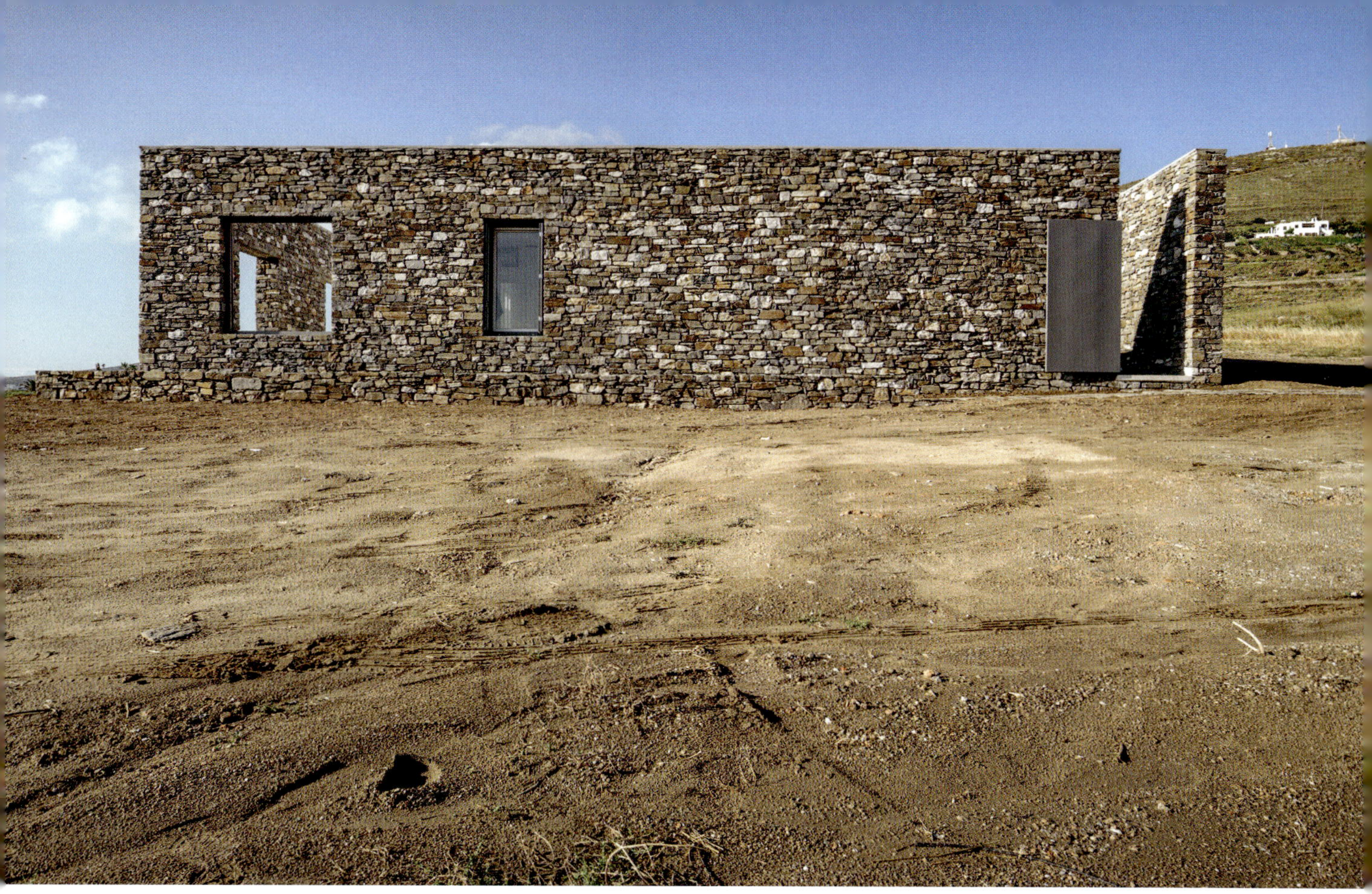

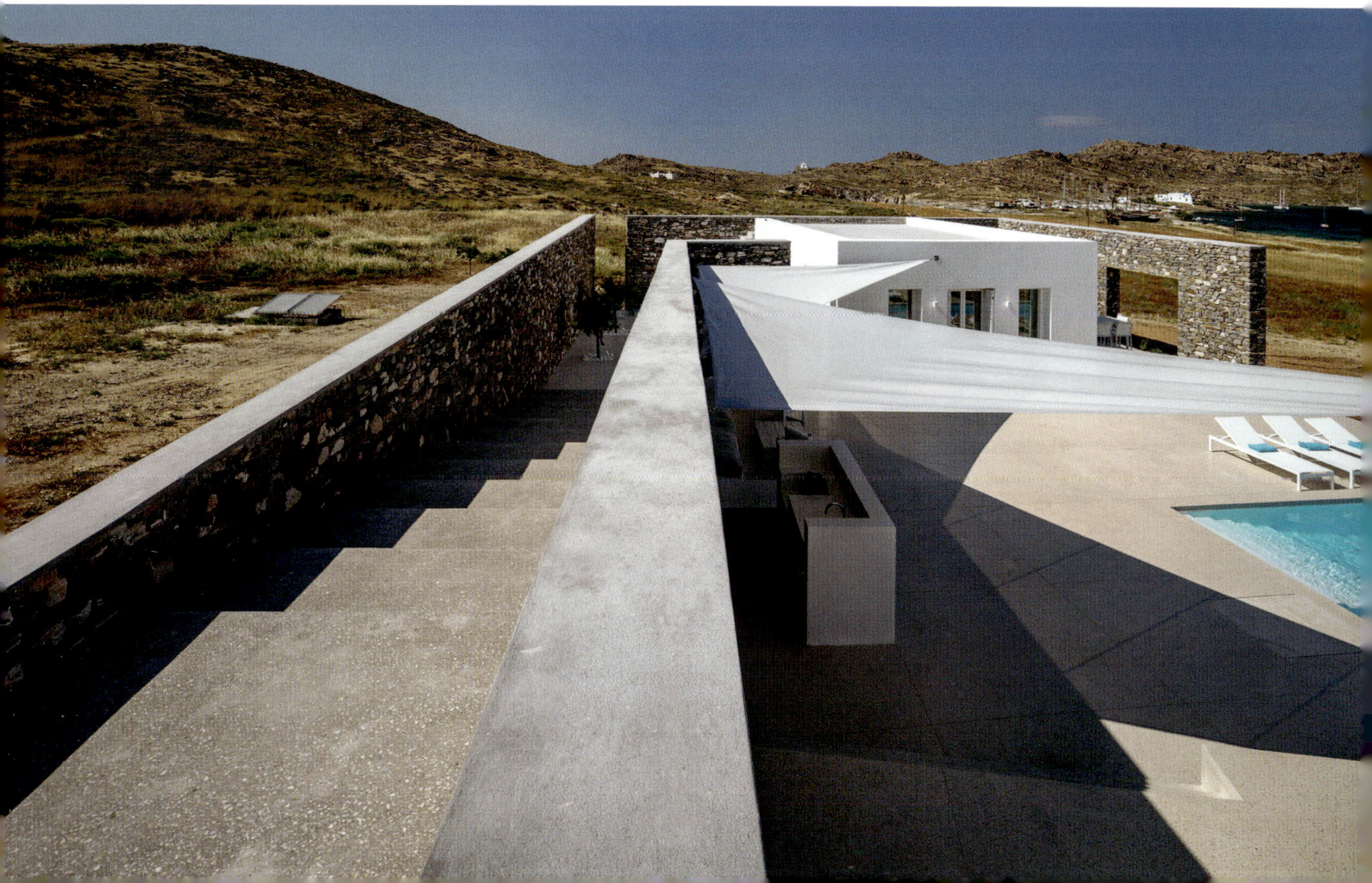

East elevation

North elevation

Sections

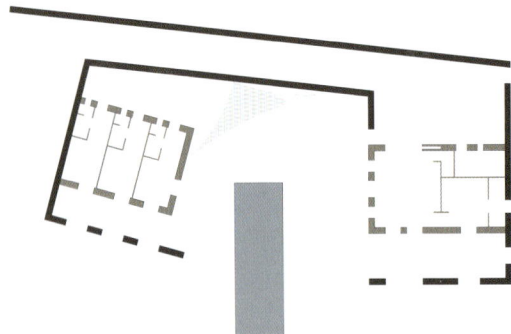

Floor plan

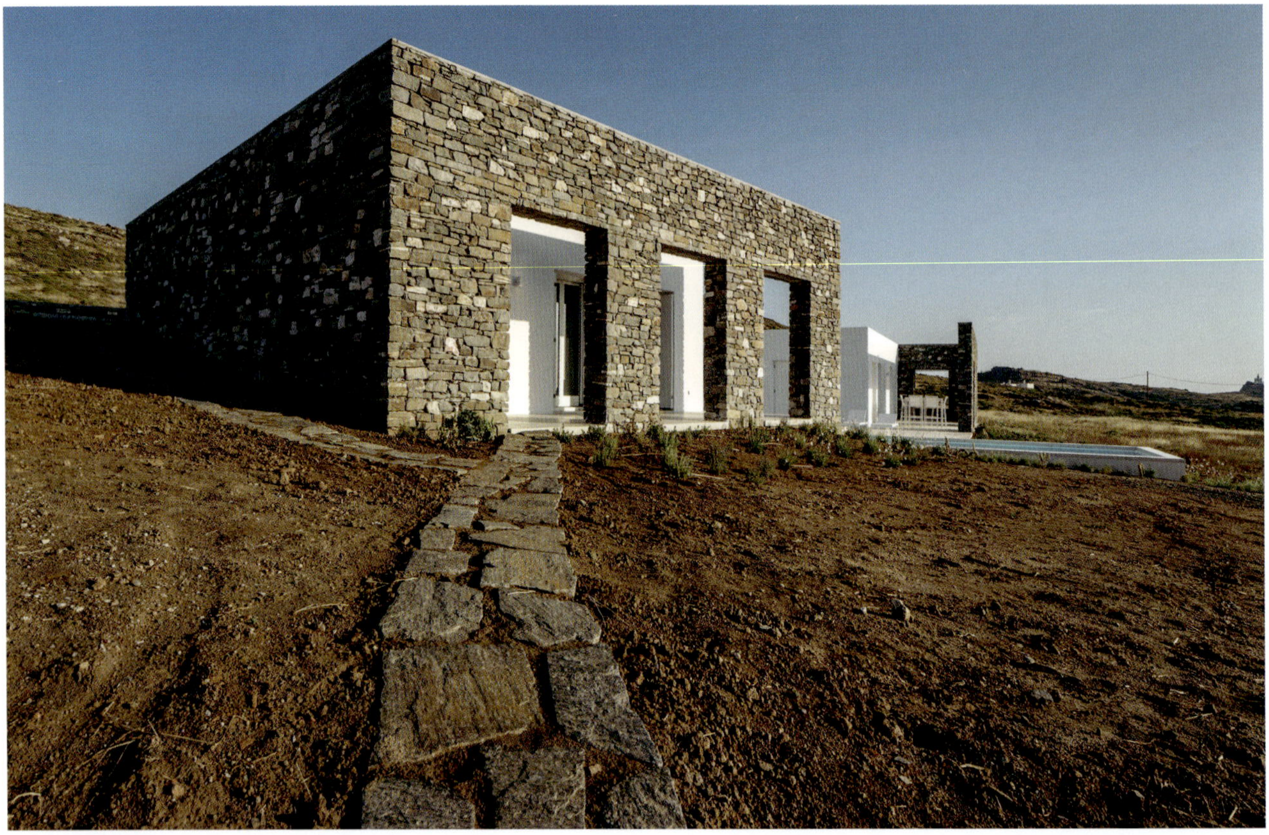

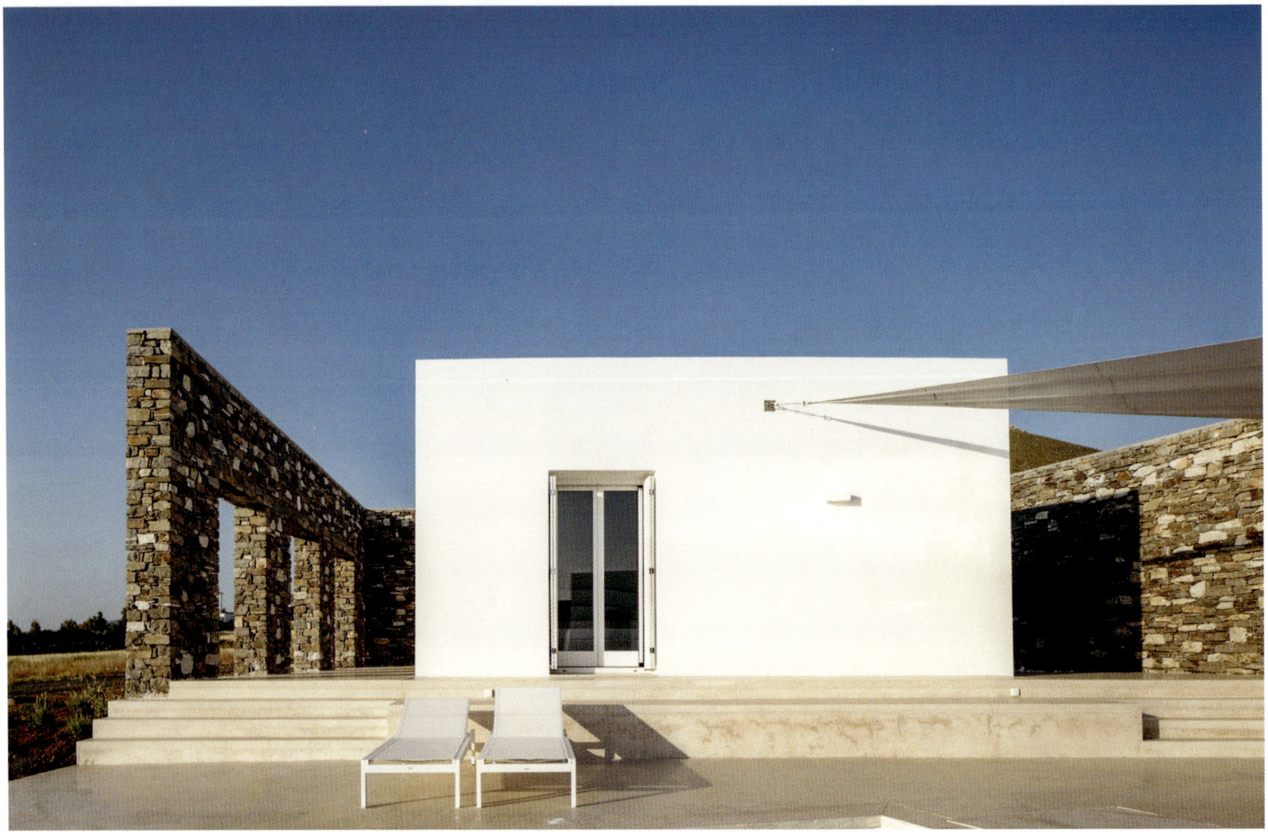

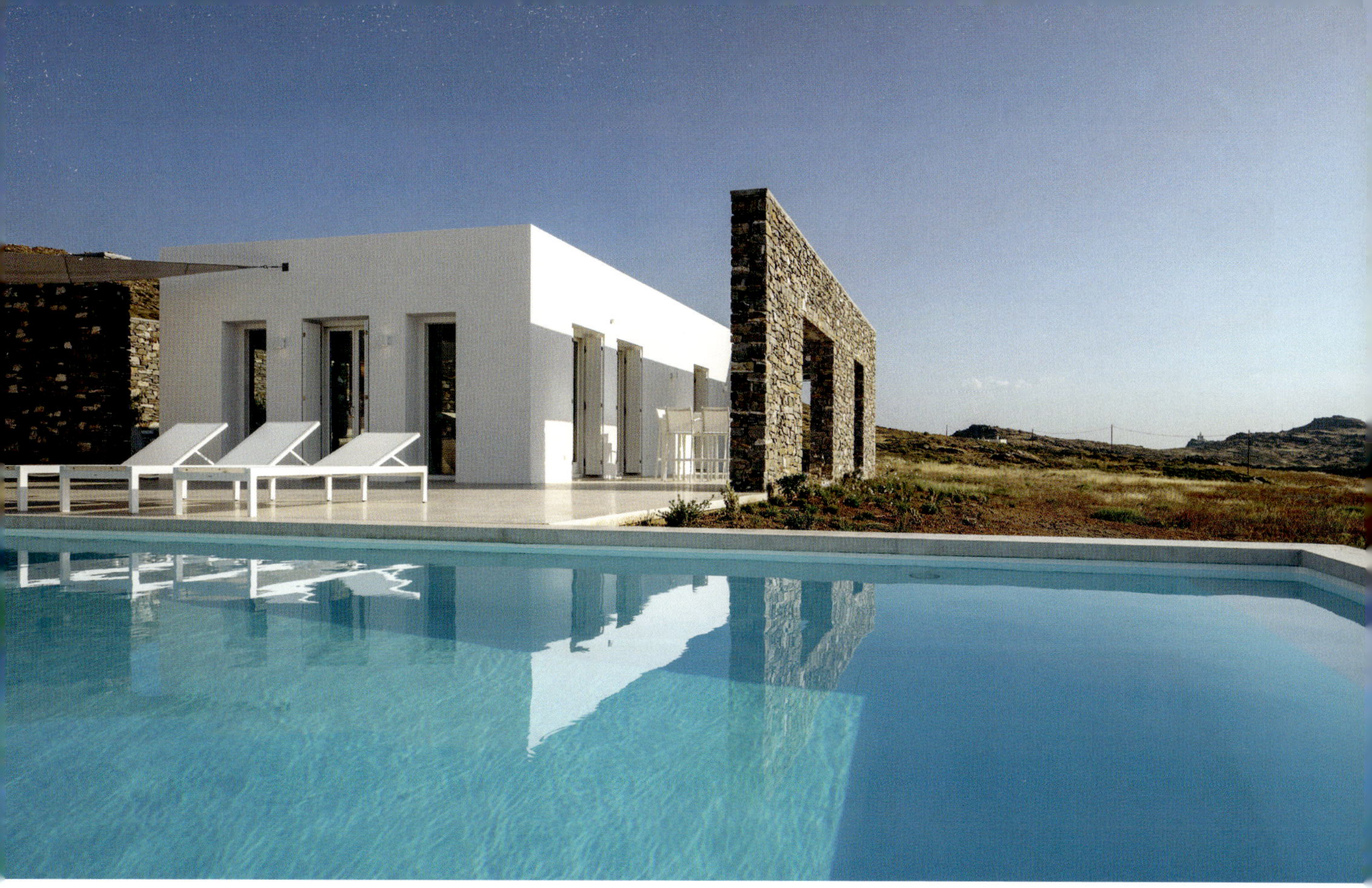

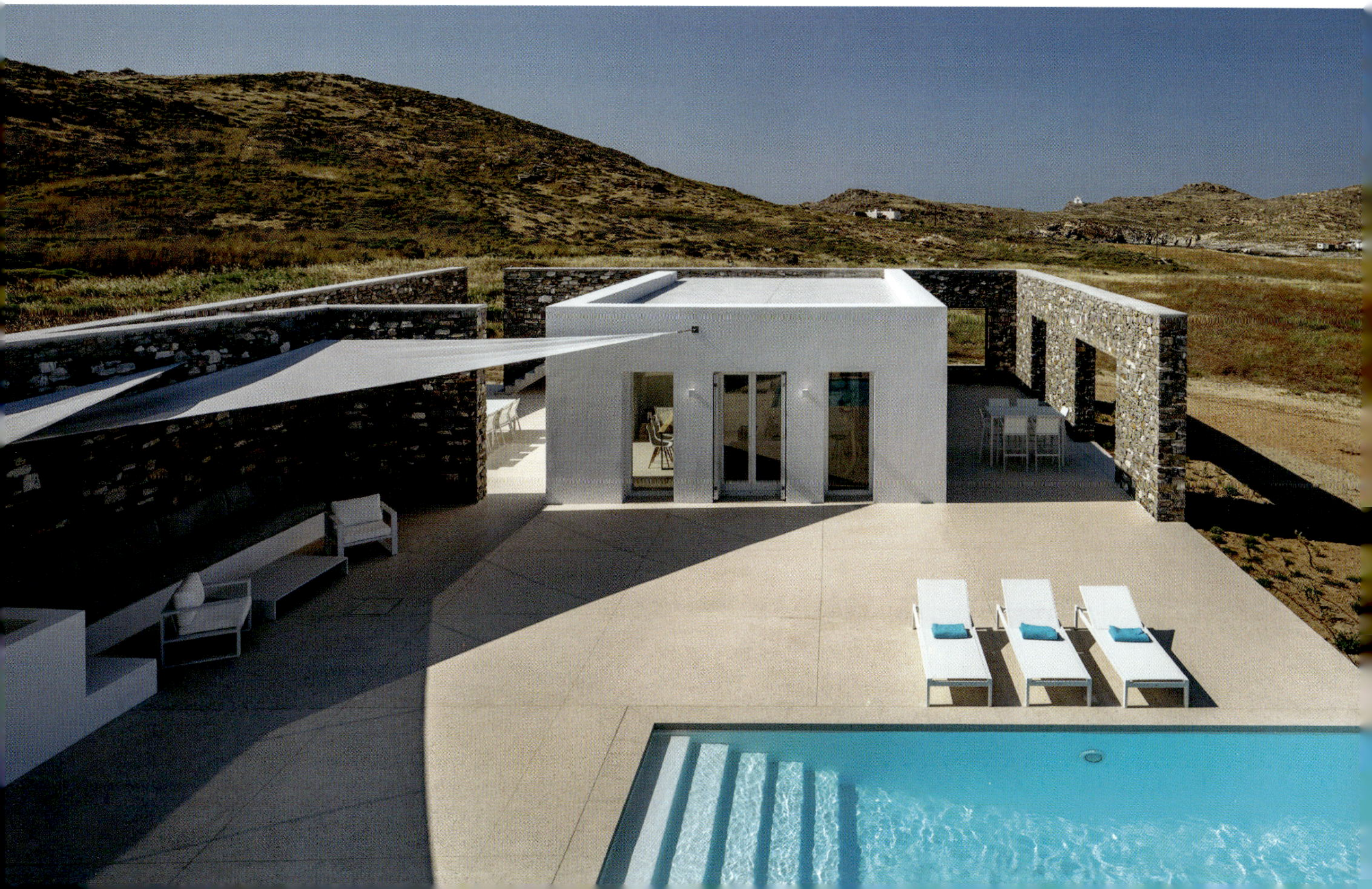

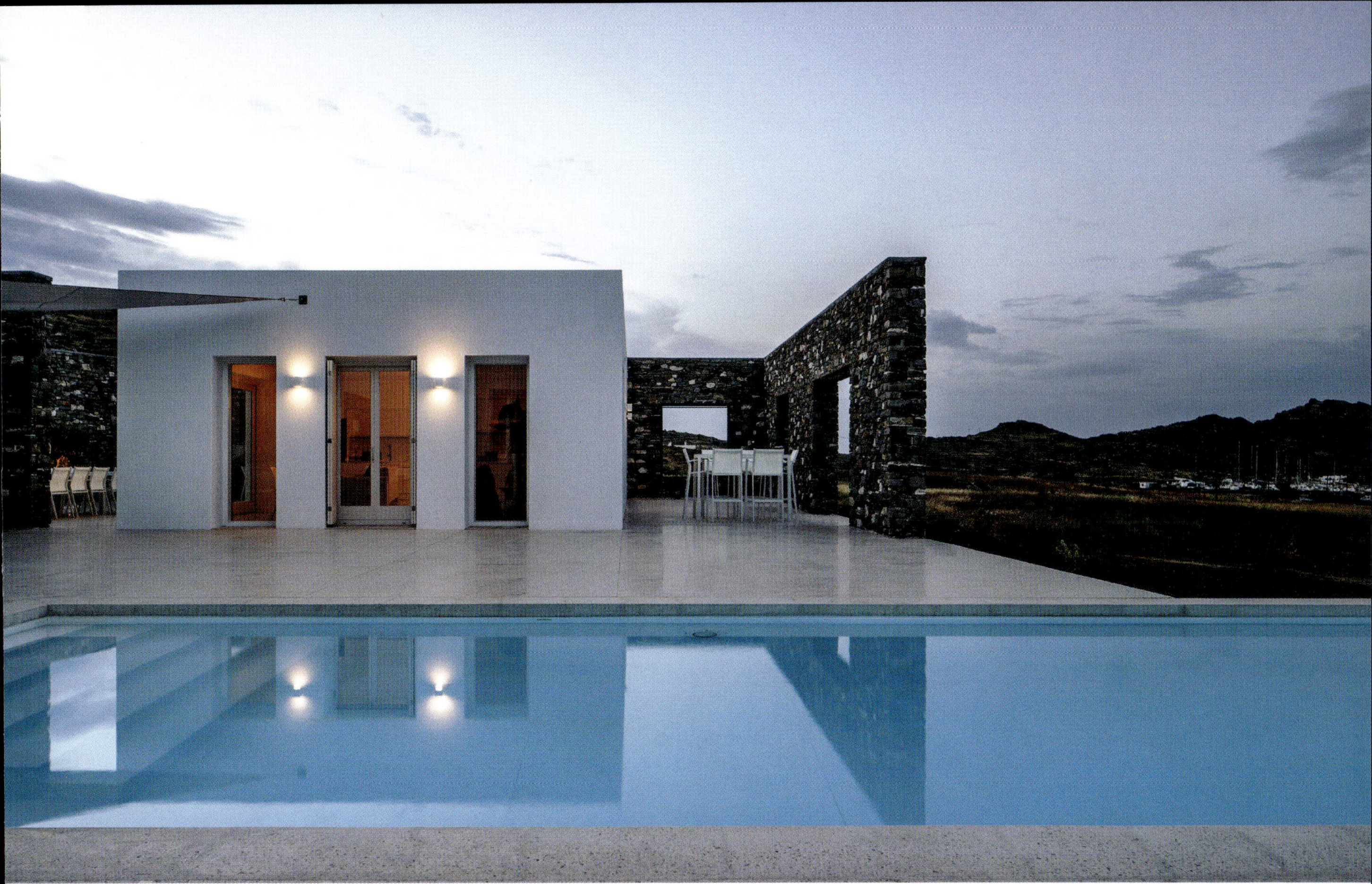
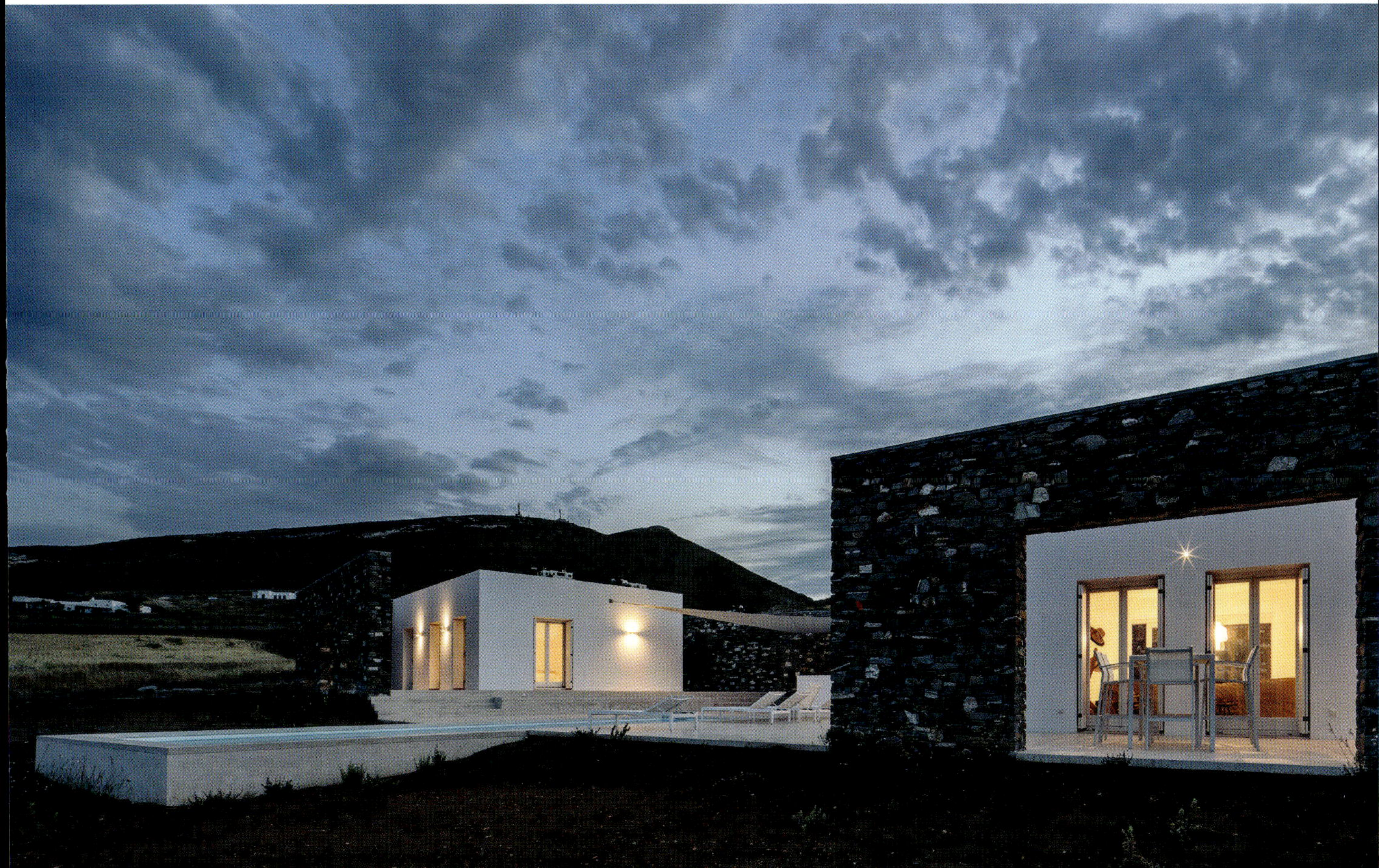

ARCHITECT'S STUDIO

RUETEMPLE

DARIA BUTAHINA, ALEXANDRE KUDIMOV

WWW.RUETEMPLE.RU

Ruetemple is an architectural bureau founded in 2011. Our area of interest is everything about the space that surrounds us, whether interiors or urban environments. Our projects include houses, interiors, landscape features, and furniture.

Ruetemple ist ein im Jahr 2011 gegründetes Architekturbüro. Unser Interessengebiet ist alles, was mit dem Raum zu tun hat, der uns umgibt, seien es Innenräume oder urbane Umgebungen. Unsere Projekte umfassen Häuser, Innenräume, Landschaftselemente und Möbel.

RUETEMPLE

Ruetemple est un bureau d'architecture fondé en 2011. Notre domaine d'intérêt est tout ce qui concerne l'espace qui nous entoure, que ce soit les intérieurs ou les environnements urbains. Nos projets comprennent des maisons, des intérieurs, des éléments de paysage et du mobilier.

Ruetemple es un estudio de arquitectura fundado en 2011. Nuestro ámbito de interés es todo lo relacionado con el espacio que nos rodea, ya sean interiores o entornos urbanos. Nuestros proyectos incluyen casas, interiores, elementos de paisaje y mobiliario.

ARCHITECT'S STUDIO

35 M² // MOSCOW, RUSSIA
PHOTOS © RUETEMPLE

A stimulating environment is capable of fostering creativity. This is what the owner of this former garage must have thought when he gave it to his daughter, an architecture student. The client's main request was to concentrate a work area and a living area, which is achieved by designing a single central wooden piece of furniture that generates several zones for different functions, integrating a multitude of shelves, a desk, a sofa and even a loft bed. The shelving system is open to maintain the open character of the space. The new studio is unique, functional and comfortable, with three types of wood used for the floor, wall panels and furniture. The use of the same material throughout the studio creates a sense of spatial continuity, but the different woods offer subtle variations in colour and texture that enrich the quality of the space.

Eine anregende Umgebung ist in der Lage, die Kreativität zu fördern. Das muss sich der Besitzer dieser ehemaligen Garage gedacht haben, als er sie seiner Tochter, einer Architekturstudentin, schenkte. Die Hauptanforderung des Kunden war es, einen Arbeits- und einen Wohnbereich zu konzentrieren, was durch den Entwurf eines einzigen zentralen Holzmöbels erreicht wird, das mehrere Zonen für verschiedene Funktionen erzeugt und eine Vielzahl von Regalen, einen Schreibtisch, ein Sofa und sogar ein Hochbett integriert. Das Regalsystem ist offen, um den diaphanen Charakter des Raumes zu erhalten. Das neue Studio ist einzigartig, funktional und komfortabel. Für den Boden, die Wandpaneele und die Möbel wurden drei verschiedene Holzarten verwendet. Die Verwendung des gleichen Materials im gesamten Studio schafft ein Gefühl der räumlichen Kontinuität, aber die verschiedenen Hölzer bieten subtile Variationen in Farbe und Textur, die die Qualität des Raums bereichern.

Un environnement stimulant est capable de favoriser la créativité. C'est ce que le propriétaire de cet ancien garage a dû penser lorsqu'il l'a donné à sa fille, étudiante en architecture. La principale demande du client était de concentrer un espace de travail et un espace de vie, ce qui est réalisé en concevant un seul meuble central en bois qui génère plusieurs zones pour différentes fonctions, intégrant une multitude d'étagères, un bureau, un canapé et même un lit mezzanine. Le système d'étagères est ouvert, afin de maintenir le caractère diaphane de l'espace. Le nouveau studio est unique, fonctionnel et confortable, avec trois types de bois utilisés pour le sol, les panneaux muraux et le mobilier. L'utilisation du même matériau dans tout le studio crée un sentiment de continuité spatiale, mais les différents bois offrent de subtiles variations de couleur et de texture qui enrichissent la qualité de l'espace.

Un entorno estimulante es capaz de fomentar la creatividad. Esto es lo que debió pensar el propietario de este antiguo garaje cuando se lo regaló a su hija, estudiante de arquitectura. La solicitud principal del cliente fue concentrar una zona de trabajo y una zona de estar, que se consigue mediante el diseño de un único mueble central de madera que genera varias zonas para diferentes funciones, integrando multitud de estanterías, un escritorio, un sofá e incluso una cama tipo *loft*. El sistema de estanterías es abierto, para mantener así el carácter abierto del espacio. El nuevo estudio es único, funcional y confortable, con tres tipos de madera utilizados para el suelo, los paneles de las paredes y el mobiliario. El uso del mismo material en todo el estudio crea una sensación de continuidad espacial, pero las diferentes maderas ofrecen sutiles variaciones de color y textura que enriquecen la calidad del espacio.

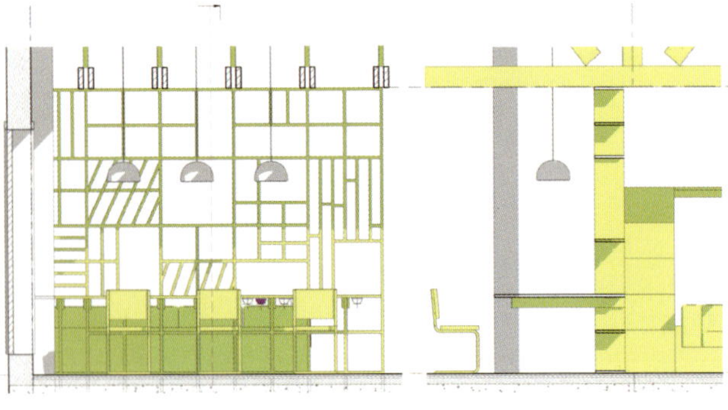

Shelving elevation

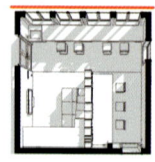

Section 1

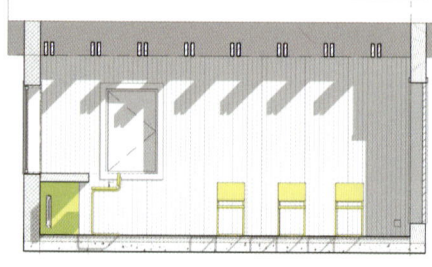
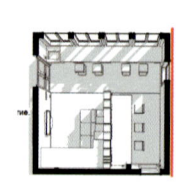

Section 2

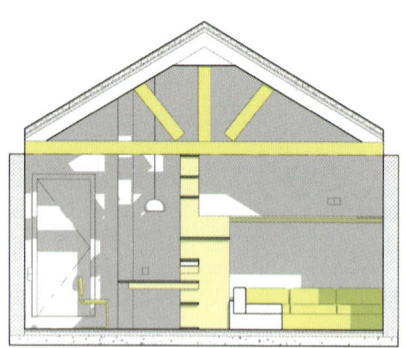
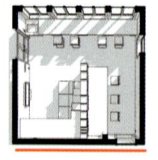

Section 3

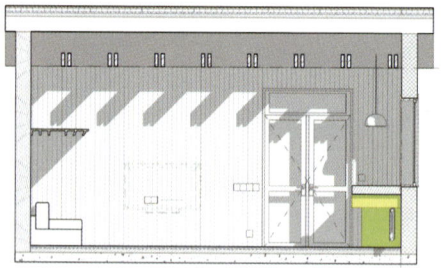
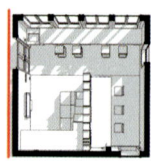

Section 4

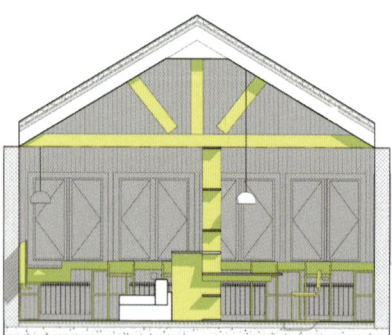

Section 5

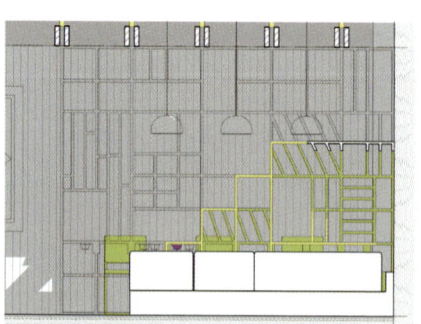
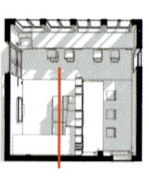

Section 6

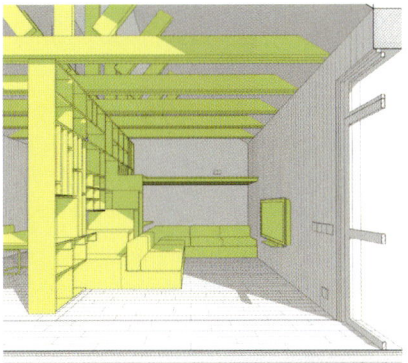

Perspective view 1

Perspective view 2

Perspective view 3

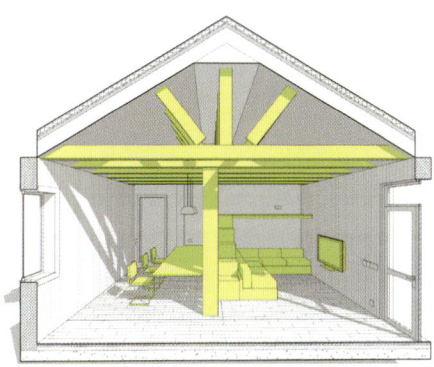

Perspective view 4

Perspective view 5

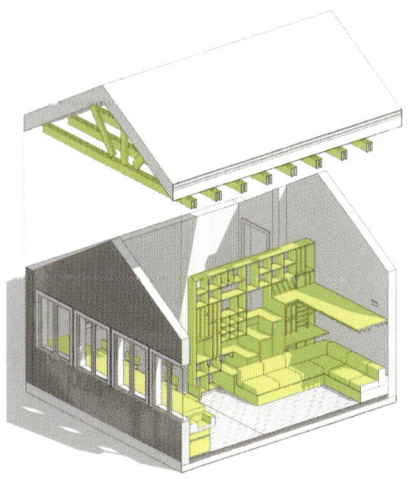

Axonometric view

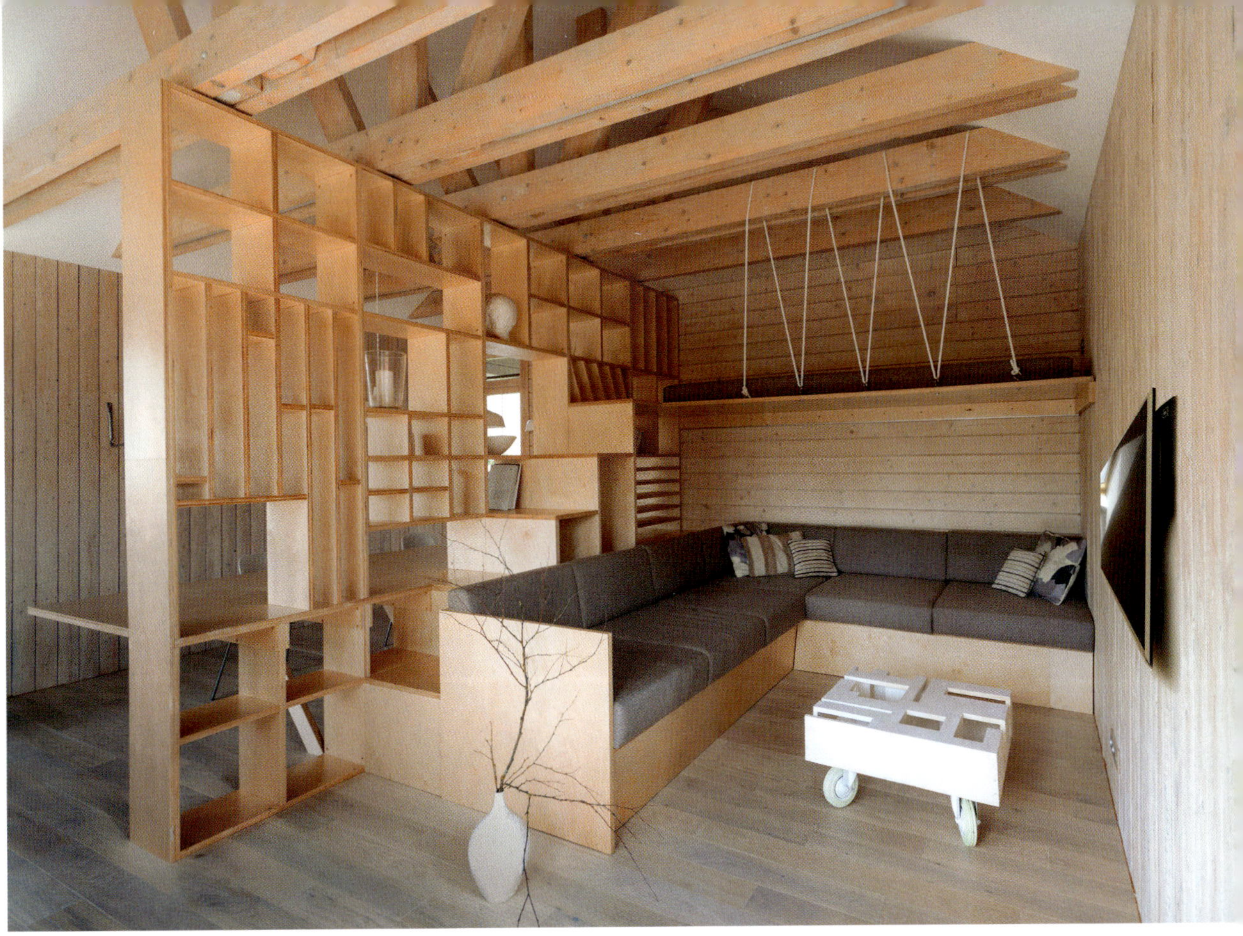

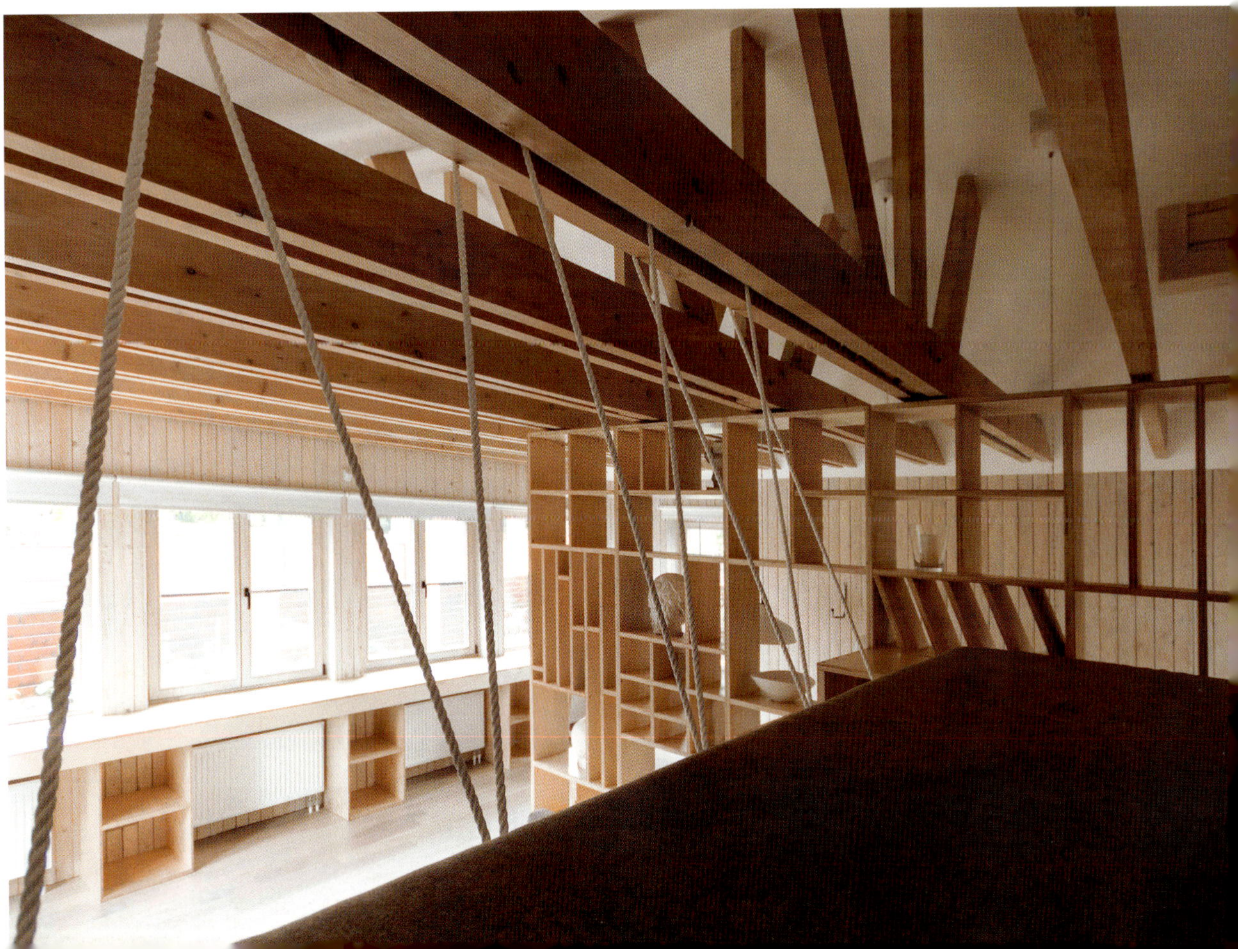

SPARROW HOUSE

SAMANTHA MINK - BODYOFWORK
SAMANTHA MINK

WWW.SAMANTHAMINK.COM

SAMANTHA MINK - BODYOFWORK is not a practice, but a discipline. It is an act of resistance. It is an exploration of the limits of the imagination. It is a pursuit, towards the poetics of architecture, through a resolute and rigorous body of work.

SAMANTHA MINK - BODYOFWORK ist keine Praxis, sondern eine Disziplin. Es ist ein Akt des Widerstands. Es ist eine Erkundung der Grenzen der Vorstellungskraft. Es ist ein Streben nach einer Poetik der Architektur durch ein entschlossenes und rigoroses Werk.

SAMANTHA MINK - BODYOFWORK

SAMANTHA MINK - BODYOFWORK n'est pas une pratique, mais une discipline. C'est un acte de résistance. C'est une exploration des limites de l'imagination. C'est une poursuite, vers la poétique de l'architecture, à travers un corps de travail résolu et rigoureux.

SAMANTHA MINK - BODYOFWORK no es una práctica, sino una disciplina. Es un acto de resistencia. Es una exploración de los límites de la imaginación. Es una búsqueda, hacia la poética de la arquitectura, a través de un cuerpo de trabajo decidido y riguroso.

SPARROW HOUSE

79 M² // CULVER CITY, CALIFORNIA, UNITED STATES

PHOTOS © SAMANTHA MINK, CHAD SLATTERY

The name of the house was inspired by a Chinese proverb: "Small as it is, the sparrow has all the essential organs." The unusual and modest lot size and configuration on the one hand, and financial budgets on the other, set the initial limitations for the scope of the project. Due to planning restrictions, the footprint and square footage of the house had to remain the same. Located on a unique street, the house came with all the great potential of "a box," mundane and ready for a transformation. The result is a sometimes stern but multi-faceted exterior, with an almost unexpectedly warm, bright, and comfortable interior. The house is small and simple, without room for stylistic and haughty gestures, but with just enough room for living.

Der Name des Hauses wurde von einem chinesischen Sprichwort inspiriert: „Wie klein der Spatz auch sein mag, er hat alle wichtigen Organe". Die bescheidene Größe des Grundstücks und seine ungewöhnliche Konfiguration einerseits und das Budget andererseits setzten die anfänglichen Grenzen für den Umfang des Projekts. An einer einzigen Straße gelegen, präsentierte sich das Haus mit all dem Potenzial einer „Big Box", bereit für eine Umgestaltung. Während aufgrund städtebaulicher Beschränkungen die Grundfläche und die Quadratmeterzahl des Hauses unverändert bleiben sollten, wurden alle Türen neu gestaltet, einschließlich des Haupteingangs, der durch einen neuen Garten zugänglich ist. Das Ergebnis ist ein etwas strenges, aber nuanciertes Äußeres mit einem unerwartet warmen, hellen und komfortablen Innenraum. Das Haus ist klein und einfach, ohne Platz für stilistische und großartige Gesten, aber mit genug Platz zum Wohnen.

Le nom de la maison est inspiré d'un proverbe chinois : « Aussi petit soit-il, le moineau possède tous les organes essentiels ». La taille modeste du site et sa configuration inhabituelle, d'une part, et le budget, d'autre part, ont fixé les limites initiales de la portée du projet. Située sur une seule rue, la maison se présentait avec tout le potentiel d'une « grosse boîte », prête à être transformée. En raison de restrictions urbanistiques, la superficie au sol et la superficie en pieds carrés de la maison devaient rester inchangées, mais toutes les portes ont été reconfigurées, y compris l'entrée principale, à laquelle on accède par un nouveau jardin. Le résultat est un extérieur un peu austère, mais nuancé, avec un intérieur étonnamment chaud, lumineux et confortable. La maison est petite et simple, sans place pour les gestes stylistiques et superbes, mais avec suffisamment d'espace pour y vivre.

El nombre de la casa se inspiró en un proverbio chino: «Por pequeño que sea, el gorrión tiene todos los órganos esenciales». El modesto tamaño del terreno y su configuración inusual, por un lado, y el presupuesto, por otro, establecieron las limitaciones iniciales para el alcance del proyecto. Ubicada en una calle única, la casa se presentó con todo el potencial de «una gran caja», lista para una transformación. Si bien debido a las restricciones urbanísticas, la huella y los metros cuadrados de la casa debían permanecer sin cambios, todas las puertas se reconfiguraron, incluso la entrada principal, a la que se accede a través de un nuevo jardín. El resultado es un exterior en cierto modo austero, pero con matices, con un interior inesperadamente cálido, luminoso y confortable. La casa es pequeña y sencilla, sin espacio para gestos estilísticos y soberbios, pero con el espacio suficiente para vivir.

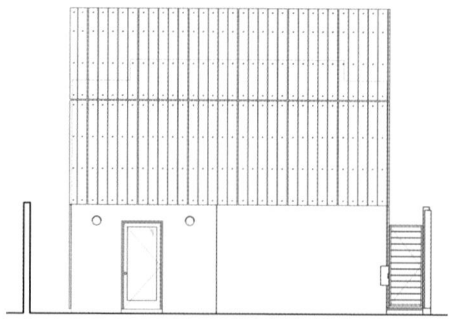

North elevation

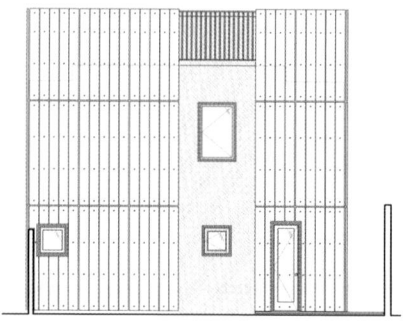

South elevation

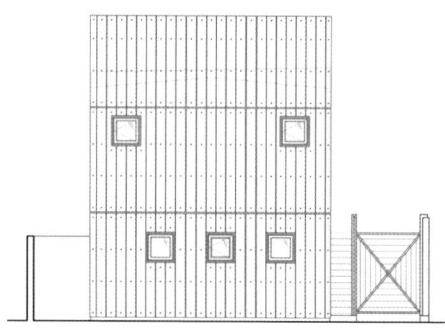

East elevation

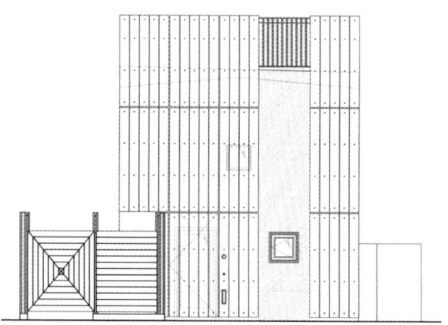

West elevation

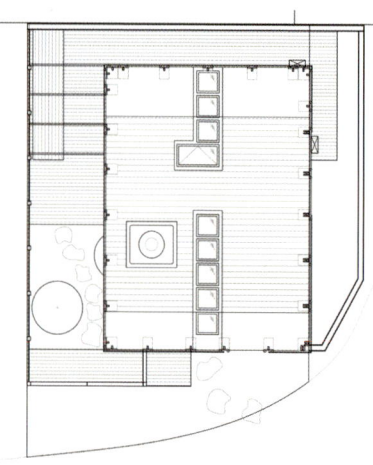

Site plan

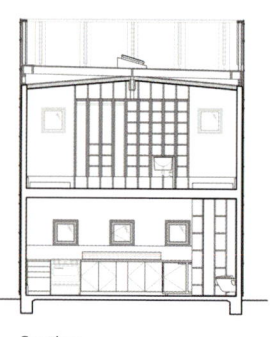
Section

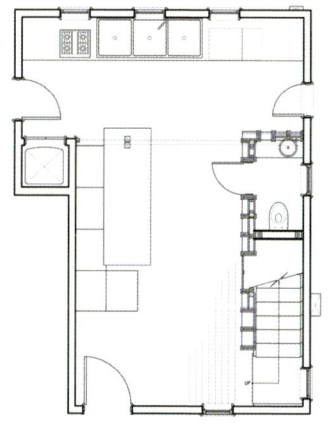

Ground floor plan

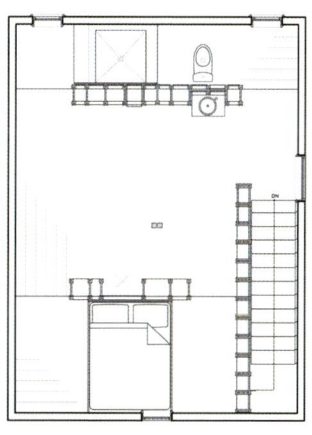

First floor plan

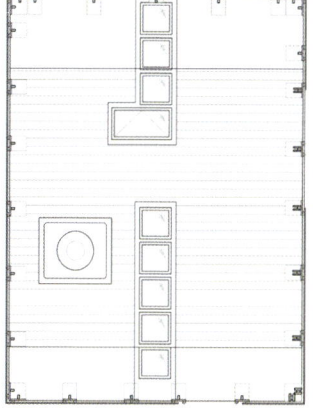

Roof deck floor plan

MANSHAUSEN

SNORRE STINESSEN ARCHITECTURE
SNORRE STINESSEN

WWW.SNORRESTINESSEN.COM

Snorre Stinessen Architecture is a small studio with offices in Norway and Italy.
The studio provides a full range of services from architecture to interior and furniture design and has received a number of international awards and has been widely published for its works.

Snorre Stinessen Architecture ist ein kleines Studio mit Büros in Norwegen und Italien.
Das Studio bietet eine breite Palette von Dienstleistungen an, die von Architektur über Innenarchitektur bis hin zu Möbeln reichen. Die Arbeiten des Studios wurden mit mehreren internationalen Preisen ausgezeichnet und sind vielfach publiziert worden.

SNORRE STINESSEN ARCHITECTURE

Snorre Stinessen Architecture est un petit studio qui a des bureaux en Norvège et en Italie.
Le studio offre une large gamme de services allant de l'architecture à la décoration intérieure et au mobilier. Il a reçu plusieurs prix internationaux et a été largement publié pour ses travaux.

Snorre Stinessen Architecture es un pequeño estudio con oficinas en Noruega e Italia.
El estudio ofrece una amplia gama de servicios desde arquitectura hasta diseño de interiores y mobiliario y ha recibido varios premios internacionales y ha sido ampliamente publicado por sus trabajos.

MANSHAUSEN

33 M² // MANSHAUSEN ISLAND, STEIGEN, NORWAY
PHOTOS © KJELL OVE STORVIK, SNORRE STINESSEN

The cabins are positioned at the tip of the rocky formations at the northern end of the Island and out over the sea. Wave heights, extreme weather conditions and also future raise in sea level were studied to determine the exact positions of the cabins. The exposure to the natural elements is extreme and aluminum sheet cladding was chosen to withstand the salinity and salt water exposure. The access to the cabins is via the rocky formations that allows you to step into and up out above the sea below. The shelter design endeavors to make a minimum environmental impact and minimum footprint. The glazing is custom made for the project and the large glasses allow for unobstructed views of the nature and the elements outside.

Die Hütten befinden sich an der Spitze der Felsformationen am nördlichen Ende der Insel und über dem Meer. Hohe Wellen, extreme Wetterbedingungen und auch der zukünftige Meeresspiegelanstieg wurden analysiert, um die genauen Positionen der Hütten zu bestimmen. Die Exposition gegenüber den natürlichen Elementen ist extrem. Daher wurde eine Verkleidung aus Aluminiumblech gewählt, die dem Salzgehalt und der Salzwasserbelastung standhält. Der Zugang zu den Hütten erfolgt durch die Felsformationen, die den Ein- und Ausstieg aus dem Meer darunter ermöglichen. Das Design des Unterstandes strebt eine geringe Umweltbelastung und einen minimalen Fußabdruck an. Die Verglasung wurde speziell für das Projekt angefertigt und die großen Glasscheiben ermöglichen einen ungehinderten Blick auf die Natur und die Elemente außerhalb des Hauses.

Les huttes sont situées à l'extrémité des formations rocheuses à l'extrémité nord de l'île et au-dessus de la mer. La hauteur des vagues, les conditions météorologiques extrêmes et aussi l'élévation future du niveau de la mer ont été étudiées pour déterminer la position exacte des huttes. L'exposition aux éléments naturels est extrême et un revêtement en tôle d'aluminium a été choisi pour résister à l'exposition à l'eau salée. L'accès aux cabanes se fait par les formations rocheuses qui permettent d'entrer et de sortir de la mer en contrebas. La conception de l'abri s'efforce d'avoir une empreinte et un impact minimaliste sur l'environnement. Pour ce projet le vitrage est fait sur mesure et les grandes vitres permettent une vue imprenable sur la nature et les éléments extérieurs.

Las cabañas están situadas en la punta de las formaciones rocosas en el extremo norte de la isla y sobre el mar. Se estudiaron las alturas de las olas, las condiciones climáticas extremas y también la futura subida del nivel del mar para determinar las posiciones exactas de las cabañas. La exposición a los elementos naturales es extrema y se eligió un revestimiento de láminas de aluminio para soportar la salinidad y la exposición al agua salada. El acceso a las cabañas es a través de las formaciones rocosas que permiten entrar y salir del mar por debajo. El diseño del refugio se esfuerza por hacer un impacto ambiental mínimo y una huella mínima. Los cristales están hechos a medida para el proyecto y los grandes vidrios permiten vistas sin obstáculos de la naturaleza y los elementos del exterior.

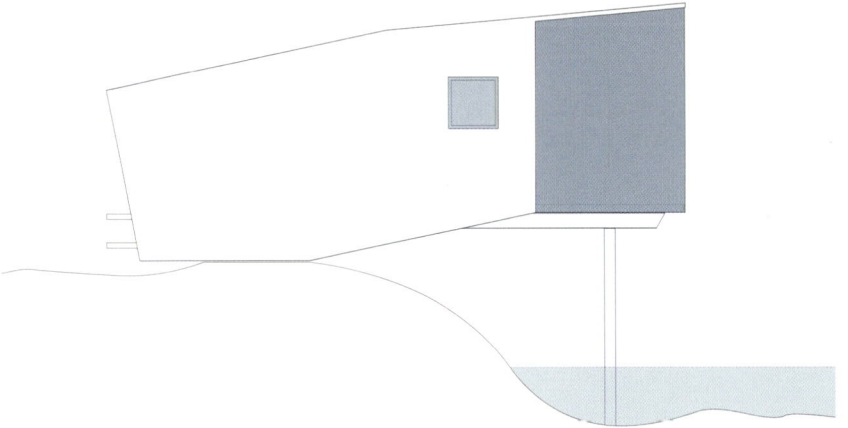

East elevation

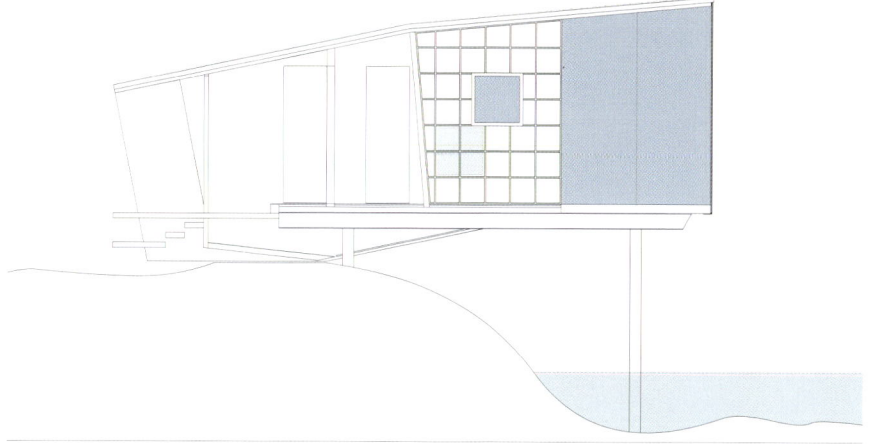

Section

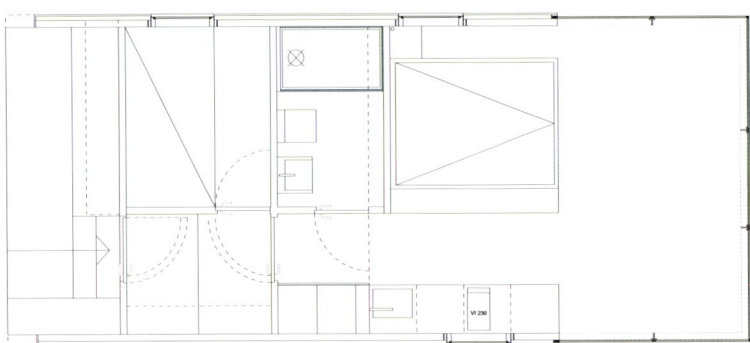

Floor plan

T-SQUARE DESIGN ASSOCIATES
SHIGERU TSUDA

WWW.T2DESIGNASSOCIATES.COM

We are a multi-disciplinary creative firm in Tokyo and Osaka, founded by architect, Shigeru Tsuda and graphic designer, Eiji Tsuda. We specialize in architecture, interior design, product design and visual communication. Tokyo studio specializes in visual communication, from brand development, communication collaterals and package design. Osaka studio specializes in developing both residential and commercial architecture, interior and product design.

Through careful research of the surrounding, the clients' needs and predictable climate condition, we try to come up with an idea that is environmental, inspirational and memorable. We also focus on how materials age, because we believe that architecture should be thought as something that ages. Aged architecture is more beautiful than something new. This is why we use stones, concrete, steel, and any other solid materials.

Wir sind ein multidisziplinäres kreativbüro in Tokio und Osaka, gegründet von architekt Shigeru Tsuda und grafikdesigner Eiji Tsuda. Wir sind spezialisiert auf architektur, innenarchitektur, produktdesign und visuelle kommunikation.

Das studio in Tokio ist spezialisiert auf visuelle kommunikation, von der markenentwicklung über kommunikationsmaterialien bis hin zum verpackungsdesign. Das studio in Osaka ist auf die entwicklung von wohn- und geschäftsarchitektur, innenarchitektur und produktdesign spezialisiert.

Durch sorgfältige untersuchung der umgebung, der bedürfnisse der kunden und der vorhersehbaren klimatischen bedingungen versuchen wir, eine idee zu entwickeln, die umweltfreundlich, inspirierend und einprägsam ist. Wir konzentrieren uns auch darauf, wie materialien altern, denn wir glauben, dass architektur als etwas gedacht sein sollte, das altert. Gealterte architektur ist schöner als etwas neues. Deshalb verwenden wir steine, beton, stahl und alle anderen soliden materialien.

T-SQUARE DESIGN ASSOCIATES

Nous sommes un cabinet de création multidisciplinaire situé à Tokyo et Osaka, fondé par l'architecte Shigeru Tsuda et le graphiste Eiji Tsuda. Nous sommes spécialisés dans l'architecture, la décoration intérieure, le design de produits et la communication visuelle.

Le studio de Tokyo est spécialisé dans la communication visuelle, qu'il s'agisse du développement de marques, de supports de communication ou de la conception d'emballages. Le studio d'Osaka est spécialisé dans l'architecture résidentielle et commerciale, l'aménagement intérieur et le design de produits.

Grâce à une étude minutieuse de l'environnement, des besoins des clients et des conditions climatiques prévisibles, nous essayons de trouver une idée qui soit environnementale, inspirante et mémorable. Nous nous concentrons également sur la façon dont les matériaux vieillissent, car nous pensons que l'architecture doit être pensée comme quelque chose qui vieillit. Une architecture vieillie est plus belle qu'une architecture neuve. C'est pourquoi nous utilisons des pierres, du béton, de l'acier et tout autre matériau solide.

Somos una empresa creativa multidisciplinar en Tokio y Osaka, fundada por el arquitecto Shigeru Tsuda y el diseñador gráfico Eiji Tsuda. Estamos especializados en arquitectura, diseño de interiores, diseño de productos y comunicación visual.

El estudio de Tokio se especializa en comunicación visual, desde el desarrollo de marcas, colaterales de comunicación y diseño de paquetes. El estudio de Osaka se especializa en el desarrollo de arquitectura residencial y comercial, diseño de interiores y de productos.

Mediante una cuidadosa investigación del entorno, de las necesidades de los clientes y de las condiciones climáticas previsibles, tratamos de dar con una idea que sea ambiental, inspiradora y memorable. También nos centramos en cómo envejecen los materiales, porque creemos que la arquitectura debe pensarse como algo que envejece. La arquitectura envejecida es más bella que algo nuevo. Por eso utilizamos piedras, hormigón, acero y cualquier otro material sólido.

FUSEIKA

113 M² // HYOGO, JAPAN

PHOTOS © SHIGEO OGAWA

This small house sits in between two rivers enabling the house free from using air conditioning by bringing the river breeze into the house. By planning a neutral zone between the interior and exterior perimeter covered with louver sliding doors, light, wind and the privacy of the house are controlled.

Concrete structure carries out strong massive image against dramatic wide openings which are covered with wooden sliding doors that make a strong connection between the house and the surroundings.

This connection with the surroundings is very important here since along with the trees that surround the house serving as a green belt for the pedestrians as well as for the owner of the house which leads the house to be connected socially to the society.

Dieses kleine Haus liegt zwischen zwei Flüssen. Indem die Flussbrise in das Haus gebracht wird, ist keine Klimaanlage notwendig. Durch die Planung einer neutralen Zone zwischen der inneren und äußeren Begrenzung, die mit Schiebelamellentüren abgedeckt ist, werden Licht, Wind und Privatsphäre des Hauses gesteuert.

Die Betonstruktur führt ein starkes, massives Bild gegen die dramatisch breiten Öffnungen aus. Diese sind mit Holzschiebetüren abgedeckt, die eine starke Verbindung zwischen dem Haus und der Umgebung herstellen.

Diese Verbindung mit der Umgebung ist hier sehr wichtig, da sie zusammen mit den Bäumen, die das Haus umgeben, als grüner Gürtel sowohl für die Fußgänger als auch für den Besitzer des Hauses dient. Auf diese Weise erfüllt das Haus auch eine soziale Funktion.

Cette petite maison est située entre deux rivières, ce qui lui permet de ne pas avoir recours à la climatisation en faisant entrer la brise de la rivière dans la maison. En prévoyant une zone neutre entre le périmètre intérieur et le périmètre extérieur, couverte de portes à persiennes coulissantes, on contrôle la lumière, le vent et l'intimité de la maison.

La structure en béton projette une image massive et forte, avec de larges ouvertures closent de portes coulissantes en bois qui établissent un lien fort entre la maison et l'environnement.

Ce lien avec l'environnement est très important ici car, avec les arbres qui entourent la maison, il sert de ceinture verte pour les piétons ainsi que pour le propriétaire de la maison, ce qui permet à celle-ci d'être socialement connectée à la société.

Esta pequeña casa se encuentra entre dos ríos, lo que permite que la casa se libere del uso del aire acondicionado al traer la brisa del río a la casa. Planeando una zona neutral entre el perímetro interior y exterior cubierta con puertas correderas de persiana, se controla la luz, el viento y la privacidad de la casa.

La estructura de hormigón lleva a cabo una fuerte imagen masiva contra las dramáticas aberturas amplias que están cubiertas con puertas deslizantes de madera que hacen una fuerte conexión entre la casa y los alrededores.

Esta conexión con el entorno es muy importante aquí ya que junto con los árboles que rodean la casa sirven como un cinturón verde para los peatones así como para el dueño de la casa lo que lleva a la casa a estar conectada socialmente con la sociedad.

Site plan

East elevation

West elevation

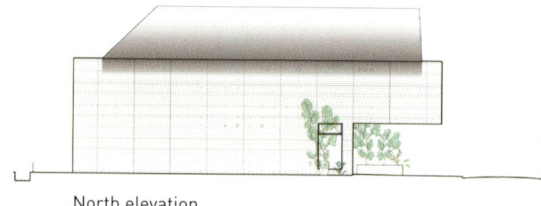

North elevation

South elevation

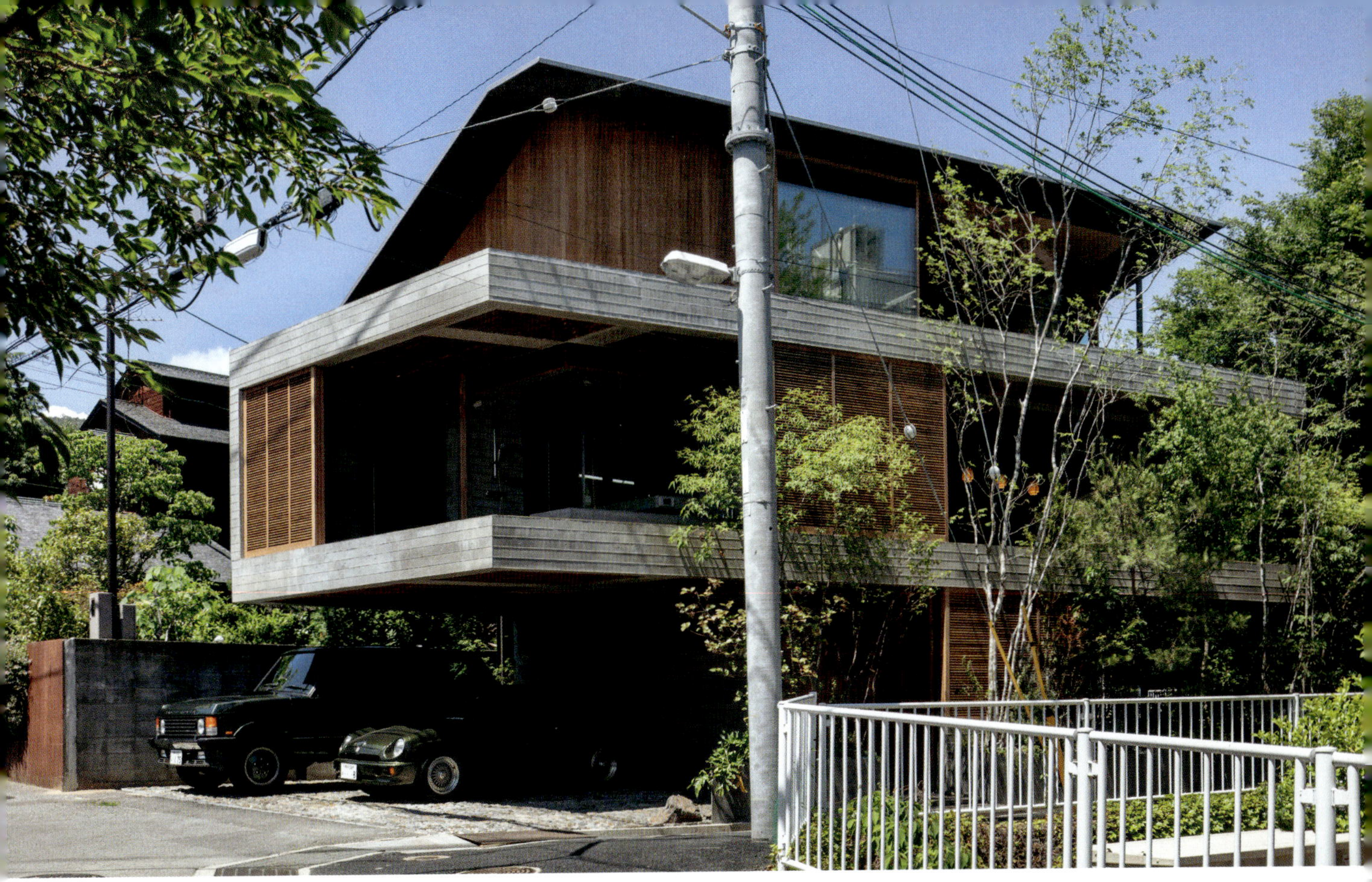
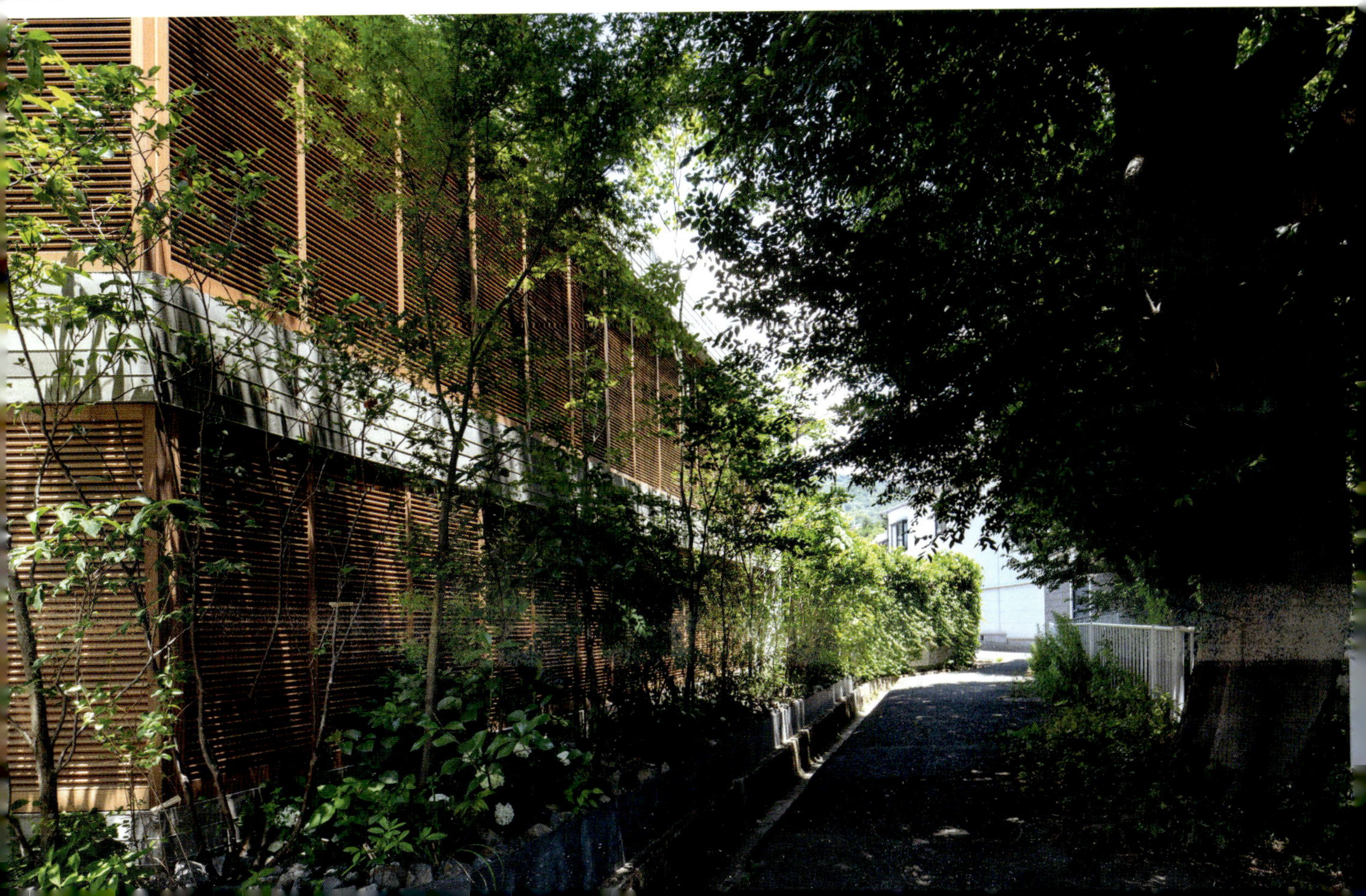

Section

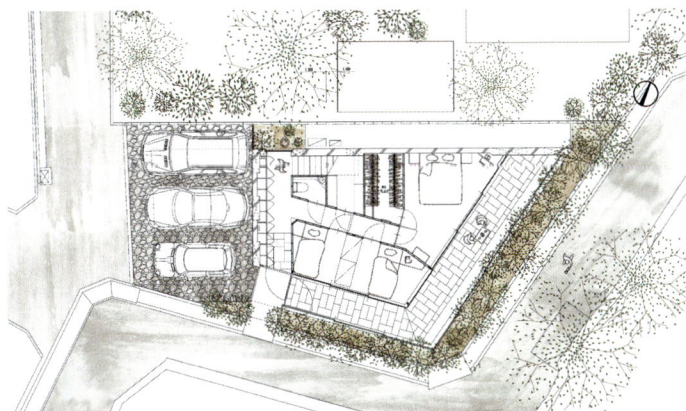

Ground floor plan

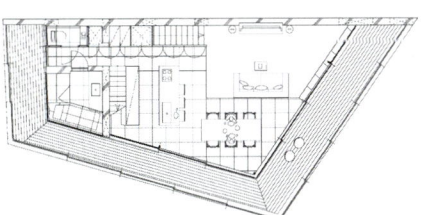

First floor plan

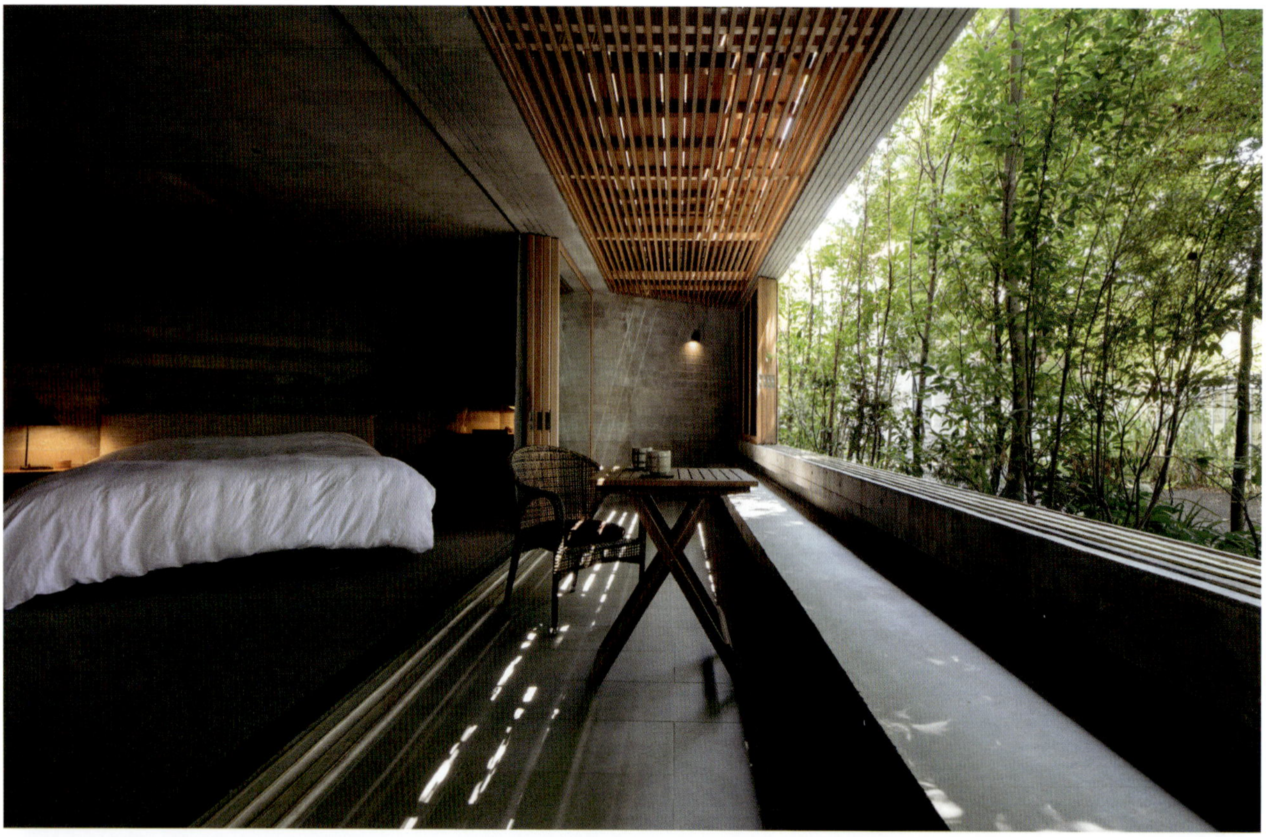

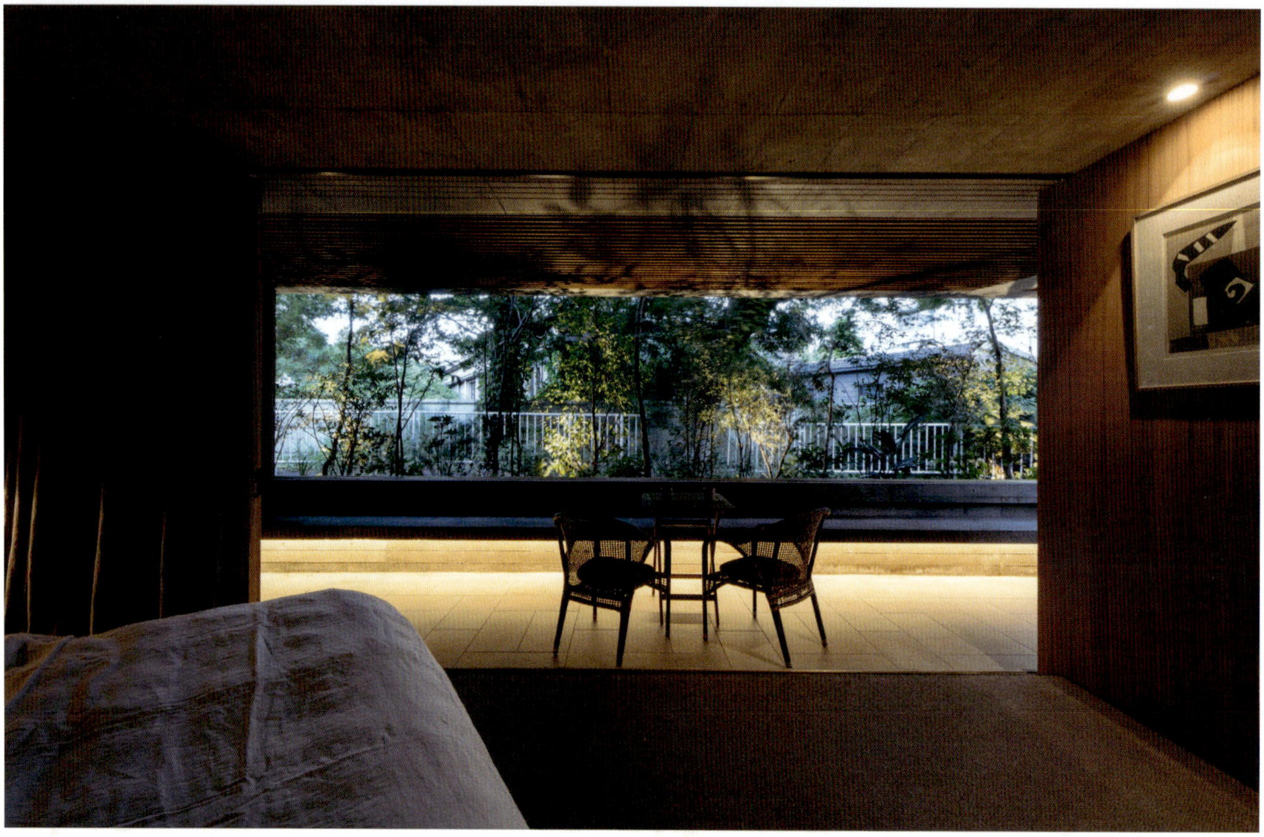

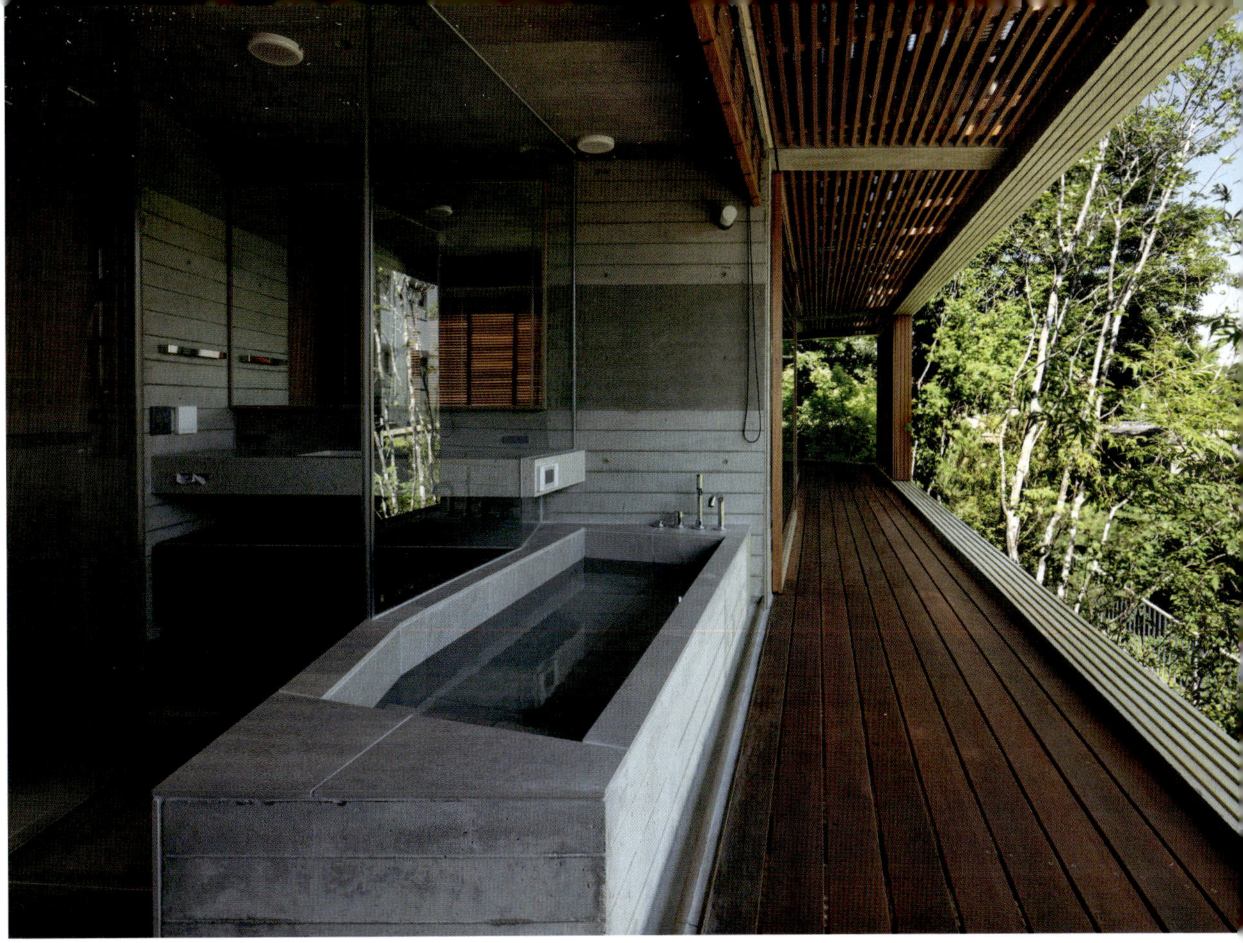

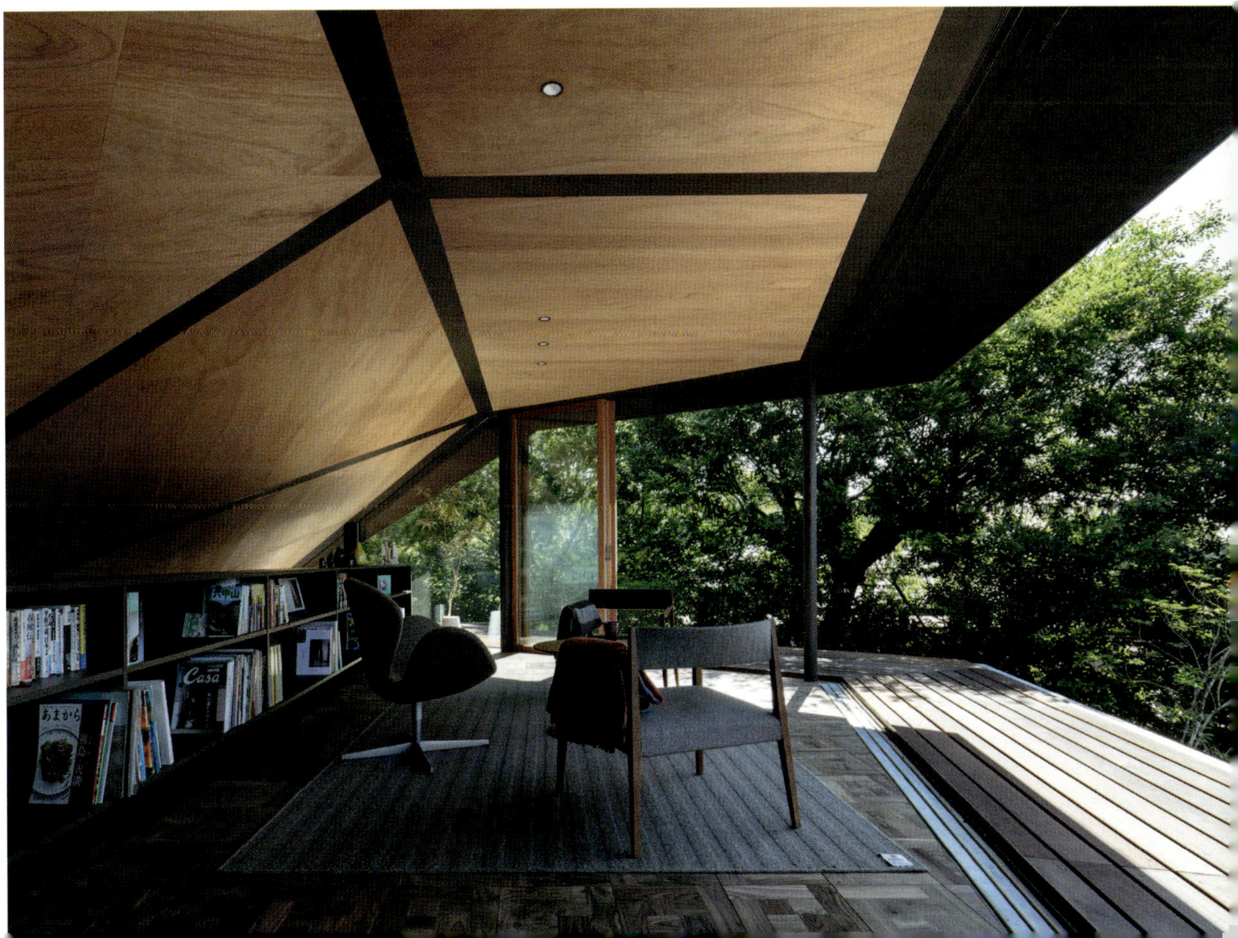
Casa
あまから

MILL VALLEY GUEST HOUSE

TURNBULL GRIFFIN HAESLOOP ARCHITECTS
ERIC HAESLOOP FAIA

WWW.TGHARCHITECTS.COM

Turnbull Griffin Haesloop is an award-winning architecture firm led by Eric Haesloop FAIA from the Berkeley Studio. We believe architecture is primarily concerned with establishing a "sense of place," inspired by the uniqueness of each site and each client. We listen carefully to the aspirations and requirements of our clients and together look for unique qualities to tailor the project. We are particularly attentive to topography, microclimate, water management, fire safety, vegetation and solar orientation since the concept for each of our buildings is rooted in its environment.

Turnbull Griffin Haesloop ist ein preisgekröntes Architekturbüro unter der Leitung von Eric Haesloop FAIA von Berkeley Studio. Wir glauben, dass es in der Architektur in erster Linie darum geht, einen „sense of place" zu schaffen, inspiriert von der Einzigartigkeit jedes Ortes und jedes Kunden. Wir hören genau auf die Wünsche und Anforderungen unserer Kunden und suchen gemeinsam nach einzigartigen Qualitäten, um das Projekt maßgeschneidert zu gestalten. Wir achten besonders auf Topografie, Mikroklima, Wassermanagement, Brandschutz, Vegetation und Sonnenausrichtung, da das Konzept jedes unserer Gebäude in seiner Umgebung verwurzelt ist.

TURNBULL GRIFFIN HAESLOOP ARCHITECTS

Turnbull Griffin Haesloop est un cabinet d'architecture primé, dirigé par Eric Haesloop FAIA du Berkeley Studio. Nous pensons que l'architecture se préoccupe avant tout d'établir un « sens du lieu », inspiré par le caractère unique de chaque site et de chaque client. Nous écoutons attentivement les aspirations et les exigences de nos clients et recherchons ensemble des qualités uniques pour adapter le projet. Nous sommes particulièrement attentifs à la topographie, au microclimat, à la gestion de l'eau, à la sécurité incendie, à la végétation et à l'orientation solaire, car le concept de chacun de nos bâtiments est ancré dans son environnement.

Turnbull Griffin Haesloop es una galardonada firma de arquitectura dirigida por Eric Haesloop FAIA del Estudio Berkeley. Creemos que la arquitectura está principalmente preocupada por establecer un «sentido de lugar», inspirado por la singularidad de cada sitio y cada cliente. Escuchamos cuidadosamente las aspiraciones y requerimientos de nuestros clientes y juntos buscarmos cualidades únicas para adaptar el proyecto. Prestamos especial atención a la topografía, al microclima, a la gestión del agua, a la seguridad contra incendios, a la vegetación y a la orientación solar, ya que el concepto de cada uno de nuestros edificios está enraizado en su entorno.

MILL VALLEY GUEST HOUSE

59 M² // MILL VALLEY, CALIFORNIA, UNITED STATES
PHOTOS © DAVID WAKELY

Sited on a small level clearing at the top of a steeply sloping lot surrounded by mature cedar and redwood trees, this guest house is designed to serve multiple generations and functions: a guest room for visiting parents and friends, a media room, and a hangout space for teenage children. The porch and media room are situated on the more open side of the site and the guest room is tucked into the trees. The flat roof punctuated by round skylights extends the dappled light of the surrounding tree canopies over the expansive porch and indoor spaces. Wood siding lets the walls blend in with the trees while the porch ceiling and skylight pattern become a playful façade as seen from the house and backyard below. The porch, cool roof, closed cell insulation, LED lighting and a high efficiency boiler keep the energy loads minimal exceeding CA Energy Code by 33%.

Auf einer kleinen Lichtung am oberen Ende eines steil abfallenden Grundstücks, umgeben von alten Zedern und Mammutbäumen, liegt dieses 640 Quadratmeter große Gästehaus, das für mehrere Generationen und Funktionen ausgelegt ist: ein Gästezimmer für Eltern oder Freunde, die zu Besuch sind, ein Medienraum und ein Raum für Jugendliche. Das flache Dach, das von runden Oberlichtern unterbrochen wird, verbreitet gedämpftes Licht aus den umliegenden Baumkronen über die weitläufige Veranda und die Innenräume. Die Holzverkleidung lässt die Wände mit den Bäumen verschmelzen, während das Verandadach und das Oberlichtmuster zu einer dynamischen Fassade werden, die vom Haus und vom Hinterhof aus betrachtet wird. Die Veranda, das Dach, die geschlossenzellige Isolierung, die LED-Beleuchtung und ein hocheffizienter Heizkessel halten die Energielasten minimal und übertreffen den AC Energy Code um 33%.

Située dans une petite clairière au sommet d'un terrain en forte pente, entourée de cèdres et de séquoias matures, cette maison d'hôtes est conçue pour accueillir plusieurs générations et fonctions : une chambre d'hôtes est réservée pour les parents ou amis en visite, une salle de réunion et un espace pour les adolescents. Le toit plat ponctué de lucarnes rondes diffuse la lumière entre les cimes des arbres environnants sur le vaste porche et les espaces intérieurs. Les murs de la facade en bois permettent de se fondre dans les arbres, tandis que le toit du porche et le motif de la lucarne deviennent une façade dynamique vue de la maison et de la cour arrière. Le porche, le toit, l'isolation à cellules fermées, l'éclairage LED et une chaudière à haut rendement permettent de réduire au minimum les charges énergétiques, dépassant de 33% le code de l'énergie CA.

Situada en un pequeño claro en la parte superior de un terreno de gran pendiente rodeado de cedros maduros y secoyas, esta casa de huéspedes está diseñada para albergar a múltiples generaciones y funciones: una habitación de invitados para las visitas de los padres o de los amigos, una sala multimedia y un espacio para los adolescentes. El tejado plano, salpicado por tragaluces redondos, extiende la luz moteada de las copas de los árboles de alrededor sobre el amplio porche y los espacios interiores. El revestimiento de madera permite que las paredes se fundan con los árboles, mientras que el techo del porche y el patrón de los tragaluces se convierten en una fachada dinámica vista desde la casa y el patio trasero. El porche, el tejado, el aislamiento de células cerradas, la iluminación LED y una caldera de alta eficiencia mantienen las cargas de energía mínimas superando el Código de Energía de CA en un 33%.

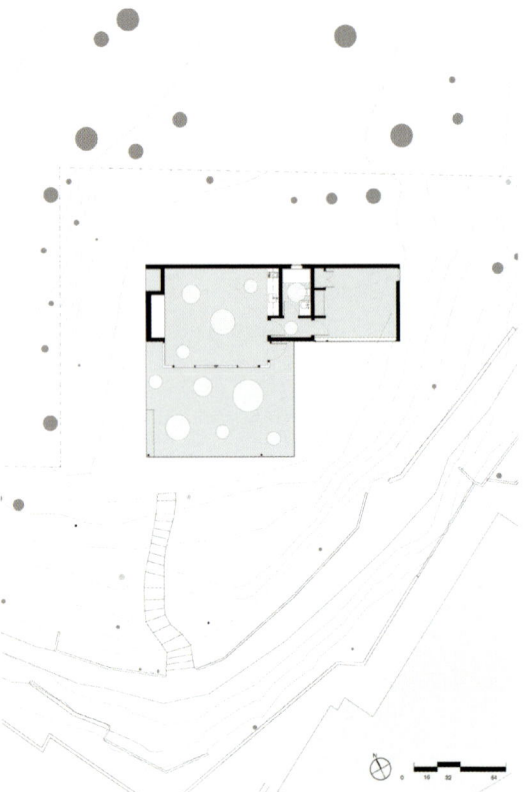

Site plan

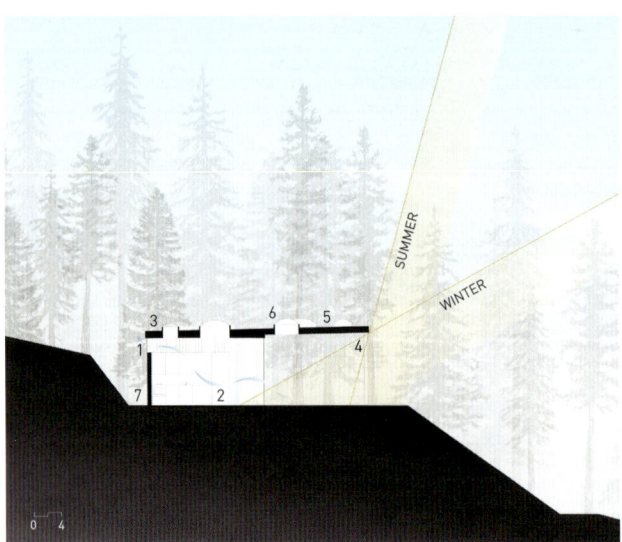

Section

1. High operable windows for cross-ventilation
2. Concrete floor with radiant heating
3. Closed-cell insulation for maximum thermal perfomance
4. Roof overhang designed to minimize solar heat gain during summer months
5. White "cool" roof
6. Modulated daylight
7. High efficiency boiler

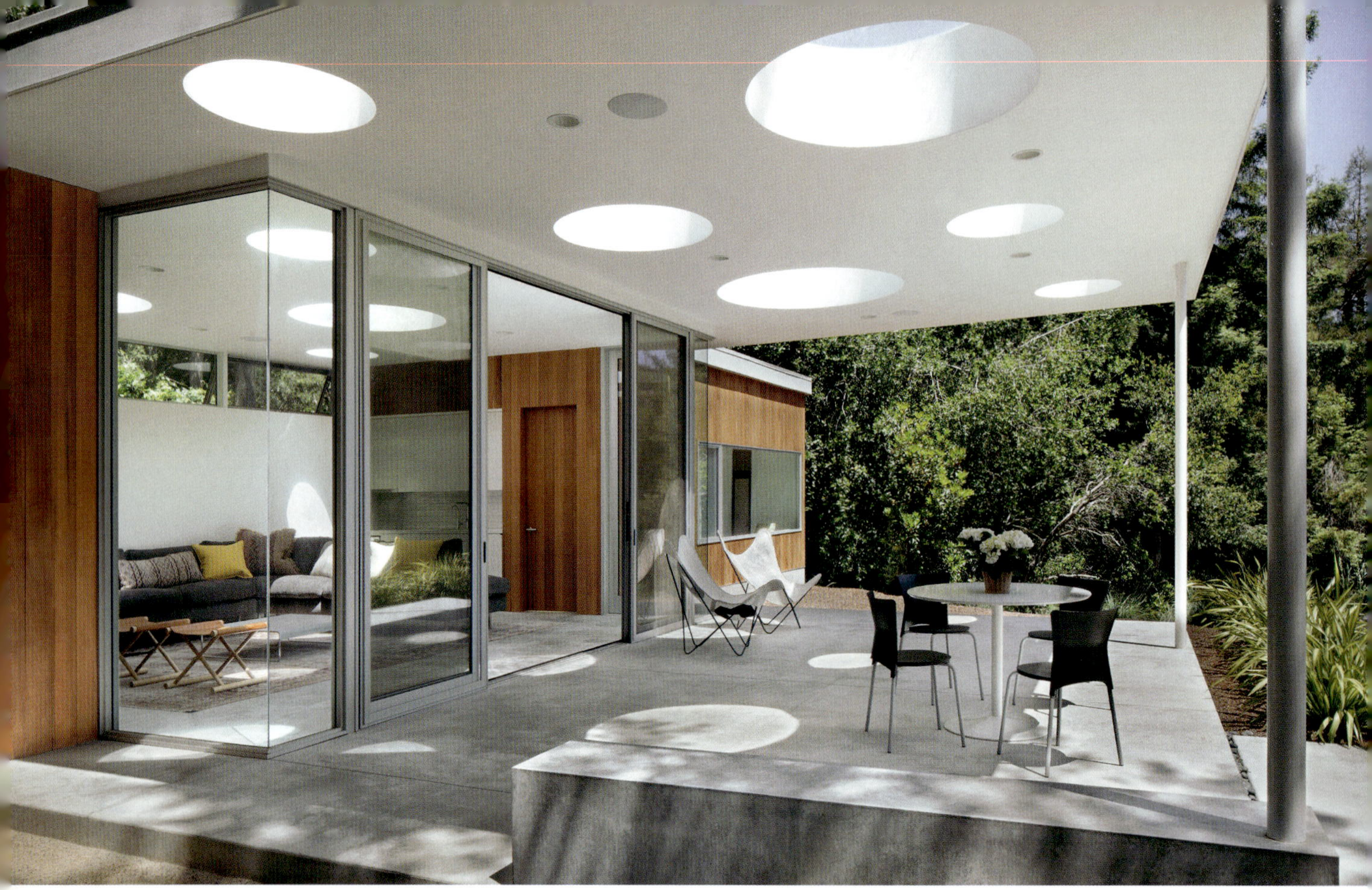

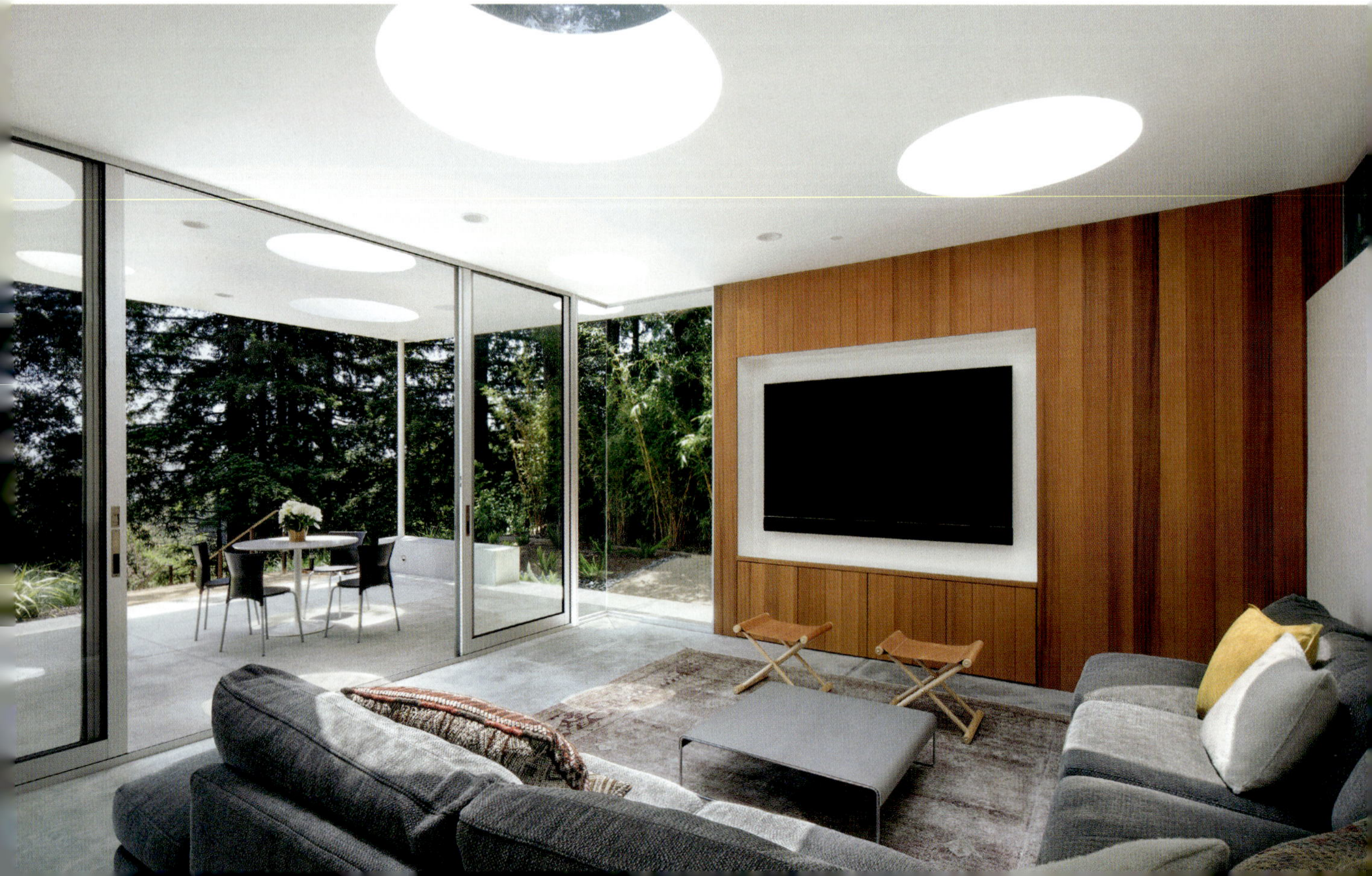

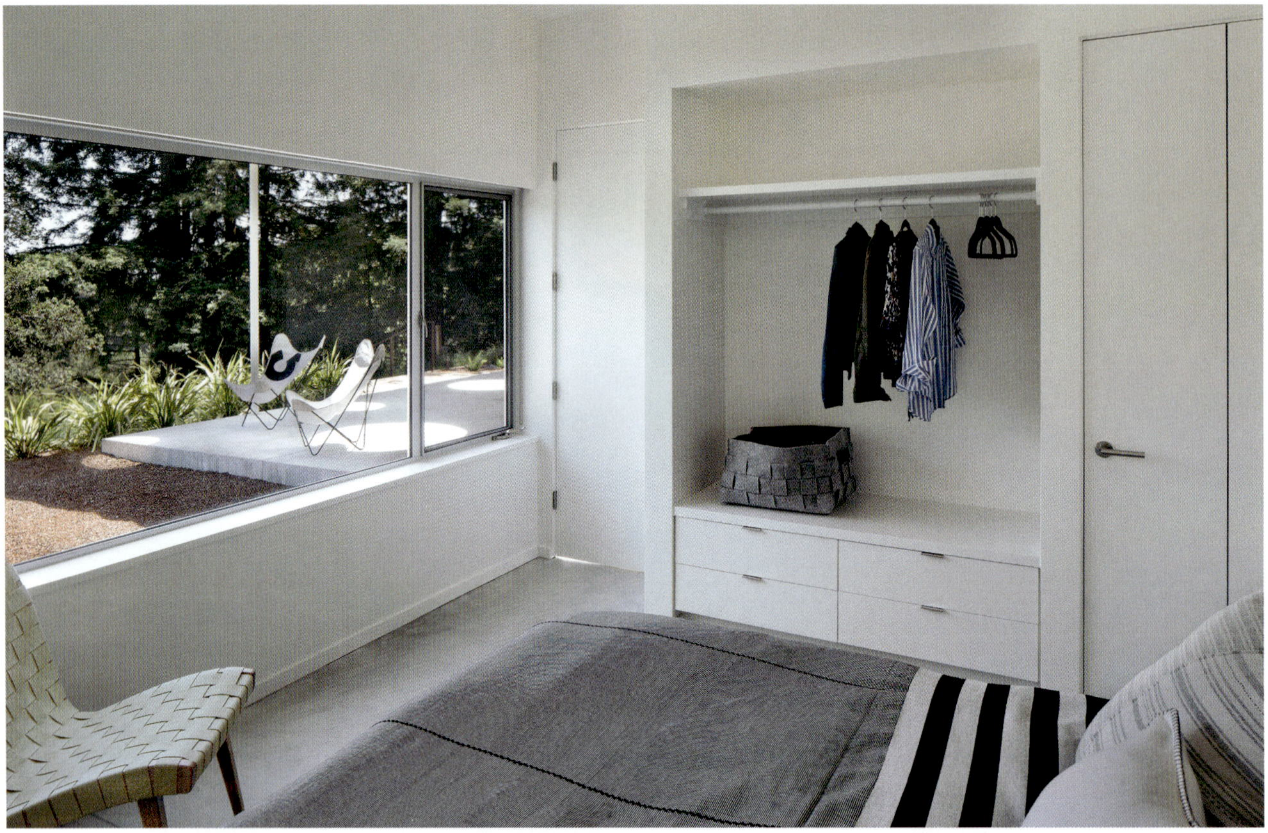

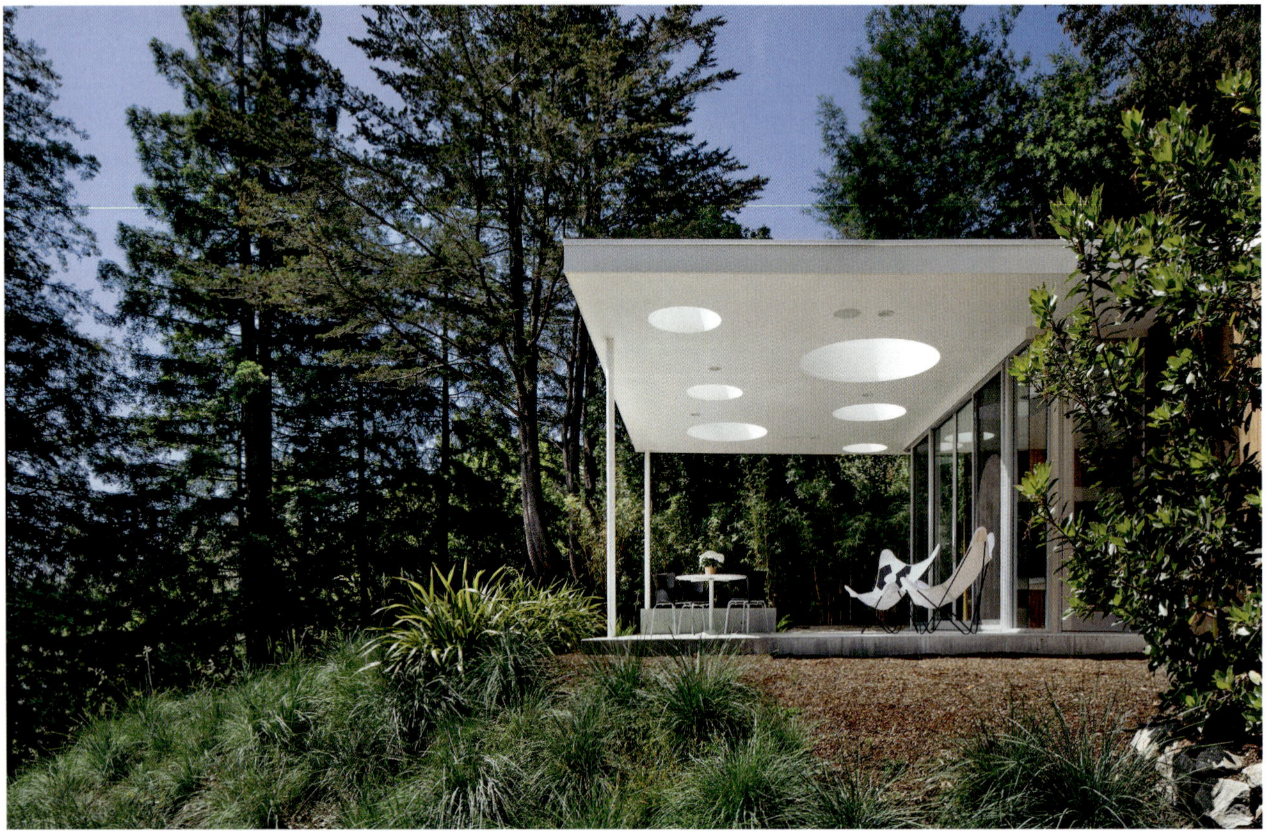